RELOCATION DISPUTES

Relocation cases are disputes between separated parents which arise when one parent proposes to move to a new geographic location with their child and the other parent objects to the proposal. Relocation disputes are widely recognised as being amongst the most difficult cases facing Family Courts, and the law governing them is increasingly a cause for debate at both national and international levels.

In *Relocation Disputes: Law and Practice in England and New Zealand*, Rob George looks at the different ways in which the legal systems of England and New Zealand currently deal with relocation cases. Drawing on case law, literature and the views of legal practitioners in the two jurisdictions, *Relocation Disputes* represents a major contribution to our understanding of the everyday practice of relocation cases. The empirical data reported in this book reveal the practical differences between the English and New Zealand approaches to relocation, along with a detailed analysis of the pros and cons of each system as seen by judges, lawyers and court experts who deal with these cases in practice. This analysis leads to detailed criticisms and lessons that can be learnt, together with practical suggestions about possible reforms of relocation law.

Relocation Disputes

Law and Practice in England and New Zealand

Rob George

·HART·
PUBLISHING
OXFORD AND PORTLAND, OREGON
2014

Published in the United Kingdom by Hart Publishing Ltd
16C Worcester Place, Oxford, OX1 2JW
Telephone: +44 (0)1865 517530
Fax: +44 (0)1865 510710
E-mail: mail@hartpub.co.uk
Website: http://www.hartpub.co.uk

Published in North America (US and Canada) by
Hart Publishing
c/o International Specialized Book Services
920 NE 58th Avenue, Suite 300
Portland, OR 97213-3786
USA
Tel: +1 503 287 3093 or toll-free: (1) 800 944 6190
Fax: +1 503 280 8832
E-mail: orders@isbs.com
Website: http://www.isbs.com

Hart Publishing is an imprint of Bloomsbury Publishing plc.

British Library Cataloguing in Publication Data
Data Available

ISBN: 978-1-84946-466-6

Typeset by Hope Services Ltd, Abingdon
Printed and bound in Great Britain by
Lightning Source UK Ltd

FOREWORD
by The Rt Hon Lord Justice Thorpe

The scale of human migration in the twenty-first century challenges global society to develop principles and remedies both to protect the welfare of minors caught up in family migration and also to deliver fair outcomes to the adults who invoke international or domestic law where compromise within the family escapes them.

The abduction of a child is a gross form of abuse and the Hague Convention of 1980 has done inestimable good over decades in providing an international legal remedy. But the Permanent Bureau has always emphasised the importance of prevention. Preventative measures include promoting public awareness of the means to a lawful removal, namely an application to the court of the country of habitual residence for a relocation order. The interrelationship between the international remedy and the domestic law route to lawful cross-border movement is obvious.

Hence the investment of the Hague Conference in exploring the possibility of an international consensus on how relocation applications should be resolved judicially. The difficulty of the task is well illustrated by the outcome of the Washington Conference in 2010, in the form of the Washington Declaration on International Family Relocation. The diversity of the approaches of the many jurisdictions represented resulted in a list of factors which, to be of much utility, would have required a great deal of refinement and distillation. A mandate to continue this work was effectively vetoed by Canada, the USA and Australia at the 6th Special Commission in January 2012.

Accordingly the next stage is likely to be individual and interdisciplinary endeavours. Such an interdisciplinary group involving experts from England and New Zealand is already constituted and a similar group pooling Canadian and Australian expertise is also contemplated. Chapter 6 of this book will be of particular importance to these initiatives.

Academics and researchers offer a vital contribution. The number of academics specialising in this field could be counted on the fingers of two hands and Rob George has rapidly established himself as the Young Turk. The exceptionally valuable study published in this book makes more widely available much of what he has so far accomplished. The research that he has done amidst the practitioners of England and New Zealand is particularly relevant.

Research so often raises many new questions, and this book is no different. The Washington Declaration called in particular for further work on trends and outcomes of relocation cases, and following the work reported in this book, Dr George has gone on to study case outcomes in contested relocation cases in

England and Wales in 2012. With the support of the President, my office promoted and co-ordinated the collection of nearly 100 first instance cases for his analysis. We look forward to his future conclusions, which will surely inform debate both within our interdisciplinary working group and beyond.

We are fortunate in having in our midst a young scholar who has chosen to devote his talent to a highly specialised but highly important topic.

Mathew Thorpe

ACKNOWLEDGEMENTS

The research reported in this book was conducted as part of my doctoral thesis in the Law Faculty at the University of Oxford, generously funded by the Arts and Humanities Research Council (Grant Number 135597).

Many people helped me along the way, not least my family and friends who supported and encouraged me. My colleagues at Jesus College, Oxford (where I worked while doing my DPhil) and at University College, Oxford (where I worked while transforming the DPhil into this book) were kind and supportive in many important ways, as were many family law colleagues in Oxford and beyond. Mark Henaghan and Stephen Gilmore deserve particular mention, along with my DPhil examiners, John Eekelaar and Gillian Douglas. Most especially, I would like to thank my supervisor, Mavis Maclean, for her wisdom, insight and friendship.

Much of this book is based on empirical research with 44 family law professionals in England and Wales and in New Zealand. I am immensely grateful to them for giving up their time to share their experiences with me, and I hope the optimism which many of them expressed that this research would bear interesting and useful fruit is justified by the findings that I present.

Finally, I would like to acknowledge the invaluable help of Eliza Eagling in the final stages of preparing the book manuscript, and to offer my thanks to Lord Justice Thorpe for writing the foreword and for his kind words therein.

Rob George
University College, Oxford
August 2013

CONTENTS

TABLE OF CASES

Australia

Canada

England and Wales

European Court of Human Rights

New Zealand

South Africa

United States of America

TABLE OF LEGISLATION

European Union

France

Germany

New Zealand

United States of America

International

INTRODUCTION

Relocation disputes arise between separated parents when one of them proposes to move to a new geographic location and take their child with him or her, and the other parent objects to the proposal. Compared with many parenting disputes, particularly about children's residence and contact arrangements, relocation disputes are rare. Nonetheless, the seriousness of the consequences of the decision, coupled with the fact that both parents usually have compelling arguments in support of their positions, makes relocation one of the most difficult issues that Family Courts address.

It is perhaps because of these difficulties that different jurisdictions around the world have adopted a wide variety of approaches to resolving relocation cases, and there is an increasingly global debate about the best way to resolve them. The law in most countries is subject to discussion and criticism, with commentators and practitioners looking to the approaches adopted elsewhere to see if legislators or judges in other countries have found better solutions.

Relocation Disputes: Law and Practice in England and New Zealand focuses on a comparison of relocation law and its practice in England and Wales[1] and in New Zealand. These two jurisdictions, which are in many ways very similar, have markedly different approaches to relocation disputes. The book draws on case law, literature and empirical interviews with judges, lawyers and court welfare advisers to explore and evaluate the ways in which relocation law is applied on the ground in these two countries. In doing so, the aim is both to understand more clearly the everyday reality of relocation cases as seen by practitioners, and also to learn from the experiences of those who use the law in order to comment on possible reforms.

The empirical interviews with family law professionals in England and New Zealand which underpin this work were conducted between October 2008 and June 2009. Inevitably, by now quite a lot of water has passed under the bridge. Some things have changed in both jurisdictions,[2] but informal follow-up discussions with some participants from the study suggest that the changes have been sufficiently modest that the core findings of this research remain important and valid. In particular, the New Zealand Supreme Court decision in *Kacem v Bashir* is widely thought to have re-affirmed the position which had been established by the New

[1] Throughout this book, the legal jurisdiction of England and Wales is referred to as 'England' in order to simplify the language used.

[2] For example, the important decisions of *K v K (Relocation: Shared Residence Arrangement)* [2011] EWCA Civ 793, [2012] 2 FLR 880, and *Kacem v Bashir* [2010] NZSC 112, [2010] NZFLR 884, both post-date the interviews.

Zealand Court of Appeal a decade earlier rather than instigating any change;[3] conversely, the UK Supreme Court's refusal of permission to appeal *Re F (Relocation)*[4] confirmed that, for now at least, the guidance set out by the English Court of Appeal in *Payne v Payne* remains valid.[5]

Indeed, as a result of luck more than judgement, the interviews reported in this book may have caught something of a transition moment in both jurisdictions. In England, this transition seems, for now, to have related primarily to the 'rigour' with which judges are thought to be assessing relocation applications within the guidance offered by *Payne v Payne*,[6] with the possible effect that relocation applications are now looked upon less favourably than they were a few years ago. In New Zealand, the transition has gone 'the other way', marking a shift from an initial view that the Care of Children Act 2004 militated against relocation applications, to a view now that the Act simply highlights factors to take into account with no predetermined effect on relocation law.

Both of these changes of emphasis were being picked up by some practitioners in 2008–09 and are reported in this book, but they found fuller expression in reported judgments given in the months and years after these interviews were conducted.[7] So far as possible, I have discussed those later changes and assessed the extent to which they may be reflected in the interview data gathered for this research. Where later shifts in judicial thinking appear to call findings of the research into question, I have endeavoured to make that clear and to discuss the possible consequences. At its core, though, this book is a report of the views and assessments of 44 experienced family law professionals about the state of relocation law in 2008–09, and readers will need to bear in mind that some of those practitioners may have revised their views to some extent as a result of subsequent events.

I have endeavoured to make all references to the law accurate as at 31 August 2013.

[3] *Kacem v Bashir* [2010] NZSC 112, [2010] NZFLR 884.

[4] *Re F (Relocation)* [2012] EWCA Civ 1364, [2013] 1 FLR 645; permission to appeal was refused on 4 February 2013.

[5] *Payne v Payne* [2001] EWCA Civ 166, [2001] 1 FLR 1052.

[6] ibid.

[7] In England and Wales, see in particular *Re H (Leave to Remove)* [2010] EWCA Civ 915, [2010] 2 FLR 1875; *J v S (Leave to Remove)* [2010] EWHC 2098, [2011] 1 FLR 1694; *Re W (Relocation: Removal Outside Jurisdiction)* [2011] EWCA Civ 345, [2011] 2 FLR 409; *K v K (Relocation: Shared Care Arrangement)* [2011] EWCA Civ 793, [2012] 2 FLR 880; and *Re F (Relocation)* [2012] EWCA Civ 1364, [2013] 1 FLR 645. In New Zealand, see in particular *Kacem v Bashir* [2010] NZSC 112, [2010] NZFLR 884; and *Millett v Clyde* [2012] NZFLR 351 (NZHC).

1

Locating Relocation

> The jurisdiction in [cases concerning the welfare of children] is one of great difficulty, as every judge who has had to exercise it must be aware. The main reason is that in most of these cases there is no right answer. All practicable answers are to some extent unsatisfactory and therefore to some extent wrong, and the best that can be done is to find an answer that is reasonably satisfactory.[1]

Separated parents often find themselves in dispute. For most couples, separation is a fraught and emotional experience, and the renegotiation of the former conjugal relationship into a new separated parenting relationship is challenging at the best of times. It is likely that parental relationships after separation have always been complicated, but as it becomes increasingly normal for both parents to remain actively involved in their children's lives after the separation,[2] so the myriad of complexities increases. Disagreements about aspects of the children's upbringing are common, ranging from questions about the child's main care arrangements and about what contact he or she should have with other important people, to questions about schooling, religious upbringing or even the child's name.[3]

Most of the time parents manage to resolve these disputes themselves, muddling through and working things out as they go. However, some questions are too important and the consequences too far-reaching for agreement to be possible, and the family finds itself turning to lawyers and to courts for help. Never is this truer than in cases where one parent proposes to move to a new geographic location and take the child to live there with them. The law in many countries has come to call these cases *relocation disputes*,[4] and judges around the world note that '[r]elocation disputes are widely regarded as one of the most controversial and difficult issues for the Family Court'.[5]

[1] *G v G (Minors: Custody Appeal)* [1985] FLR 894 (UKHL) 897–98.

[2] See generally P Amato, C Meyers and R Emery, 'Changes in Nonresident Father-Child Contact from 1976 to 2002' (2009) 58 *Family Relations* 41; P Parkinson, *Family Law and the Indissolubility of Parenthood* (Cambridge, Cambridge University Press, 2011).

[3] See generally R Probert, S Gilmore and J Herring (eds), *Responsible Parents and Parental Responsibility* (Oxford, Hart Publishing, 2009).

[4] The terms 'leave to remove cases', 'mobility cases' and 'move-away cases' are also used.

[5] *Bashir v Kacem* [2010] NZCA 96, [2010] NZFLR 865 [1], quoting P Tapp and N Taylor, 'Relocation: A Problem Or A Dilemma?' [2008] *New Zealand Family Law Journal* 94, 94; see similarly *Payne v Payne* [2001] EWCA Civ 166, [2001] 1 FLR 1052; *Tropea v Tropea* 665 NE 2d 145 (1996) (Court of Appeals, New York, USA); *Ford v Ford* Case No 52/05 (Supreme Court of Appeal, South Africa); *U v U* (2002) 191 ALR 289 (High Court, Australia).

Relocation is a topic of increasing global debate,[6] and legal approaches to relocation disputes vary significantly between countries, despite general agreement that the welfare and best interests of the children concerned should be the guiding principle. This book offers an empirically based examination of the ways in which the courts in England[7] and New Zealand address relocation disputes, these countries representing two of the major legal approaches found in the common law world. The book draws on reported case law, literature, and interviews with legal practitioners in the two countries to examine the reality of relocation law in practice. The analysis raises questions about the approaches currently taken in both countries.

Introduction

The first complication with relocation law is in deciding what constitutes a relocation case, with few universally accepted definitions available.[8] Defining a relocation dispute is difficult, because the key issue is the effect which the move would have on the child, rather than the geographic distance involved. One proposal, which may usefully capture the point, is to say that relocation is any move involving 'a shift of the child's residence which affects the child's relationship with his or her parents, both practically and emotionally, and/or gives rise to other changes which raise guardianship issues'.[9] With that definition in mind, it is unsurprising that relocation disputes vary considerably, encompassing moves between different suburbs of the same city, between different parts of the same country, and between different countries, depending on the facts of the case.

In legal terms, relocation disputes form part of private child law, which governs disputes between family members about the upbringing of children. In most Western and common law countries, the guiding principle for courts adjudicating private child law disputes is that the welfare and best interests of the child concerned should be the paramount consideration.[10] In the leading interpretation of this provision, Lord MacDermott held that once all relevant factors had been con-

[6] For an overview of recent international discussions, see R George, 'The International Relocation Debate' [2012] *Journal of Social Welfare and Family Law* 141.

[7] Throughout this book, the term 'England' is used as shorthand to signify the legal jurisdiction of England and Wales.

[8] Some commentators suggest that there is no need to be overly precise when defining a relocation case, since there can be a rather blurred line between relocation cases and other parenting disputes: see, eg, P Parkinson, J Cashmore and J Single, 'The Need for Reality Testing in Relocation Cases' (2010) 44 *Family Law Quarterly* 1, 6.

[9] *AJL v BSO* [2010] NZFLR 476 (NZFC) [18].

[10] See, eg, Children Act 1989 (England), s 1; Care of Children Act 2004 (New Zealand), s 4; Family Law Act 1975 (Cth) (Australia), s 60CA; Divorce Act 1985 (Canada), s 16; Code civil, Art 373-2 (France); Bürgerliches Gesetzbuch, § 1627 (Germany). International documents contain similar provisions: see, eg, United Nations Convention on the Rights of the Child 1989, Art 3; Washington Declaration on International Family Relocation 2010 [3].

sidered, 'the course to be followed will be that which is most in the interest of the child's welfare'.[11] Put simply, factors 'are only relevant in a case involving the upbringing of children in so far as they affect the welfare of the child'.[12]

It is difficult to assess how many families a year are affected by relocation law. Looking at England, records are not specific enough to know how many litigated cases there are each year,[13] though a number in the low hundreds seems likely in terms of judicially determined cases.[14] Even if we knew that information, it would tell us nothing about the number of cases which are not adjudicated in court, because they settle either without any litigation or before a final determination is made by a judge – though there is reason to think that the number of cases where this is true, especially for international relocation, is proportionately fairly low. For international relocation cases, practitioners in this study reported that most cases which reached the stage of obtaining legal advice would reach a final hearing,[15] and subsequent research suggests that the figure may be around 85 per cent.[16]

In terms of internal relocation, on the other hand, most English practitioners in this study reported seeing few such cases, and thought that the issue which reached

[11] *J v C* [1970] AC 668 (UKHL) 711.

[12] J Herring, 'The Welfare Principle and the Rights of Parents' in A Bainham, S Day Sclater and M Richards (eds), *What Is A Parent? A Socio-Legal Analysis* (Oxford, Hart Publishing, 1999) 92.

[13] The number is impossible to ascertain from official data, because those records do not distinguish between categories of private law cases in such a way as to identify relocation disputes. While MoJ data from 2011 onwards include records of children whom the court permitted to be removed from the jurisdiction, the information includes both permanent international relocation and temporary removals (for holidays, usually); more importantly, the data record only those children involved in relocation cases that were allowed and therefore miss the crucial group of children who were involved in applications that were refused.

[14] As part of a subsequent research project (hereafter, the 2012 Study), I collected first instance orders and judgments from all trial courts in England and Wales for a year, resulting in 96 international relocation cases: see R George, 'Relocation Disputes in England and Wales: First Findings from the 2012 Study' (Oxford Legal Studies Research Paper, 2013), online at http://ssrn.com/abstract=2306097. Inevitably, this research will not have gathered all such cases; but even pessimistically assuming a 25% collection rate, that would give an estimated total of 384 international relocation cases which were judicially determined in 2012, and something in the range 200–250 litigated cases a year seems more likely. (That says nothing about cases not judicially determined.) By contrast, a number of sources around 2007 cited the family solicitors' organisation Resolution as saying that '[t]he number of contested court applications for "leave to remove" children has risen to more than 1,200 a year from only a few cases in the 1990s': L Rogers, 'Fathers to Fight Removal of Children Overseas', *The Telegraph* (11 Feb 2007); the same figure is quoted in M Freeman, *Relocation: The Reunite Research* (London, Reunite, 2009) 3. When asked about how this number was reached, Resolution officials reported that the work had been done some years earlier and that they now had no information about its provenance.

[15] See below, p 26.

[16] As part of the 2012 study, family lawyers were given questionnaires about relocation cases. Of the 63 completed international cases from 2012 about which the questionnaires gave information, 52 (85%) were resolved by judicial determination: R George, 'Relocation Disputes in England and Wales: First Findings from the 2012 Study (Oxford Legal Studies Research Paper, 2013), online at http://ssrn.com/abstract=2306097, [3.29]. By comparison, it is estimated that a little over 12% of separating families obtain final orders from a judge over issues to do with children: J Hunt with C Roberts, *Child Contact With Non-Resident Parents* (Oxford, University of Oxford, 2004). Similarly, in an Australian empirical study, 59% of relocation cases were resolved by judicial determination, whereas looking at family law disputes in Australia overall only 13% reach a final hearing and only 6% are eventually resolved by judicial determination: P Parkinson, J Cashmore and J Single, 'The Need for Reality Testing in Relocation Cases' (2010) 44 *Family Law Quarterly* 1, 14.

them when there was a move within the country was about contact arrangements rather than about the move itself.[17] However, subsequent research suggests that this view may be, in part at least, a result of the sample of participants. Because of the way in which most participants were recruited,[18] relatively experienced lawyers and relatively senior judges (High Court Judges and Designated Family Judges in the County Courts) were recruited to the study, and in terms of studying international relocation this approach worked well. But since internal relocation cases are often dealt with by more junior lawyers and, importantly, by District Judges in the County Courts, it may be that participants in this study simply did not see many of those cases which do exist. In later research, questionnaire responses from 115 family lawyers who had been involved with a relocation case in 2012 were split at a rate of 85 international cases to 30 domestic ones.[19]

That position may be compared with New Zealand. Although records there are also unable to give much indication of the total number of cases each year, New Zealand participants estimated that between a half and two thirds of the relocation cases that they dealt with were internal moves within New Zealand.[20] It may be that there is a difference between the two countries in terms of the frequency of internal versus international cases; but another possibility is that New Zealand's single Family Court, with no hierarchy of judges or cases within it,[21] means that a 'typical' Family Court judge sees the full range of relocation cases, whereas English judges tend to see either internal or international ones, but not many see both.

Regardless of these variations, it seems to be generally accepted that the frequency of disputes over post-separation migration is increasing, and is likely to continue increasing as time goes on.[22] One reason for this is increasing mobility amongst the population in general. Not only do people move more frequently within countries,[23] but over recent years 'the phenomenon of what may be called "cross-border families" and the frequency of consequential litigation has undoubtedly dramatically increased'.[24] Another reason relates to changing family practices after parental separation, with an increasing trend in Western countries for both parents to have a hands-on role in children's upbringing.[25] We have also

[17] See below, pp 91–92.

[18] See Methodological Appendix.

[19] R George, 'Relocation Disputes in England and Wales: First Findings from the 2012 Study' (Oxford Legal Studies Research Paper, 2013), online at http://ssrn.com/abstract=2306097.

[20] See below, p 117.

[21] For more about the court structures in New Zealand and in England, see below, pp 26–28.

[22] For similar analysis focused on Australia and the United States, see P Parkinson, J Cashmore and J Single, 'The Need for Reality Testing in Relocation Cases' (2010) 44 *Family Law Quarterly* 1, 2–4.

[23] See, eg, T Champion, 'Population Movement within the UK' in *Focus on People and Migration* (London, Office for National Statistics, 2005).

[24] N Lowe, 'Where in the World Is International Family Law Going Next?' in G Douglas and N Lowe (eds), *The Continuing Evolution of Family Law* (Bristol, Jordan Publishing, 2009) 261.

[25] This trend is seen to differing extents in different countries: see, eg, R Collier and S Sheldon, *Fragmenting Fatherhood: A Socio-Legal Study* (Oxford, Hart Publishing, 2008); P Amato, C Meyers and R Emery, 'Changes in Nonresident Father-Child Contact from 1976 to 2002' (2009) 58 *Family Relations* 41; P Parkinson, *Family Law and the Indissolubility of Parenthood* (Cambridge, Cambridge University Press, 2011).

seen increasing focus by courts[26] and legislatures[27] around the world on the importance of both parents remaining involved in their children's lives after separation. These trends fit with international provisions relating to children having the right to maintain direct personal relations with both parents (whether the parents live in the same country as one another or not) save in exceptional circumstances.[28]

These changes combine to mean that, as migration becomes more frequent, so too non-moving parents have more incentive to litigate in opposition to proposed moves, and more powerful arguments that their children's welfare might be better served by their remaining where they are than by moving. It may be in part because of these factors that relocation is becoming a politicised issue.[29] In England,[30] relocation is increasingly a topic of concern for fathers' groups and others.[31] A report commissioned by the child abduction charity Reunite noted the increasing number of relocation cases reported to its helpline,[32] which led David Maclean MP to put forward an Early Day Motion on relocation in December 2009.[33] The online organisation The Custody Minefield then began a campaign aimed at changing the approach to relocation disputes taken by the English

[26] See, eg, *Re A (Joint Residence: Parental Responsibility)* [2008] EWCA Civ 867, [2008] 2 FLR 1593; *H v C* [2009] NZFLR 414 (NZHC); *MRR v GR* [2010] HCA 4, (2010) 263 ALR 368 (High Court, Australia).

[27] See, eg, Care of Children Act 2004 (New Zealand); Children and Adoption Act 2006 (England); Family Law Amendment (Shared Parental Responsibility) Act 2006 (Cth) (Australia). The Children and Families Bill 2013 (England) was before Parliament when this book went to press.

[28] United Nations Convention on the Rights of the Child 1989, Arts 9(3) and 10(2).

[29] For newspaper coverage, see, eg, L Rogers, 'Fathers to Fight Removal of Children Overseas', *The Telegraph* (11 February 2007); C Overington, 'Divorced Mums Forced to Stay Put', *The Australian* (1 June 2009); J Bingham, '"Barbaric" Family Courts Behind "State Sponsored Kidnap" – Bob Geldof', *The Telegraph* (7 December 2009); S Doughty, 'Bob Geldof Accuses "Barbaric" Family Courts of "Kidnapping Children from Their Fathers"', *The Daily Mail* (8 December 2009); L Salkeld, 'Let Them Use Skype! Judge Sends Children to Australia with Mother and Tells Father to Talk to Them Via the Internet', *The Daily Mail* (31 March 2011); A Hill, 'Mothers Lose Out as Expat Parents Fight for Custody in Foreign Courts', *The Guardian* (20 October 2012).

[30] Again, the trend is seen to differing extents in different countries.

[31] See, eg, J Junk, 'Your Number's Up, Payne v Payne: Time for Change?' (2010) online at http://www.mckenziefriend.com/2010/04/27/your-numbers-up-payne-v-payne-time-for-change (last accessed 27 August 2013).

[32] M Freeman, *Relocation: The Reunite Research* (London, Reunite, 2009) 1. There were 122 cases reported to Reunite in 2008.

[33] Early Day Motion 373: 'That this House believes that a child's relationship with its parents requires greater legislative protection with regard to the Family Court's current application of precedent in international and national relocation cases; further believes that the Family Courts of England and Wales' position on the importance of the father/child relationship does not reflect the current authoritative research on the importance of father involvement in educational and psychological development in relocation cases; further believes that the courts in practice place too great an emphasis on the unsubstantiated emotional risk to the child from the mother's possible distress and disappointment if not allowed to relocate; considers that this emphasis over-rides all other considerations including the needs and rights of the child; and calls on the Government to respond positively to the research report by the charity Reunite, entitled Relocation, funded by the Ministry of Justice and published in July 2009': see http://www.parliament.uk/edm/2009-10/373 (last accessed 11 February 2013).

courts,[34] which was supported by Sir Bob Geldof and the fathers' group Families Need Fathers.

It is not surprising, therefore, that relocation has become an increasingly important issue for academics, lawyers and judges as the law in different countries responds to these disputes. The last few years have seen an increase in the academic attention given to relocation in many countries, and previous studies in England now provide excellent insight into the approach taken to relocation by the higher courts.[35] However, this research is unable to examine the day-to-day application of this legal approach in the trial courts because the main source used tends to be reported cases which, in turn, almost inevitably come from the High Court or the appeal courts.[36] Reliance on reported cases has two consequences. First, cases are filed in the High Court because they are complex, and are appealed either because there is something very unusual about their facts, or because it is arguable that the judge made an appealable error.[37] Second, there is the issue of reporting cases: cases are reported because of their significance to the law or its practice,[38] meaning that it is difficult to assess the extent to which such cases reflect the experience of everyday litigation.

Relocation Disputes: Law and Practice in England and New Zealand starts to address this information gap by examining relocation disputes from the perspective of legal practitioners who work with these cases, analysing relocation from a comparative socio-legal perspective. The book draws on interviews with Family Court judges, barristers, solicitors and court welfare advisers in England and New Zealand to examine the everyday practice of relocation law in these two countries.

The Context of Relocation Disputes

One of the reasons that relocation disputes are thought to be amongst the most difficult cases that Family Courts face, and amongst the most difficult issues that family law as a whole faces, is their contextual complexity.[39] Indeed, discussing 'relocation cases' as a group risks overlooking their heterogeneity. For example,

[34] See www.relocationcampaign.co.uk (last accessed 27 August 2013).

[35] Below, pp 15–17.

[36] The Family Law Reports provide 'case reports of . . . Family Division, Court of Appeal, Supreme Court and European Court of Justice case[s]', while the Family Court Reports cover 'cases in the High Court, Court of Appeal and Supreme Court'.

[37] CPR, r 52.3(6).

[38] The Family Law Reports cover 'every important . . . case', while the Family Court Reports cover 'cases . . . which are of interest to family law practitioners'.

[39] See, eg, N Taylor, M Gollop and M Henaghan, *Relocation Following Parental Separation: The Welfare and Best Interests of Children* (Dunedin, University of Otago, 2010); R Kaspiew, J Behrens and B Smyth, 'Relocation Disputes in Separated Families Prior to the 2006 Reforms: An Empirical Study' (2011) 86 *Family Matters* 72.

relocation disputes arise for many reasons,[40] at different stages in the family's post-separation lives,[41] with different family members involved,[42] and with different aged children.

Consider the difference between cases involving a 2-year-old and a 12-year-old, for example. Sometimes younger children are said to be more 'portable' because their welfare is dependent more on their main carer than on their geographic location.[43] The effect of refusing leave on the applicant parent (whatever that effect may be) may also last longer since the child's minority still has many years to run. On the other hand, relocation over any significant distance risks the child losing all meaningful links with the other parent; the younger child is less well able to maintain relationships through indirect means (Skype, telephone, etc); and travel for contact will be more difficult while the child is young. With the older child, on the other hand, the child's own views will start to take on more significance, though knowing what weight to give views about a potential relocation (when the consequences of the decision either way are hard to conceptualise) is difficult. Maintaining a strong relationship with the other parent after relocation may be easier than with the younger child; on the other hand, the older child will increasingly be entering a stage of life where spending time with friends and other activities separate from either parent becomes important,[44] meaning that in practice contact may be less easy to manage.

Separate from these aspects, relocation can be seen as a socio-political issue. One aspect of this discussion is the gender dimension of relocation cases.[45] One side of this gender argument is explained well by Juliet Behrens, whose feminist

[40] Many applicants have a range of reasons for seeking relocation. For example, of 38 applicant mothers interviewed in an Australian study, nine reported a single reason for seeking relocation, 17 reported two reasons and 12 reported three: P Parkinson, J Cashmore and J Single, 'Mothers Wishing to Relocate with Children: Actual and Perceived Reasons' (2011) 27 *Canadian Family Law Journal* 11.

[41] Sometimes cases arise as part of the parents' separation; other times they come about years later.

[42] The 'typical' case involves the two parents of the child involved, with the mother applying to relocate and the father opposing the move, but there are many variations: grandparents and other family members are often involved in a supporting role, but can also be applicants or respondents depending on the existing care arrangements for the child.

[43] A New Zealand barrister in this research, discussing the age that children tend to be in relocation disputes, summarised it as 'what I suppose you would call the more portable child, whatever that is' (NB7). Some children interviewed for a New Zealand research project thought that moving was easier for younger children: N Taylor, M Gollop and M Henaghan, *Relocation Following Parental Separation: The Welfare and Best Interests of Children* (Dunedin, University of Otago, 2010) 112.

[44] On the importance of friends for older children in relocation cases, see N Taylor, M Gollop and M Henaghan, *Relocation Following Parental Separation: The Welfare and Best Interests of Children* (University of Otago, Dunedin, 2010) 108–10.

[45] See, eg, S Boyd, 'Gendering the Best Interests Principle: Custody, Access and Relocation in a Mobile Society' in H Niman and G Sadvari (eds), *Family Law: 'The Best Interests of the Child'* (Ottawa, Law Society of Upper Canada, 2000); F Mackenzie, *Uneasy Trends in Relocation Law* (unpublished LLM Thesis, Victoria University of Wellington, 2009) 55–60; S Boyd, 'Autonomy for Mothers? Relational Theory and Parenting Apart' (2010) 18 *Feminist Legal Studies* 137; L Young, 'Resolving Relocation Disputes: The "Interventionist" Approach in Australia' [2011] *Child and Family Law Quarterly* 203; N Taylor and M Freeman, 'The Gender Agenda and Relocation Disputes' [2012] *International Family Law* 184.

commentaries on relocation law are broadly supportive of relocation applications being allowed. Behrens says that relocation has potentially huge gender implications, and that 'restrictions on residence parents argued for by contact parents are usually restrictions on women argued for by men'.[46] Moreover, 'restrictions on relocation operate unfairly against the person who is likely to be providing the majority of care to a child. In doing so, they compound the social and economic disadvantages that accompany the provision of care, particularly where the caregiver is a woman'.[47]

Behrens suggests that relocation law in Australia implies that 'residence parents (usually mothers) should be expected to sacrifice their interests to what a judge perceives as being in their child's best interests, but contact parents (typically fathers) should not'.[48] Of course, if a non-resident parent wishes to maintain a strong relationship with his child, his freedom to relocate as he wishes is also limited.[49] However, the position is not entirely equal, because a parent who proposes to move without taking the child with him cannot be compelled to stay if he chooses to leave, whereas as a question of fact (though not of law) a parent seeking to move with the child can usually be so compelled.[50]

On the other side of the gender debate, when relocation law is (or is perceived to be) broadly in favour of relocation applications, this can be seen as legal or judicial bias against fathers,[51] as seen in the English context.[52] The vast majority of relocation applications in all jurisdictions are brought by mothers, so outcomes which favour relocation can be interpreted by some commentators as diminishing the importance of fathers compared with mothers. Fathers' groups point out that relocation often has the effect of depriving the child of any meaningful relationship with his or her father, and claim that the courts often give inadequate

[46] J Behrens, 'A Feminist Perspective on *B and B* (The Family Court and Mobility)' (1997) 2 *Sister in Law* 65, 66.

[47] J Behrens, '*U v U*: The High Court on Relocation' [2003] *Melbourne University Law Rev* 572, 584.

[48] ibid 585.

[49] P Parkinson, 'Freedom of Movement in an Era of Shared Parenting: The Differences in Judicial Approaches to Relocation' (2008) 36 *Federal Law Review* 145.

[50] See further L Young, 'Resolving Relocation Disputes: The "Interventionist" Approach in Australia' [2011] *Child and Family Law Quarterly* 203, 220–22. Most jurisdictions consider that contact orders cannot be made or enforced against an unwilling parent, and the UK Government specifically rejected the idea of introducing a power to require a parent to have contact against his will: see *Re L, V, M and H (Contact: Domestic Violence)* [2000] 2 FLR 334 (EWCA) 364; N Lowe and G Douglas, *Bromley's Family Law*, 10th edn (Oxford, Oxford University Press, 2007) 521 and 572–73. The Family Court of Australia once said that it had power under Australia's Family Law Act 1975 (Cth), s 114(3), 'to enjoin a parent from relocating or to relocate, provided that that injunction is no more than is necessary to secure the best interests of a child': *Sampson v Hartnett* (No 10) [2007] Fam CA 1365 (Full Court of the Family Court, Australia) [58]; for comment, see R Chisholm, 'To What Extent Can the Court Make Orders that Inhibit a Parent's Right to Relocate?' [2008] *Australian Journal of Family Law* 154.

[51] See also the views of parents reported in M Freeman, *Relocation: The Reunite Research* (London, Reunite, 2009), discussed below, pp 21–22.

[52] For a summary of a seminar discussing this issue in November 2010, see 'House of Commons Seminar Calls for Reform of Poel and Payne', online at http://www.familylaw.co.uk/articles/FNF10112010-458 (last accessed 27 August 2013).

attention to this factor compared with the effect of the relocation decision on the applicant.[53]

This sense that mothers are given an importance which is denied to fathers is, perhaps, reinforced by the occasional reported case of a primary carer father whose application to relocate appears to have been treated less favourably than a mother in an equivalent position would have been. *Re H (Children) (Residence Order: Condition)* is a particularly vivid example,[54] where the primary carer father was refused permission to relocate to Northern Ireland. Despite the Court of Appeal's insistence that a male primary carer was in an equal position to a female one, there was a notable focus on evidence that 'the effect [of relocation] on the [non-moving] mother would be devastating . . . [T]o devastate the mother would be to indirectly devastate the children'.[55] It is hard to think of an equivalent statement in a case involving an applicant mother, where the effect of relocation on the respondent father was thought so significant to the welfare analysis.[56]

The more recent decision in *Re F (Relocation)* might raise similar concerns.[57] Put shortly, the parents had moved to the UK from Spain in 2009. When the relationship broke down in 2011, the mother returned to Spain, leaving the child (then aged 6) with the father. When, nearly a year later, the mother instigated relocation proceedings, the trial judge found that the father was, by then, the primary carer. Nonetheless, when assessing the mother's application, the judge proceeded by following judicial guidance from *Payne v Payne*[58] which is premised on the applicant being the primary carer, and granted her leave to relocate with the child. The father appealed on the basis that, since he had been recognised as the child's primary carer, the *Payne* guidance ought not to have been applied; the case was more akin to an application for a change of residence, which should normally be considered only if the care provided by an existing primary carer is inadequate.[59] The Court of Appeal dismissed the father's appeal, and the Supreme Court subsequently refused his application to appeal further. Again, some may

53 See, eg, M Robinson, *Relocation: The Case for Reform* (The Custody Minefield/Families Need Fathers, 2010) online at http://www.thecustodyminefield.com/Reports/FamilyLaw-Relocation_The_Need_For_Reform.pdf (last accessed 27 August 2013).

54 *Re H (Children) (Residence Order: Condition)* [2001] EWCA Civ 1338, [2001] 2 FLR 1277.

55 ibid [25]–[26].

56 A rare exception might be May LJ's short concurring judgment in *Re B (Leave to Remove: Impact of Refusal)* [2004] EWCA Civ 956, [2005] 2 FLR 239 [25]: 'I have no doubt but that the mother would be devastated if she cannot [relocate] with the children and that this would be likely to be detrimental to the welfare of the children themselves. Equally, I have no doubt but that the father would be devastated if the children do [relocate]. That, too, may have a detrimental effect on the children's welfare and the necessary radical change in their contact with him is an obvious detriment to their welfare which may well not be alleviated by alternative arrangements.' Nonetheless, the trial judge's decision to refuse the mother's relocation application was overturned and, at the subsequent re-trial, the mother was given permission to relocate: see M Hayes, 'Relocation Cases: Is the Court of Appeal Applying the Correct Principles?' [2006] *Child and Family Law Quarterly* 351, fn 68.

57 *Re F (Relocation)* [2012] EWCA Civ 1364, [2013] 1 FLR 645.

58 *Payne v Payne* [2001] EWCA Civ 166, [2001] 1 FLR 1052; the guidance is set out below, p 39.

59 In argument, the father cited *Re B (A Child)* [2009] UKSC 5, [2010] 1 FLR 551 in support of this position. The trial judge said that the father was providing good care for his son.

look at this case and think that matters would not have proceeded in the same way had a father been applying to remove the child from the established primary care of a mother in order to take him or her to another country.[60]

Alongside the factual variation of relocation cases and the socio-political background, further complexity is introduced to the discussion by the interconnection between relocation and other parenting issues. The way in which the law approaches relocation cases in general, and the way in which any particular relocation case is approached by the court, will depend on background questions about the child's care arrangements before the relocation question arises. The changing approach to post-separation parenting in recent decades – the rise of shared parental responsibility, the increasingly hands-on role that both parents retain in their children's upbringing after separation – creates challenges for relocation law. Different countries have responded to these challenges in different ways, and the next section of this chapter provides a brief overview of some of the major legal approaches to relocation.

Legal Approaches to Relocation Disputes

Most jurisdictions address relocation cases using the same underlying objective – to promote the welfare and best interests of the child concerned – but in the relocation context, different countries currently vary in their interpretation of that principle. There are also national and international human rights documents setting out various rights which are directly relevant to the determination of relocation cases, including most importantly the right to respect for private and family life,[61] the right of a child to maintain direct contact with both parents regardless of whether they live in the same country or not,[62] and the right to free movement within countries and internationally.[63] The aim of this section is to give an understanding of the different ways in which relocation disputes are approached by different legal systems, and it is not intended to provide a complete picture on what is always a complex issue.

While it is difficult to divide jurisdictions precisely, there are said to be three broad categories:[64] pro-relocation, anti-relocation, and neutral, with both common

[60] See further R George, 'International Relocation, Care Arrangements, and Case Taxonomy' [2012] *Family Law* 1478.

[61] See, eg, European Convention on Human Rights and Fundamental Freedoms 1950, Art 8; Human Rights Act 1998 (England).

[62] See, eg, United Nations Convention on the Rights of the Child 1989, Arts 9(3) and 10(2).

[63] See, eg, Bill of Rights Act 1993 (New Zealand), s 18; Treaty on the Functioning of the European Union 2010, Arts 21 and 45.

[64] T Foley, 'International Child Relocation: Varying Approaches Among Member States to the 1980 Hague Convention on Child Abduction' (London, Court of Appeal, 2006) 33; J Morley and J Maguire, 'International Relocation of Children: American and English Approaches' [2006] *International Family Law* 77. For an overview of the law in England, France and Germany, see H Baker, J Hirsch and N Sauvage, 'International Family Relocation from an English, French and German Perspective' [2012] *International Family Law* 97.

law and civil law jurisdictions falling into each category. Fuller discussion of two of these legal approaches – the law of England, which is said to be pro-relocation and the law of New Zealand, which is said to be anti-relocation – are set out in full in Chapter 2. For now, a general overview of the three core approaches will suffice.

Jurisdictions which are described as pro-relocation typically give especial consideration to the link between a primary carer's well-being and the welfare of the child. They tend to look favourably on well-planned and bona fide applications to relocate, because they consider that the effect on a primary carer of restricting his or (more commonly) her life choices will impact on the child more adversely in the long term than the reduction of contact with the other parent and the other upheavals of relocation. Examples of this approach are said to be England, Ireland, France, Germany, South Africa and some US States, including New Jersey, Washington and Minnesota.

At the other end of the spectrum, anti-relocation jurisdictions tend to focus their enquiries on the importance to children's welfare of having a strong relationship with both parents, viewing it as a matter of concern that relocation proposals often involve the risk of significant disruption to the child's relationship with the non-moving parent. These jurisdictions tend to be sceptical of relocation applications in cases where the non-moving parent has (or is seeking) a strong relationship with his or her child, because this relationship is thought to be more important to the child's overall welfare than the well-being of a primary carer (if there is one such person). Jurisdictions in this category might include Australia, New Zealand, Sweden, Norway and some US States, such as Pennsylvania, Alabama, Virginia and Connecticut.

Between these two are the so-called neutral countries. Neutral countries have no starting point and assess each case on its individual facts to try to work out whether relocation will be in each particular child's interests or not. Countries typically said to be neutral about relocation include Canada, Belgium and US States such as New York, California and Florida. The difficulty with this approach is that it tends to make the law unpredictable, and prone to variation between different judges or different regions.[65]

It is important to note, as a caveat to this discussion, that one significant complication of trying to categorise approaches in this way is that many of the countries which are classified as pro- or anti-relocation would likely describe themselves in the same way as the neutral countries – that they take into account all factors relevant to the child's welfare in deciding the best outcome. While some jurisdictions have explicit pro- or anti-relocation approaches, usually in statutory form,[66]

[65] See, eg, criticism of the Canadian law in R Thompson, 'Ten Years After Gordon: No Law, Nowhere' (2007) 35 *Reports of Family Law* (6th) 307.

[66] See, eg, the pro-relocation presumption in the Revised Code of Washington, § 26.09.520 ('There is a rebuttable presumption that the intended relocation of the child will be permitted') and the anti-relocation presumption in the General Statutes of Connecticut, § 46b–56d ('the relocating parent shall bear the burden of proving, by a preponderance of the evidence, that (1) the relocation is for a legitimate purpose, (2) the proposed location is reasonable in light of such purpose, and (3) the relocation is in the best interests of the child').

in many cases it is only when those approaches are applied to actual cases that the potential differences become apparent. The categorisation is therefore rather 'rough and ready', based mainly on impression.

Having thus seen, in summary, the ways in which the law might address relocation disputes, we are now in a position to turn to previous literature and to see what is known about relocation already. Because this study is focused on the approaches to relocation in England and New Zealand, the literature review will primarily cover existing research in those jurisdictions. However, since relocation disputes have significant commonalities across the common law world, relevant literature from other jurisdictions is also discussed, especially that in Australia, with which New Zealand has strong ties.

Relocation Literature

As we have seen, relocation disputes are part of the law's approach to private law child disputes, governed by the welfare principle – that is, that the child's welfare and best interests are the court's paramount consideration. Within this field, there are three particular areas of study with which relocation overlaps. First, there is a sizeable literature on the welfare principle itself. Some of that literature relates specifically to relocation, and some relocation literature links to the welfare principle more broadly.

Second, relocation disputes are closely connected to the general area of private child law, focused on issues of residence and contact (known in some jurisdictions as custody and access). Australian research suggests that relocation is often 'part of an on-going story' of litigation, preceded by high levels of conflict over various aspects of parenting.[67] In addition, many relocation applications are met with a cross-application for residence by the non-moving parent,[68] and the reason for most opposition to relocation is the damage to the child's relationship with the non-moving parent which relocation would produce.[69] Relocation disputes therefore sit as part of a spectrum of private law disputes about children's upbringing, interwoven with residence, contact and other family law issues (most notably domestic violence).

Finally, there is significant overlap between international relocation and international parental child abduction,[70] both of which involve the cross-border movement of children with one parent. The factual connection between these classes of case is obvious: both involve the movement of a child across an inter-

[67] R Kaspiew, J Behrens and B Smyth, 'Relocation Disputes in Separated Families Prior to the 2006 Reforms: An Empirical Study' (2011) 86 *Family Matters* 72.

[68] *Payne v Payne* [2001] EWCA Civ 166, [2001] 1 FLR 1052 [42].

[69] ibid [27].

[70] See generally N Lowe, M Everall and M Nicholls, *International Movement of Children: Law Practice and Procedure* (Bristol, Jordan Publishing, 2004) chs 12–19.

national border with one of his or her parents. However, studies relating to abduction are of only tangential relevance to relocation because, despite the factual similarity between the two issues, there are important distinctions. Relocation cases are requests for permission to relocate *prior to the event* in the absence of consent from the other parent, whereas abduction cases are requests for a court to return a child where removal has *already taken place* without consent. This difference is crucial in legal terms: relocation cases are part of the domestic law of the country in which the child was originally habitually resident, whereas abduction cases are governed either by international law[71] or the national law of the country to which the child has been taken,[72] depending on whether the destination country is a signatory of a relevant international Treaty or not.[73] This legal difference distinguishes abduction from relocation as a topic of legal enquiry and therefore, although we will see occasional reference to abduction throughout this book, it is not a main area of focus.[74]

Alongside these adjacent areas of scholarship, there is a growing literature on relocation itself. This literature has primarily been doctrinal in its approach, focusing in particular on reported appeal cases. However, there is a developing body of work, especially in New Zealand and Australia, involving empirical research specifically focused on relocation.[75] This section starts with a brief discussion about the role of empirical research in general, and then looks at some of the key research that has been done already on relocation disputes, starting with doctrinal analysis and then looking at empirical studies.

The Role of Research on Relocation

As a preliminary point, while lawyers have a strong understanding of the value of doctrinal work, most lawyers (both practitioners and academic lawyers) are not trained in empirical research and therefore sometimes struggle to understand both its value and its limitations. It may therefore be valuable to consider briefly the purpose of empirical research and the potential uses that it may have.[76]

[71] ibid.

[72] ibid 457–62.

[73] The main Treaty is the Hague Convention on the Civil Aspects of International Child Abduction 1980, which has 82 contracting states.

[74] The connection between these two issues in practice is apparent from the number of relocation cases which have previously involved abduction proceedings. In other words, the applicant parent initially took or retained the child in the foreign country without obtaining the requisite permission and subsequently, having been returned to the original country, applied for permission to move as a relocation case.

[75] There are also debates, especially in the US, about the utility of general psychological and sociological research to relocation scholarship. For a useful summary, see B Horsfall and R Kaspiew, 'Relocation in Separated and Non-Separated Families: Equivocal Evidence from the Social Science Literature' [2010] *Australian Journal of Family Law* 34.

[76] Some of this discussion appeared previously in R George, 'Reviewing Relocation?' [2012] *Child and Family Law Quarterly* 110, 126–29. See also M Freeman and N Taylor, 'The Reign of Payne' (2011) 2 *Journal of Family Law and Practice* 20, 24–25; Z Rathus, 'A Call for Clarity in the Use of Social Science Research in Family Law Decision-Making' [2012] *Australian Journal of Family Law* 81.

Put simply, empirical legal research tends to ask either about what is happening in the day-to-day practice of the law itself, or what effects the law is having on the world more broadly. In the relocation context, those two categories are realised as, on the one hand, research into the legal process of resolving relocation cases[77] and, on the other, research into the effects of relocation law on parents and children.[78] Both categories of research have similar potential: they can identify strengths and weaknesses of the existing law or its practice; they can highlight risks and trends; they can point to relevant considerations when making decisions or evaluating the law; and they can demonstrate, in general, that particular outcomes might be associated with particular combinations of those risks and considerations. All of this is highly valuable, both in terms of understanding what is now happening and in terms of informing debates about the development of the law.[79]

Despite this value, though, empirical research is not a panacea for all the problems faced by lawyers and judges. In particular, no research study will be able to answer the question which is before the judge in a particular case, namely, what is the best thing to do *in this case*. As I explained previously:

> If a study were to show, for example, that 90% of children are harmed by doing X, that does not mean that X should never be ordered by a judge – the case before the judge might be one of the 10%. The judge can use the research as a basis for cross-checking the decision to order X; but if the facts of the case support X, the research is not a reason to refuse it. Cases are inevitably fact-sensitive and call for a careful determination by decision-makers who are aware of and informed by research evidence, but not constrained or unduly restricted by it.[80]

The aim of research into relocation cases is to tell us more about the people involved, about what kinds of considerations arise in their disputes, about how the law 'deals with' those disputes (both in terms of court outcomes and also, importantly, in terms of legal advice), and about the consequences once the law's involvement ends. With these points in mind, we can now consider the work which has been done on relocation already.

Doctrinal Research

Doctrinal analyses tend to be specific to one jurisdiction, and we start with the literature in England. Relocation is not a new phenomenon in English law,[81] but

[77] The research reported in this book is one example; see also work by Fiona Mackenzie, discussed below, p 21.

[78] See, eg, the work by Nicola Taylor, Megan Gollop and Mark Henaghan, discussed below, pp 22–23.

[79] Note that 'informing debates about the development of the law' is different from determining whether or how the law should be changed.

[80] R George, 'Reviewing Relocation?' [2012] *Child and Family Law Quarterly* 110, 128.

[81] See below, p 31.

as a subject of academic enquiry it is a relative newcomer.[82] The first publications specifically on relocation, other than brief case commentaries,[83] were two short articles in the 1980s.[84] There followed sporadic commentary through the 1990s,[85] culminating at the end of that decade with a suggestion that 'the bandwagon may be beginning to roll' in relation to relocation.[86] This prediction was borne out in the literature, though the real trigger for scholars appears to have been the Court of Appeal's decision in *Payne v Payne* in February 2001,[87] which is discussed in Chapter 2.[88]

Looking at the post-*Payne* literature, a number of approaches can be discerned. One group of commentators can be seen as being in broad support of the approach to relocation set out in that case.[89] For example,[90] District Judge Glenn Brasse suggested extra-judicially that '[t]here are sound psychological, emotional and policy considerations to support [the English] approach'.[91] The judge points out that the law 'offers a high degree of predictability which facilitates the task of advising the parties' and 'may also encourage constructive definition of post-location contact, preserving and helping to adapt family relationships to the new situation'.[92]

Another group of commentators challenges the way in which the welfare principle is interpreted by the English courts in the relocation context,[93] or critically

[82] Moreover, the literature focuses almost entirely on international relocation; on internal relocation, see R George, 'Re L (Internal Relocation: Shared Residence Order) [2009] EWCA Civ 20, [2009] 1 FLR 1157' (casenote) [2010] *Journal of Social Welfare and Family Law* 71; R George, 'Re F (Children) (Internal Relocation) [2010] EWCA Civ 1428' (casenote) [2011] *Journal of Social Welfare and Family Law* 169.

[83] See, eg, L Polak, 'Note on Bevan v Bevan' [1974] *Family Law* 127; N Lowe, 'Note on Lonslow v Hennig (Formerly Lonslow)' [1986] *Family Law* 304.

[84] J Holman, 'Emigration and Leave to Remove from the Jurisdiction' [1983] *Family Law* 92; M Mears, 'Removal of Children from the Jurisdiction' [1989] *Family Law* 322.

[85] See, eg, C Barton, 'Emigration After Divorce: (Not) the Children Act 1989' (1990) 24 *The Law Teacher* 81; G Bishop, 'Brookside or Stateside: A Residence Battle' (1993) 137 *Solicitors Journal* 556; M Hayes and C Williams, *Family Law: Principles, Policy and Practice*, 1st edn (London, Butterworths, 1995) 243–48; C Barton, 'When Did You Next See Your Father? Emigration and the One-Parent Family' [1997] *Child and Family Law Quarterly* 73.

[86] A Kirkconel, 'Removing Children From The Jurisdiction' [1999] *Family Law* 333, 334.

[87] *Payne v Payne* [2001] EWCA Civ 166, [2001] 1 FLR 1052. Two case commentaries were written about *Payne* at the time: A Perry, 'Leave to Remove Children from the Jurisdiction: Payne v Payne' [2001] *Child and Family Law Quarterly* 455; A Bainham, 'Taking Children Abroad: Human Rights, Welfare and the Courts' [2001] *Cambridge Law Journal* 489.

[88] See below, p 37.

[89] See, eg, K Beatson and S Turrell, 'Leave to Remove: The Carer's Prerogative?' (2005–06) 52 (Dec/Jan) *Family Law Journal* 9.

[90] See also P Pressdee, 'Relocation, Relocation, Relocation: Rigorous Scrutiny Revisited' [2008] *Family Law* 220.

[91] G Brasse, 'The Payne Threshold: Leaving the Jurisdiction' [2005] *Family Law* 780, 782.

[92] ibid 783.

[93] See, eg, A Perry, 'Leave to Remove Children from the Jurisdiction: Payne v Payne' [2001] *Child and Family Law Quarterly* 455; R Spon-Smith, 'Relocation Revisited' [2004] *Family Law* 191; M Robinson, 'Relocation and Leave to Remove' (2009) online at www.thecustodyminefield.com, 12; D Hodson, 'Every Family Matters: An In-Depth Review of Family Law in Britain' (London, Centre for Social Justice, 2009) 165; R George, 'The Shifting Law: Relocation Disputes in New Zealand and England' [2009] *Otago Law Review* 107.

addresses particular issues arising from the case law.[94] The leading work in this area is a detailed case law analysis by Mary Hayes.[95] From a review of nearly four decades of reported relocation decisions, Hayes argues that 'the court has focused on too narrow a range of questions when determining a child's best interests [in relocation cases]'.[96] She provides a critique of *Payne*, suggesting that it 'imposes a gloss on the welfare principle' by being overly directive as to the considerations relevant to relocation decisions.[97] The result of this guidance, Hayes says, is to require trial judges to give especial weight to considerations that favour applicants, which 'offends the fundamental principle that justice should be even-handed'.[98]

According to Hayes, this 'deeply flawed' English approach to relocation is worsened by the Court of Appeal's insistence that judges should 'treat discretion-based [relocation] rulings as "authoritative"';[99] this enables the appeal court to interfere with judges' decisions by ruling that discretionary decisions refusing relocation involve an error of law. Hayes considers that this approach robs trial judges of any real discretion in relocation cases.[100] This analysis tells us a lot about the development of relocation law. However, as is inevitable for any analysis based on reported cases, it is difficult to know whether these criticisms apply more generally, or are confined to the reported cases themselves. It is that broader question that this book starts to address by talking to practitioners about their experiences of relocation law in practice.

A third area of literature on relocation in England uses relocation to examine the welfare principle and its application to child law disputes more broadly. John Eekelaar's work shows how relocation cases can be employed in this way.[101] Eekelaar describes a number of existing criticisms of the welfare principle, one of which he calls 'the *lack of transparency* objection': using the welfare principle 'conceals the fact that the interests of others, or, perhaps, untested assumptions about what is good for children, actually drive the decision'.[102] Eekelaar highlights relocation cases as 'demonstrat[ing] the classic signs of the lack of transparency objection': the interests of resident parents are promoted under the guise of the interests of children.[103]

Jonathan Herring and Rachel Taylor draw on work like Eekelaar's when they use relocation as a case study to argue that the English courts have taken inadequate account of the introduction of the Human Rights Act 1998 in the family law

[94] See, eg, C Geekie, 'Relocation and Shared Residence: One Route or Two?' [2008] *Family Law* 446; S Gilmore, 'The Payne Saga: Precedent and Family Law Cases' [2011] *Family Law* 970.

[95] M Hayes, 'Relocation Cases: Is the Court of Appeal Applying the Correct Principles?' [2006] *Child and Family Law Quarterly* 351.

[96] ibid 351.

[97] ibid 362.

[98] ibid 364.

[99] ibid 366.

[100] ibid 370.

[101] J Eekelaar, 'Beyond the Welfare Principle' [2002] *Child and Family Law Quarterly* 237.

[102] ibid 237.

[103] ibid 242.

context.[104] They suggest that 'the problem with the relocation cases is . . . that the welfare principle prevents a full analysis of the interests of all those affected by the decision'.[105] In particular, they argue that resident parents have 'three important interests . . . financial, emotional and autonomy',[106] while for non-resident parents the key interest is 'the right to maintain and develop a relationship with his child'.[107] The welfare approach, Herring and Taylor say, 'automatically assumes that *any* interference with the rights of family members is justified in order to protect the welfare of the child'.[108] By contrast, a rights-based approach under the Human Rights Act would enable the court to give attention to all the 'underlying values raised in each particular case'.[109] While it may be possible to address some of these concerns without abandoning the welfare approach entirely,[110] it is valuable to have the clear understanding of the various interests involved which this work offers.

Some doctrinal analysis in other countries focuses on what might be called a 'pure' legal approach.[111] For example, in New Zealand Mark Henaghan has produced detailed studies, analysing the outcomes of trial court decisions over many years. His work maps shifts in the weight given by courts to different factual considerations,[112] suggesting that different factors are treated as more or less significant at different points in time,[113] but without passing comment on those developments.

Other doctrinal work adopts particular approaches to the analysis of relocation cases. One perspective, taken by several scholars, draws on a feminist approach to emphasise the gender dimension of relocation law, which we discussed earlier in this chapter.[114] On this view, it is claimed that restrictions on relocation should be rare, because of the generally greater impact that they have on women compared with men. This work contrasts with doctrinal work by others, a good example

[104] J Herring and R Taylor, 'Relocating Relocation' [2006] *Child and Family Law Quarterly* 517; see similarly A Bainham, 'Taking Children Abroad: Human Rights, Welfare and the Courts' [2001] *Cambridge Law Journal* 489; S Choudhry and J Herring, *European Human Rights and Family Law* (Oxford, Hart Publishing, 2010) 282–85.

[105] J Herring and R Taylor, 'Relocating Relocation' [2006] *Child and Family Law Quarterly* 517, 522.

[106] ibid 523.

[107] ibid 525.

[108] ibid 527.

[109] ibid 531.

[110] See below, pp 160–63.

[111] In Australia, see P Easteal and K Harkins, 'Are We There Yet? An Analysis of Relocation Judgments in Light of Changes to the Family Law Act' [2008] *Australian Journal of Family Law* 259; P Parkinson, 'The Realities of Relocation: Messages from Judicial Decisions' [2008] *Australian Journal of Family Law* 35. In Canada, see R Thompson, 'Ten Years After Gordon: No Law, Nowhere' (2007) 35 *Reports of Family Law* (6th) 307; E Jollimore and R Sladic, 'Mobility: Are We There Yet?' [2008] *Canadian Family Law Quarterly* 341; R Thompson, 'Heading for the Light: International Relocation from Canada' [2011] *Canadian Family Law Quarterly* 1.

[112] Such as the health and wellbeing of the relocating parent, the child's relationship with the non-moving parent, parental conflict, the child's views, etc.

[113] M Henaghan, B Klippel and D Matherson, 'Relocation Cases' (*New Zealand Law Society Seminar*, Wellington, 2000); although unattributed, Henaghan is also the author of the relevant section of D Webb *et al*, *Family Law in New Zealand*, 14th edn (Wellington, LexisNexis, 2009) 271–300.

[114] See above, pp 7–10.

being Patrick Parkinson. Parkinson has written several articles on relocation, making what the Chief Justice of the Family Court of Australia has aptly described as an 'erudite and incisive, but not uncontroversial, contribution to the relocation "debate" in Australia'.[115]

In a major contribution to the current thinking on relocation, Parkinson locates relocation disputes within a conception of parenthood as an 'indissoluble' tie which, he argues, means that although adult relationships can be ended, 'the freedom which that dissolution brings is limited by the connection of parenthood'.[116] Parkinson suggests that relocation 'can only be resolved by developing a prima facie policy position on where the balance is to be found between post-divorce autonomy and the importance to both the child and to the non-resident parent of their parent-child relationship'.[117] Parkinson says that being honest about the relocation debate requires us to recognise 'that relocation cases raise fundamental issues about the importance which should be given to the best interests of children in the post-separation family'.[118]

Similar themes are found in another of Parkinson's articles, which proposes to give guidance to judges that 'an outcome that allows the child to form and maintain strong attachments with both parents, and to spend time on a frequent basis with both parents . . . shall be preferred'.[119] Elsewhere, Parkinson suggests that relocation is 'an inherently risky activity' for both parent and child in terms of emotional and psychological well-being,[120] implying that these risks are given inadequate attention in judicial analysis.

However, although these articles offer a useful discussion, they may also imply certain assumptions, namely that most parents who seek to move do so for their own purposes, and that maximal contact with both parents is always in children's best interests. With those assumptions in place, Parkinson might be thought to present relocation as an anti-welfare decision, and as one which promotes the interests of the relocating parent at the expense of those of the child. These assumptions may risk a loss of focus on some of the issues being discussed. For example, while relocating may be 'an inherently risky activity',[121] a more telling question might be to ask whether this risk is justified. That question requires thought to be given to the reality of those 'risks' – returning 'home' after a short time away involves very different risks from setting off into the relative unknown

[115] D Bryant, 'Freedom of Movement in an Era of Shared Parenting: The Difference in Judicial Approaches: A Critique' [2010] *International Family Law* 11, 11.

[116] P Parkinson, 'Family Law and the Indissolubility of Parenthood' (2006) 40 *Family Law Quarterly* 237, 281; see further P Parkinson, *Family Law and the Indissolubility of Parenthood* (Cambridge, Cambridge University Press, 2011) ch 7.

[117] P Parkinson, 'Family Law and the Indissolubility of Parenthood' (2006) 40 *Family Law Quarterly* 237, 266.

[118] ibid 267.

[119] P Parkinson, 'Freedom of Movement in an Era of Shared Parenting: The Differences in Judicial Approaches to Relocation' (2008) 36 *Federal Law Review* 145, 170.

[120] P Parkinson, 'The Realities of Relocation: Messages from Judicial Decisions' [2008] *Australian Journal of Family Law* 35.

[121] ibid.

to follow a new partner, for example – as well as the counter-risks of not relocating. An individual's values and circumstances play an important part in determining the size of one risk compared with another, and in deciding whether a risk is worth taking or not, and it is difficult to be sure that any generalisations about risk will hold true in a majority of cases.[122]

Similarly, Parkinson's construction of the relocation question as being about 'a parent's wishes' versus 'a child's welfare' presents a questionable dichotomy.[123] One could say that relocation is about a number of competing aspects of child welfare, such as the likely benefit of having strong relationships with both parents, the likely benefit of having parents who are happy and fulfilled in their lives, the likely benefit of living in a family with sufficient resources to keep them above the poverty line, and so on. Alternatively, relocation could be constructed as a question about individual's interests (or rights) more generally, in which case the interests of the child and of each parent need to be presented separately.[124] Parkinson's writing appears to combine these comparators – the child's welfare interest in strong parental relationships compared with the relocating parent's personal desire to relocate – and that might be thought to imply an assumption against relocation. A relocation application appears to be presented as placing the parent's wishes in conflict with the child's welfare, and that comparison risks side-tracking the debate.

For these reasons amongst others, Parkinson's view is thought by some to be controversial,[125] and could be said to represent what Eekelaar calls an 'objectivized' approach to children's best interests.[126] This approach 'draws on beliefs which indicate conditions which are deemed to be in the child's best interests' and 'presuppose[s] various states of affairs the experience of which are thought to have beneficial or adverse results for the child'.[127] If one accepts that frequent time

[122] The complexity of 'risk' should not be underestimated, particularly since it is used in different ways by psychologists when talking about 'risk factors' and by philosophers and the public at large. For the former, 'risk factors' are elements related to the increased likelihood of a negative outcome occurring, and are contrasted with 'protective factors'. More generally, 'risk' relates to 'chance', modifiable with either positive or negative adjectives (a good risk or a bad risk, for example). A nuanced view of risk in the sense of the chance of gaining or losing something of value requires acknowledgement of the fact that different people will assess risks differently depending on which outcomes they value. Even taking that variation into account, there will still be a complex calculation (or estimation) of what the overall risk is, which draws on the likelihood of the risk occurring (chance) and the consequences of it (magnitude), which then must be compared (inevitably imperfectly) with other possible decisions. See generally B Fischhoff and J Kadvany, *Risk: A Very Short Introduction* (Oxford, Oxford University Press, 2011).

[123] For similar criticism of this 'unfair comparison', see M Henaghan, 'Relocation Cases in Australia Post The Family Law Amendment (Shared Parental Responsibility) Act 2006 – Considerations Not Rules Determine the Best Interests of the Child' (*Sixth Annual Family Law Summit*, Brisbane, 2009).

[124] See J Herring and R Taylor, 'Relocating Relocation' [2006] *Child and Family Law Quarterly* 517.

[125] See, eg, R Chisholm, 'A Brief Reply to Professor Parkinson' [2007] *Australian Journal of Family Law* 229; D Bryant, 'Freedom of Movement in an Era of Shared Parenting: The Difference in Judicial Approaches: A Critique' [2010] *International Family Law* 11; L Young, 'Resolving Relocation Disputes: The "Interventionist" Approach in Australia' [2011] *Child and Family Law Quarterly* 203, 220–22.

[126] J Eekelaar, 'The Interests of the Child and the Child's Wishes: The Role of Dynamic Self-Determinism' [1994] *International Journal of Law and the Family* 42, 46.

[127] ibid 46–47.

with both parents should be favoured as being in a child's best interests 'in the absence of abuse, violence, or very high conflict',[128] relocation might indeed appear as a debate between the best interests of the child and the wishes of the would-be relocating parent. However, if one does not accept this 'objectivized' construction of best interests, instead taking the view that the significance of different factors to different children's welfare will vary,[129] then relocation is not a debate about children's interests versus adults' interests, but is rather a debate about which factors best promote each individual child's interests given the particular circumstances.

Doctrinal work is clearly important and underpins much of our understanding and analysis of relocation law. However, while such analysis is important, it inevitably struggles to account for a number of key aspects. First, reported case law is not a representative sample, and is unlikely to reflect 'normal' cases in the trial courts. Second, discussions of reported cases cannot account for the role of the 'shadow of the law' in which pre-trial bargaining occurs,[130] and in particular the role of lawyers as 'gatekeepers'.[131] It is in recognition of these limitations that scholars have started to use interdisciplinary empirical research in the relocation context.

Empirical Research

Perhaps the first step in going beyond an analysis of reported cases was Mark Henaghan's work on case outcomes in New Zealand. His research, looking at virtually all first instance relocation decisions, considered the 'success rate' for New Zealand relocation applicants over a number of years.[132] Henaghan found, for example, that in 1999–2000 48 per cent of adjudicated applications succeeded,[133] whereas in the three years from 2005 to 2008, following the introduction of the Care of Children Act 2004, the success rate fell to 35 per cent.[134] Later research suggested that the success rate in relocation applications in New Zealand then returned to

[128] P Parkinson, J Cashmore and J Single, 'The Need for Reality Testing in Relocation Cases' (2010) 44 *Family Law Quarterly* 1, 1.

[129] See, eg, J Eekelaar, 'The Interests of the Child and the Child's Wishes: The Role of Dynamic Self-Determinism' [1994] *International Journal of Law and the Family* 42; R Chisholm, 'Making It Work: The Family Law Amendment (Shared Parental Responsibility) Act 2006' [2007] *Australian Journal of Family Law* 143.

[130] R Mnookin and L Kornhauser, 'Bargaining in the Shadow of the Law: The Case of Divorce' (1979) 88 *Yale Law Journal* 950.

[131] J Behrens, B Smyth and R Kaspiew, 'Outcomes in Relocation Decisions: Some New Data' [2010] *Australian Journal of Family Law* 97, 100.

[132] For similar work in Canada, see R Thompson, 'Ten Years After Gordon: No Law, Nowhere' (2007) 35 *Reports of Family Law* (6th) 307; N Bala and A Wheeler, 'Canadian Relocation Cases: Heading Towards Guidelines' [2012] *Canadian Family Law Quarterly* 27. For discussion of the Bala and Wheeler work, see below, pp 149–151.

[133] M Henaghan, B Klippel and D Matherson, 'Relocation Cases' (*New Zealand Law Society Seminar*, Wellington, 2000); the success rate from 1988 to 1998 was 62%.

[134] M Henaghan, 'Care of Children Act Cases: Where Are We, Where Are We Going?' (*LexisNexis Annual Child Law Conference*, Auckland, 2008).

around 50 per cent,[135] but this figure requires further explanation to be understood fully, and this is where the empirical work is used to good effect.

The limitation of looking at success rates in litigated cases is that case outcomes, as with an analysis of reported cases, do not allow the researcher to assess the role of legal advisers and pre-litigation decision making.[136] This is where work with legal advisers and with parents involved in relocation cases can help, allowing us better to understand the context of doctrinal analysis or case outcomes. For example, as one Australian study observed, it is possible that cases being litigated now are substantially different from those seen in earlier studies:

> It may well be that lawyers are 'gatekeeping' many relocation disputes out of court by advising clients that it will be harder to relocate . . . or that, even without legal advice, potential 'relocators' are making that assumption. This might mean that the cases actually getting to court are ones in which there is a stronger case for relocation than in the typical [earlier] case.[137]

In other words, in the Australian context, it may be that cases which are now litigated would previously have been settled in favour of relocation, while those which would previously have litigated are now settled in favour of staying in the current location.

Fiona Mackenzie's questionnaire research with lawyers and judges in New Zealand reached similar conclusions with regard to the effects of the introduction of the Care of Children Act 2004 on relocation law.[138] As she explains:

> There has been a shift in judicial thinking in the Family Court with respect to relocation cases, resulting in increased weight being given to the factor of the importance of a child's relationship with the non-relocating parent. There also appears to have been decreased weight given to the factor of the relocating parent's (usually the mother's) emotional health and happiness within the matrix of a welfare and best interests enquiry. The outcome has led to an increasing difficulty in achieving a successful relocation in the Family Court. [Footnote omitted.][139]

Alongside these projects, a number of studies have looked at the experiences of parents involved in relocation cases. In England, a study by Marilyn Freeman looked at the experiences of parties involved in relocation disputes between 1999 and 2009.[140] 25 fathers and 11 mothers who were involved in relocation litigation in that period were interviewed, and reported considerable concern about the way

[135] M Henaghan, 'Going, Going . . . Gone – To Relocate Or Not To Relocate, That Is The Question' (*New Zealand Family Law Conference*, Auckland, 2009).

[136] One should recognise, of course, that not all parents have legal representation in relocation cases, though the law's 'shadow' affects the decisions that parents make to some extent whether they are legally advised or not.

[137] J Behrens, B Smyth and R Kaspiew, 'Outcomes in Relocation Decisions: Some New Data' [2010] *Australian Journal of Family Law* 97, 100. See similarly the views of New Zealand practitioners in this study, discussed in ch 5.

[138] F Mackenzie, *Uneasy Trends in Relocation Law* (unpublished LLM Thesis, Victoria University of Wellington, 2009) 69–92.

[139] ibid 2.

[140] M Freeman, *Relocation: The Reunite Research* (London, Reunite, 2009).

in which the law appeared to prioritise the interests of applicants over those of respondents. The legal advice which participants in this study reported having received was that applicants 'will inevitably be granted leave to remove from the jurisdiction, and that fathers should not bother to defend such applications as it is better to try to make good contact arrangements'.[141] Concerns were expressed about the practicality of the contact ordered by the court,[142] along with doubt about the perceived prioritisation of applicant parents' well-being over other factors in the welfare assessment.[143] Despite the significant difficulties associated with recruiting participants in the short time-frame available for this research project,[144] and the consequent limitations on the conclusions that can be drawn from it,[145] Freeman's study offers an interesting first insight into the experiences of some of those involved in relocation disputes.

A larger scale study has been conducted in New Zealand, offering invaluable insights into the experience of parents there. Nicola Taylor, Megan Gollop and Mark Henaghan conducted research with 100 families where the mother, the father or both were interviewed; in 30 of those families the children were also interviewed.[146] While it is difficult to summarise such rich empirical research, a number of key findings emerge.

A particularly significant point is the huge importance of the relocation decision to all those involved. Applicants (mostly mothers) whose relocations were prevented by the courts (N=20) often saw this as an infringement of their rights and spoke about applying again in the future (which, indeed, a third of them did).[147] On the other side, where applications were allowed, the respondents (N=22, mostly fathers) talked of their 'uncertainty and distress', and of being

[141] ibid 20.

[142] ibid 14–16.

[143] ibid 16–17.

[144] A particular difficulty which arises when participants have to be recruited quickly is that there is little scope to be selective. Consequently, to obtain a reasonably sized sample, Freeman interviewed parents who had been involved in relocation disputes anywhere between 1999 and 2009. This long time-frame has two consequences: first, many interviewees will have been reporting experiences from many years ago, which creates a high risk of recollection error; and second, the law itself is not static, meaning that it is difficult to know whether participants were reporting about experiences in the same legal climate or not. Another difficulty that Freeman experienced with her sample is that, although both applicants and respondents to relocation disputes participated, parents who were unsuccessful in court were over-sampled. Those who are dissatisfied with any state of affairs are often most willing to participate in a research project, but it is perhaps unsurprising that a group of litigants who lost in court in a matter as highly personal and emotionally charged as relocation would be dissatisfied with the law.

[145] The report goes beyond the data available from the research when it calls for reforms which 'may result in a readjustment to the "pro-relocation" attitude which is routinely adopted by [the English] courts': see C O'Flinn, 'Back in the Fold' (2009) 159 *New Law Journal* 1416; F Judd and R George, 'International Relocation: Do We Stand Alone?' [2010] *Family Law* 63, 66.

[146] N Taylor, M Gollop and M Henaghan, *Relocation Following Parental Separation: The Welfare and Best Interests of Children* (Dunedin, University of Otago, 2010). Key findings of this project are summarised in M Henaghan, 'Relocation Cases: The Rhetoric and the Reality of a Child's Best Interests: A View from the Bottom of the World' [2011] *Child and Family Law Quarterly* 226, 236–38.

[147] N Taylor, M Gollop and M Henaghan, *Relocation Following Parental Separation: The Welfare and Best Interests of Children* (Dunedin, University of Otago, 2010) 95.

made to feel 'like expendable accessories in their children's lives'.[148] In part because of these issues, cases were likely to end in litigation (unlike most parenting disputes), and the average amount of money spent by each parent on litigation was more than New Zealand's average annual salary.[149]

The authors' conclusion is that the key determinant of whether post-dispute arrangements worked or not is the parents' attitude:

> Where parents could be creative in promoting and maintaining direct (face-to-face visits) and indirect means of contact (eg, reading story books to their children over the phone; marking a calendar with the child so they knew when the next visit/phone call would be; allowing children the flexibility to contact their non-resident parent whenever they wished) then relocation could be a more positive experience. When inter-parental relations are marked by ongoing bitterness, hostility and conflict then it may be immaterial whether the child is in the same locality as both parents, or has relocated elsewhere with one, as such detrimental influences can impact on them wherever they live.[150]

The researchers highlight a number of areas arising from their data which require further debate, and suggest the need to reconsider whether an appropriate balance has been struck between the tensions implicit in relocation cases. This important project offers fascinating insights into families' experiences of life after relocation disputes and, as the authors suggest, helps to 'provide an informed basis for applying the best interests principle in relocation disputes'.[151] A five-year longitudinal study with 80 parents in Australia seems to be producing similar results.[152]

Overview of the Book

A number of gaps within the existing research in England have been identified. First, English scholars have produced excellent doctrinal analyses of reported cases, but these discussions are inevitably limited by the fact that reported cases are unlikely to be representative of 'normal' cases in the trial courts. Second, while some comparative work has been undertaken, the studies are small and descriptive,

[148] ibid.

[149] M Henaghan, 'Relocation Cases: The Rhetoric and the Reality of a Child's Best Interests: A View from the Bottom of the World' [2011] *Child and Family Law Quarterly* 226, 236. The average amount spent by participants was just under NZ$30,000 (including parents who did not go to court as well as those who did), while the average salary in New Zealand is NZ$27,500.

[150] N Taylor, M Gollop and M Henaghan, *Relocation Following Parental Separation: The Welfare and Best Interests of Children* (Dunedin, University of Otago, 2010) 96–97.

[151] ibid 145.

[152] This study is being led by Patrick Parkinson and Judy Cashmore. Most of the data from their project is still being analysed at the time of going to press, but for early publications see P Parkinson, J Cashmore and J Single, 'The Need for Reality Testing in Relocation Cases' (2010) 44 *Family Law Quarterly* 1; P Parkinson, J Cashmore and J Single, 'Mothers Wishing to Relocate with Children: Actual and Perceived Reasons' (2011) 27 *Canadian Family Law Journal* 11.

suggesting that detailed evaluative comparison may usefully be added. Third, many jurisdictions are examining outcomes of litigated cases, but it is acknowledged that such data are unable to account for the role of advisers in 'gatekeeping' the cases that reach trial, meaning that the statistics themselves may be an unreliable indicator of changing practices over time. These analyses are also unable to compare approaches between countries. We know that different jurisdictions have approaches which, on paper, look different, but we are unable to tell whether those differences are likely to cause individual cases to be treated differently. It is this information gap that the research reported in this book starts to fill, though it should be recognised that the gap is large and this study is only a first step in providing the missing information. In contributing to filling those gaps, five main questions are addressed by this book.

The first question asks how relocation law has developed and, in particular, why it might be that countries with social and legal backgrounds as similar as England and New Zealand have developed such different approaches to relocation disputes. The second question is whether these differences in legal approach cause individual cases to be treated differently. Would the same set of facts lead to a different outcome if it were decided in New Zealand as opposed to in England?

Third, we can ask whether our understanding of the law at the moment, based as it is primarily on reported cases which originate mainly in appeal courts, is reflective of the law in practice in the trial courts. Are cases 'on the ground' following the same approaches as are set out by the appeal courts? The fourth question asks how practitioners who are experienced in dealing with these daily realities of relocation law evaluate that law. Does the law work well, from the point of view of the professionals who apply it, or are there concerns? Finally, what lessons might be learned from this study and how might the law approach relocation disputes more satisfactorily?

Relocation Disputes: Law and Practice in England and New Zealand addresses these questions in the following chapters. Chapter 2 looks at the development of the legal provisions relating to relocation disputes in England and New Zealand, critically examining the reported case law and mapping their divergent developments. Chapters 3, 4 and 5 report findings from interviews with practitioners in England and New Zealand.[153] Chapter 3 looks at how the differences in legal approach seen in Chapter 2 might affect individual cases, by asking practitioners to analyse three hypothetical disputes. Chapter 4 looks in detail at English practitioners' experiences of relocation law, examining the reality of day-to-day practice from their perspective and assessing the evaluations of the law offered by those who use it on a daily basis. Chapter 5 turns to New Zealand practitioners' perspectives on their law, offering an equivalent analysis to that seen in Chapter 4. The book concludes, in Chapter 6, by suggesting some lessons that might be learnt from this study, and discussing some possible alternative approaches to relocation disputes which might take those lessons into account.

[153] For methodology, see Methodological Appendix.

2

Changes in 'the Tides of Chance and Life': The Development of Relocation Law in England and New Zealand

Lord Justice Thorpe once said that post-separation parenting relationships are governed in part by 'the tides of chance and life'.[1] In the relocation context, it might be said (continuing the metaphor) that the law acts as the moon in affecting those tides, waxing and waning over time. This chapter explores the different ways in which the legal principles governing relocation disputes have evolved in England and in New Zealand.

We start by explaining aspects of the court structures and legislation relevant to relocation law. We then look at *Poel v Poel*,[2] the long-time leading case in both England and New Zealand. Put simply, *Poel* suggested that courts should not normally interfere with the reasonable plans of a primary carer because of the adverse consequences which were likely to flow from such interference. The next section of the chapter focuses on the English law, which continued to build on *Poel* to the now-leading case of *Payne v Payne*,[3] together with two subsidiary strands of relocation law.

The chapter then turns to New Zealand which, by contrast with England, rejected the *Poel* approach in 1995. At first, New Zealand law simply required all factors to be assessed without a priori weight being given to any one consideration. However, statutory change in 2004 led to a degree of confusion about whether factors favouring children having strong relationships with both parents should be dominant in the welfare analysis, and whether this would militate against a relocation application.

[1] *Re B (Removal from Jurisdiction); Re S (Removal from Jurisdiction)* [2003] EWCA Civ 1149, [2003] 2 FLR 1043 [12].

[2] *Poel v Poel* [1970] 1 WLR 1469 (EWCA) (hereafter, *Poel*).

[3] *Payne v Payne* [2001] EWCA Civ 166, [2001] 1 FLR 1052 (hereafter, *Payne*).

Court Structures

In order to understand some of the development of relocation law, it is necessary to have an overview of the family justice systems within which these disputes are adjudicated. Despite a suggestion on high authority that there is no reason why relocation disputes should not be mediated,[4] it is thought that most contested relocations end up before a judge.[5] According to lawyers interviewed as part of this research, almost all cases which get as far as seeking legal advice proceed to trial. One English solicitor described relocation as 'the one area of family work that I do where I start the case with the expectation of going to trial' (ES3). There are two reasons why this may be so. One is that relocation is 'an issue where it's very difficult to compromise. You either go and live [somewhere else] or you don't – there's no halfway point' (EB3). The other is that 'the stakes are high for both sides . . . [so] quite often people don't agree even when they know they're going to lose' (EB7). While there are undoubtedly proposed relocations which are not litigated, either because the move is not opposed using legal means or because the dispute is settled before trial, it seems likely that a high proportion of relocation cases are adjudicated in court. Consequently, the focus of this discussion is on court structures.

In England, international relocation cases should be heard either in the Family Division of the High Court,[6] in the Principal Registry of the Family Division, or by a Circuit Judge in a County Court (or, of course, by a Deputy High Court Judge or a Recorder).[7] Internal relocation cases, on the other hand, are rarely heard in the High Court, and are predominantly heard by District Judges in the County Courts. Consequently, relocation disputes are heard by a large and partially non-specialist family bench, with many judges lacking prior experience of

[4] B Hale, 'Relocation' (*International Child Abduction, Forced Marriage and Relocation Conference*, London Metropolitan University, 2010); see also A Thomas, 'Relocation Dispute Resolution Hearings' [2010] *Family Law* 872.

[5] In later research based on lawyer questionnaires, around 85% of international relocation cases and 65% of domestic relocation cases seen by legal advisers were resolved by judicial determination rather than by settlement: R George, 'Relocation Disputes in England and Wales: First Findings from the 2012 Study' (Oxford Legal Studies Research Paper, 2013), online at http://ssrn.com/abstract=2306097, [3.29].

[6] If the proposed relocation is to a country which is not a signatory of the Hague Convention on the Civil Aspects of International Child Abduction 1980, the case should go before a High Court Judge: see Practice Direction: Allocation and Transfer of Proceedings [2009] 1 FLR 365 [5.2(6)]. Note that many circuit judges can sit as High Court Judges under the Senior Courts Act 1981 (England), s 9.

[7] While the Practice Direction: Allocation and Transfer of Proceedings [2009] 1 FLR 365 says nothing about how relocation cases should be allocated within the County Court, Wall LJ once said that international cases should not normally be heard by District Judges: see *Re D (Children)* [2009] EWCA Civ 957 [3]. Nonetheless, a number of participants in this research reported (with some criticism) having had international relocation cases tried by District Judges in the County Courts; in later research, almost 20% of international cases were tried by District Judges in the County Courts: R George, 'Relocation Disputes in England and Wales: First Findings from the 2012 Study' (Oxford Legal Studies Research Paper, 2013), online at http://ssrn.com/abstract=2306097 [3.19].

such cases. Clear appellate guidance may therefore be particularly important in the English system, helping judges who have limited expertise in child law to ask themselves the right questions in a relocation case. Appeals from international relocation cases are generally heard in the Court of Appeal,[8] which is a generalist bench sitting in panels of two or three;[9] panels hearing appeals from family cases usually include at least one judge experienced in family work. In England, judicial decisions about children's upbringing are said to be 'discretionary' and therefore, although appeals are based only on an assessment of whether the decision was 'wrong' or not,[10] the appeal court's jurisdiction to intervene with the outcomes favoured by trial judges is constrained by a degree of deference to the first instance tribunal.[11]

Turning to New Zealand, relocation cases are heard in the specialist Family Court. There are just 48 Family Court judges, selected by virtue of 'training, experience, and personality, [such as make them] suitable person[s] to deal with matters of family law',[12] and the Family Court is acknowledged as having specialist experience and expertise.[13] By contrast with England, this court structure creates a limited and expert field of judges hearing relocation cases, which may mean that less guidance is needed in specific areas. Family appeals in New Zealand are heard in the High Court, usually by a single judge, with further appeals on points of law possible to the Court of Appeal and then the Supreme Court. The High Court is a generalist bench whose members are appointed from the Bar; most have limited or no experience of family work. This point is significant because New Zealand no longer considers judicial decisions about children's welfare to be discretionary,[14] meaning that appeal judges give no especial weight to the decision below except in relation to witness credibility.[15] Consequently, the non-specialist High Court may overturn the specialist Family Court even where the trial judge directed herself correctly in law and made a decision which was reasonable:

[8] Appeals from District Judges in the Principal Registry are heard by High Court Judges, while those from District Judges in the County Courts are heard by Circuit Judges: see FPR Practice Direction 30A [2.1].

[9] Further appeals to the Supreme Court on points of law are possible, but no relocation case has yet gone beyond the Court of Appeal.

[10] CPR r 52.11(3); *Re B (Care Proceedings: Appeal)* [2013] UKSC 33, [2013] 2 FLR 1075, [44], [91], [137] and [202].

[11] *G v G (Minors: Custody Appeal)* [1985] FLR 894 (UKHL) 898; *Re J (A Child) (Return to Foreign Jurisdiction: Convention Rights)* [2005] UKHL 40, [2005] 2 FLR 802, [12]; the gist of this approach appears to have survived *Re B (Care Proceedings: Appeal)* [2013] UKSC 33, [2013] 2 FLR 1075, since the judgments make clear that decisions in private law cases continue to be considered 'discretionary' and accept that the *G v G* approach continues to apply to those cases (see [45], [96] and [202]). For an argument that in the mid-2000s the Court of Appeal took a more interventionist approach in relocation appeals, see M Hayes, 'Relocation Cases: Is the Court of Appeal Applying the Correct Principles?' [2006] *Child and Family Law Quarterly* 351, 369–71; see also below, pp 110–112.

[12] Family Courts Act 1980 (New Zealand), s 5(2)(b).

[13] *SCS v GMS [Leave to Appeal]* [2009] NZCA 505, [2010] NZFLR 259 [11].

[14] *D v S (No 2)* [2003] NZFLR 81 (NZCA) [18].

[15] *B v B [Relocation]* [2008] NZFLR 1083 (NZHC) [42]; *Bashir v Kacem* [2010] NZCA 96, [2010] NZFLR 865 [37] (rev'd on other grounds *Kacem v Bashir* [2010] NZSC 112, [2010] NZFLR 884).

> If the appellate court's opinion is different from the conclusion of the tribunal appealed from, then the decision under appeal is wrong in the only sense that matters, even if it was a conclusion on which minds might reasonably differ.[16]

The family justice systems of England and New Zealand thus have key differences. England's first instance bench has both specialist and non-specialist judges, whereas New Zealand's trial judges are all specialists. By contrast, whereas English appeals are heard by a panel of judges which includes a family law expert and whose power to intervene with the first instance decision is limited, New Zealand appeals are heard by a single judge from a generalist bench, and who is entitled to reverse the decision below on the simple ground that it is not the decision she would have made. It is within these judicial structures that relocation law in England and New Zealand has developed.

Relevant Legislation

Both England and New Zealand structure their relocation law around the principle that the welfare and best interests of the child concerned should be the court's paramount consideration.[17] This core provision is then supplemented by lists of considerations, known in England as the *welfare checklist*[18] and in New Zealand as the *principles relevant to welfare and best interests.*[19]

England's *welfare checklist* provides that, when making a welfare decision, 'the court shall have regard in particular' to the following factors:

(a) the ascertainable wishes and feelings of the child concerned (considered in the light of his age and understanding);
(b) his physical, emotional and educational needs;
(c) the likely effect on him of any change in his circumstances;
(d) his age, sex, background and any characteristics of his which the court considers relevant;
(e) any harm which he has suffered or is at risk of suffering;
(f) how capable each of his parents, and any other person in relation to whom the court considers the question to be relevant, is of meeting his needs;
(g) the range of powers available to the court under this Act in the proceedings in question.[20]

[16] *Austin, Nichols & Co v Stichting Lodestar* [2007] NZSC 103, [2008] 2 NZLR 141 [16]. There is a strong view amongst many family lawyers in New Zealand that it is wrong to apply this approach to family law appeals, such that the appeal judge is effectively making the decision again rather than reviewing the decision below.

[17] Children Act 1989 (England), s 1(1); Care of Children Act 2004 (New Zealand) [hereafter, COCA 2004], s 4(1).

[18] Children Act 1989 (England), s 1(3).

[19] COCA 2004, s 5.

[20] Children Act 1989 (England), s 1(3).

Relocation disputes are divided in legal terms between international and domestic moves. Proposed moves outside the United Kingdom are addressed by the Children Act specifically in section 13(1):

> Where a residence order is in force with respect to a child, no person may—
>
> . . .
>
> (b) remove him from the United Kingdom;
>
> without either the written consent of every person who has parental responsibility for the child or the leave of the court.[21]

In other words, international moves are presumptively restricted absent the agreement of all those with parental responsibility or the permission of the court,[22] and removal of the child from the UK without consent or permission is child abduction.[23]

For moves within the United Kingdom, there are no specific legislative provisions. Such moves are presumptively allowed,[24] but can be prevented both directly (by making a *prohibited steps order*[25] or by imposing conditions on a *residence order*[26]) and indirectly (with certain types of *specific issue order*[27]). There is some confusion about whether there is any difference between a move within the legal jurisdiction of England and Wales compared with a move to Scotland or Northern Ireland,[28] but they are generally treated in the same way.[29]

[21] Children Act 1989 (England), s 13(1).

[22] There is some uncertainty about the legal powers under which the court grants such permission. One view is that the order is made under Children Act 1989 (England), s 13 itself, but there is little indication that s 13 contains any such power, and s 13(3) alludes to leave being granted under s 8. The better view therefore seems to be that s 13 is a quasi-injunctive prohibition, and leave to remove the child should be granted as a *specific issue order* under s 8: see R George, 'Changing Names, Changing Places: Reconsidering Section 13 of the Children Act 1989' [2008] *Family Law* 1121; a similar point might be read between the lines of Hale J's judgment in *Re M (Leave to Remove Child from Jurisdiction)* [1999] 2 FLR 334 (EWHC).

[23] Child Abduction Act 1984 (England), s 1.

[24] *Re E (Residence: Imposition of Conditions)* [1997] 2 FLR 638 (EWCA).

[25] Children Act 1989 (England), s 8.

[26] Children Act 1989 (England), s 8. Although this power is referred to in Children Act 1989 (England), s 11(7), the power itself is clearly under s 8: as it says in s 11(7), '[a] section 8 order may . . . impose conditions'.

[27] Children Act 1989 (England), s 8.

[28] On the one hand, Children Act 1989 (England), s 13 and Child Abduction Act 1984 (England), s 1 specify that removal of the child *from the United Kingdom* is prohibited in the absence of consent. On the other hand, the change of legal jurisdiction involved in a move to Scotland or Northern Ireland has potential consequences. For example, while a shared residence or contact order made in England and Wales would be automatically *recognised* by the courts of Scotland and Northern Ireland, such an order would need to be registered in the new jurisdiction before it could be *enforced*: Family Law Act 1986 (England), ss 25 and 27. Another potential complication arises with regard to jurisdiction, as discussed in *Re W-B (Family Proceedings: Appropriate Jurisdiction within the UK)* [2012] EWCA Civ 592, [2013] 1 FLR 394.

[29] See, eg, *Re B (Prohibited Steps Order)* [2007] EWCA Civ 1055, [2008] 1 FLR 613 [4].

New Zealand's *principles relevant to welfare and best interests* are, in some ways, quite different. The court must consider any of the following matters which are relevant,[30] as well as the views of the child[31] and any relevant unlisted considerations:[32]

(a) the child's parents and guardians should have the primary responsibility, and should be encouraged to agree to their own arrangements, for the child's care, development, and upbringing:

(b) there should be continuity in arrangements for the child's care, development, and upbringing, and the child's relationships with his or her family, family group, whā nau, hapū, or iwi,[33] should be stable and ongoing (in particular, the child should have continuing relationships with both of his or her parents):

(c) the child's care, development, and upbringing should be facilitated by ongoing consultation and co-operation among and between the child's parents and guardians and all persons exercising the role of providing day-to-day care for, or entitled to have contact with, the child:

(d) relationships between the child and members of his or her family, family group, whā nau, hapū , or iwi should be preserved and strengthened, and those members should be encouraged to participate in the child's care, development, and upbringing:

(e) the child's safety must be protected and, in particular, he or she must be protected from all forms of violence (whether by members of his or her family, family group, whānau, hapū, or iwi, or by other persons):

(f) the child's identity (including, without limitation, his or her culture, language, and religious denomination and practice) should be preserved and strengthened.[34]

The Care of Children Act makes clear that relocation is a guardianship issue,[35] which means that one parent may not move the child any significant distance without consulting the other parent and either obtaining consent for the move or permission from the court.[36] If a child is moved within New Zealand without such consent, courts often order his or her immediate return,[37] enforceable through contempt proceedings;[38] moves outside New Zealand constitute child abduction.[39]

[30] COCA 2004, s 4(5)(b).
[31] COCA 2004, s 6.
[32] COCA 2004, s 4(6).
[33] Māori terms, roughly translated as 'family' (broadly conceived), 'sub-tribe' and 'tribe'. Whānau (pronounced 'fɑːnaʊ), in particular, is a very important concept in New Zealand, for Māori and non-Māori alike.
[34] COCA 2004, s 5.
[35] COCA 2004, s 16(2)(b).
[36] COCA 2004, s 16(5).
[37] Note the rather more nuanced approach to such cases called for in *Millett v Clyde* [2012] NZFLR 351 (NZHC) [50].
[38] If the child is abducted and concealed intentionally, the Habeas Corpus Act 2001 (New Zealand) can be invoked: see *Jones v Skelton* [2006] NZSC 113, [2007] 2 NZLR 178.
[39] COCA 2004, subpart 4.

The Common Starting Point: Relocation Law, 1970–1995

The legal principles applicable to relocation cases can be traced back through the Court of Chancery's inherent jurisdiction to protect children who were wards of court.[40] The first reported case in England which fits the broad facts of a relocation dispute – a dispute between separated parents where one of them proposes to move with their children – was decided in the English Court of Appeal in 1884.[41] However, *Poel v Poel*, decided on 24 July 1970, was the first truly significant event in the development of modern relocation law.[42] For 25 years after *Poel* was decided, England and New Zealand walked much the same path in relocation law. However, since there are few reported cases from New Zealand during this period, and those that there are applied *Poel*,[43] our initial focus is on English developments.

Poel was, perhaps, an unlikely candidate to become the leading case on relocation. As Rachel Taylor has said, '[i]t is astounding that a five-page case that cites no authority and does not appear to have roused any particular argument on principle has founded a doctrine that has lasted 40 years'.[44] Indeed, an observation by FH Newark, made in a rather different context, applies aptly to *Poel*:

> Decisive cases in the development of the law are of two kinds. There is the weighty cause which passes leisurely from the High Court to the House of Lords, argued at length from a multitude of authorities at every stage of its progress, while onlookers in the Inns of Court and the universities eagerly canvass the result. Equally decisive may be the obscure case, casually decided and even more casually reported. All lawyers are familiar with half a dozen or so cases which must have appeared to the judges who tried them to be so straightforward and lacking in novelty that they were doubtless surprised when the case was reported at all, and would be astounded to learn later that they were supposed to have played a part in the formulation of new doctrines. [*Poel v Poel*] would seem to fall into this second category.[45]

[40] See *Powell v Cleaver* (1788) 2 BroCC 500, 29 ER 274; *De Manneville v De Manneville* (1804) 10 Ves 52, 32 ER 762; *Campbell v Mackay* (1837) 2 My&Cr 31, 40 ER 552; *Dawson v Jay* (1854) 2 DeGM&G 764, 43 ER 300; and generally J Seymour, 'Parens Patriae and Wardship Powers: Their Nature and Origin' [1994] *Oxford Journal of Legal Studies* 159.

[41] *Hunt v Hunt* (1884) 28 Ch D 606 (EWCA).

[42] *Poel*; for interesting commentary, see R Taylor, 'Poels Apart: Fixed Principles and Shifting Values in Relocation Law' in S Gilmore, J Herring and R Probert (eds), *Landmark Cases in Family Law* (Oxford, Hart Publishing, 2011). As Taylor remarks, there were other Court of Appeal relocation cases around the same time, and it is unclear why *Poel* was reported in both the Weekly Law Reports and the All England Reports when other cases received at most a brief summary.

[43] See, eg, *Willamson v Willamson* (HC Invercargill, M42/77, 1 Dec 1974); *Kennedy v Tyley* (1988) 4 NZFLR 708 (NZFC).

[44] R Taylor, 'Poels Apart: Fixed Principles and Shifting Values in Relocation Law' in S Gilmore, J Herring and R Probert (eds), *Landmark Cases in Family Law* (Oxford, Hart Publishing, 2011) 111.

[45] F Newark, 'Twine v Bean's Express Ltd' (casenote) (1954) 17 *Modern Law Review* 102, 102.

However, despite *Poel*'s apparent shortcomings, 'the reasoning within it continues to underpin modern thinking' in English relocation cases.[46]

In *Poel*, the mother was the primary carer, the father having weekly contact. The mother had remarried, was pregnant, and wished to emigrate to New Zealand, where her new husband had better job prospects. The trial judge refused leave, but the Court of Appeal reversed him.

The reasoning of *Poel* is not entirely straightforward. Sir Gordon Willmer treated the case as primarily about the Court of Appeal's appellate function, and questioned whether there were grounds to interfere with 'a matter very much for the discretion of the judge'.[47] However, his Lordship accepted the 'more decided view' of his colleagues that the appeal should be allowed.[48]

The other two judgments focused on substantive principles. Winn LJ noted that the welfare of the child was the guiding consideration, within which

> it is to be regarded, I think, as a very dominant factor in such a dispute that there has been an order . . . for custody in favour of the one parent . . . and . . . the custody thus ordered has been working satisfactorily in every respect; and that although, naturally, the other parent will feel . . . that the access permitted to him is not all that he would wish, in no other respect is it suggested in the slightest degree that the custody arrangements have been anything but entirely beneficial to the child and satisfactory in general to the parties concerned.[49]

The child, said Winn LJ, was now part of the stepfather's family, and the mother and stepfather had a legitimate reason for relocating.[50] His Lordship was

> very firmly of opinion that the child's happiness is directly dependent not only upon the health and happiness of his own mother but upon her freedom from the very likely repercussions, of an adverse character, which would result affecting her relations with her new husband and her ability to look after her family peacefully and in a psychological frame of ease, from the refusal of the permission to take this boy to New Zealand which I think quite clearly his welfare dictates.[51]

Much the same points were made by Sachs LJ in a passage much quoted since:

> When a marriage breaks up . . . the child of that marriage, instead of being in the joint custody of both parents, must of necessity become one who is in the custody of a single parent. Once that position has arisen and the custody is working well, this court should not lightly interfere with such reasonable way of life as is selected by that parent to whom custody has been rightly given. Any such interference may . . . produce considerable strains which would not only be unfair to the parent whose way of life is interfered

[46] M Hayes, 'Relocation Cases: Is the Court of Appeal Applying the Correct Principles?' [2006] Child and Family Law Quarterly 351, 352; see, most recently, *K v K (Relocation: Shared Care Arrangement)* [2011] EWCA Civ 793, [2012] 2 FLR 880 [46], explaining why the principles from *Poel* continue to apply.

[47] *Poel*, 1474.

[48] *Poel*, 1474.

[49] *Poel*, 1471.

[50] The reason was 'to go again to a climate which [the stepfather] has enjoyed in the past and to surroundings in an agricultural type of country which he finds pleasant and enjoyable': *Poel*, 1471.

[51] *Poel*, 1473.

> with but also to any new marriage of that parent. In that way it might well in due course reflect on the welfare of the child. The way in which the parent who properly has custody of a child may choose in a reasonable manner to order his or her way of life is one of those things which the parent who has not been given custody may well have to bear.[52]

Thus the key aspects of *Poel* were, first, that children needed a single primary carer and, second, that interfering with decisions about that parent's life would likely bring repercussions which would affect the child more adversely than the loss of 'the advice of his father from time to time' (which appears to be more or less the extent of the father's role as envisaged by the Court of Appeal).[53]

However, the precise effect of *Poel* in the years following it is not clear.[54] The recollection of one judge interviewed for this research was that, during the 1970s, *Poel* was 'thought to have been overtaken by a general consideration of welfare'.[55] For example, with one significant exception,[56] reported cases in the 1970s placed little emphasis on the 'principles' expressed in *Poel.* For instance, a judgment of Scarman LJ in 1973 was summarised as saying that 'all the circumstances were to be looked at and each factor weighed against another. One factor was not to take priority against another'.[57]

A number of cases even appeared to limit the scope of *Poel.* The clearest example is *A v A (Child: Removal from Jurisdiction)*, in which Ormrod LJ said that

> although [counsel] has argued persuasively for the test which was suggested in the case of *Poel v Poel* . . . the test which is often put on the basis of whether it is reasonable for the mother to return to her own country with the child, I myself doubt whether it provides a satisfactory answer to this question. The fundamental question is what is in the best interest of the child.[58]

In similar vein, the analysis in one unreported Court of Appeal case stands in sharp contrast to the reasoning in *Poel.* In *Godfrey v Godfrey*,[59] Walton J (with whom Orr and Ormrod LJJ agreed) thought that loss of contact with the father stemming from relocation 'must be borne very, very much in mind'.[60] The fact that the father had 'real and substantial access to and contact with his children' was significant in distinguishing the case from *Poel*: in *Poel*, Ormrod LJ said, 'the father was not playing a prominent role in the children's lives'.[61] The key consideration in *Godfrey* was

52 *Poel*, 1473.

53 ibid 1471.

54 See also R Taylor, 'Poels Apart: Fixed Principles and Shifting Values in Relocation Law' in S Gilmore, J Herring and R Probert (eds), *Landmark Cases in Family Law* (Oxford, Hart Publishing, 2011) 97.

55 See below, p 105.

56 *Nash v Nash* [1973] 2 All ER 704 (EWCA).

57 *Bevan v Bevan* [1974] *Family Law* 126 (EWCA) 127.

58 *A v A (Child: Removal from Jurisdiction)* (1980) 1 FLR 380 (EWCA) 381; see also *Hurwitt v Hurwitt* (1982) 3 FLR 194 (EWCA), decided 1979.

59 *Godfrey v Godfrey*, 31 Jan 1980 (EWCA), available from the LexisNexis Official Transcripts 1980–1989.

60 ibid [3] (my paragraph numbering).

61 ibid [21] (my paragraph numbering).

'the effect upon the children of uprooting them from the comparative placidity of life in England and subjecting them to the swirling democratic ferment of the United States of America' (which had not been a consideration in *Poel* because the child there was so young).[62] The argument that the mother would be distressed by refusing her permission to relocate was dismissed by the Court of Appeal as 'a little amateur psychology'.[63]

Despite perhaps waning in the 1970s, *Poel* was rejuvenated in the 1980s. The first indication came in the unreported case of *Moodey v Field* in 1981, in which Ormrod LJ said:

> The question therefore in each case is, is the proposed move a reasonable one from the point of view of the adults involved? If the answer is yes, then leave should only be refused if it is shown beyond any doubt that the interests of the children and the interests of the custodial parent are incompatible.[64]

Like *Godfrey*, the *Moodey* decision was not reported, but it was the latter that Ormrod LJ quoted in *Chamberlain v de la Mare* in 1983.[65] At first instance in *Chamberlain*, Balcombe J had declared *Poel* to be inconsistent with the welfare principle, but the Court of Appeal firmly endorsed *Poel* and rebuked Balcombe J for failing to follow authority which was binding upon him. With reference to the judgments in *Poel*, Ormrod LJ said that he 'would be sorry to think that anything should be said to throw doubt on them as authority for the approach of the courts to this very difficult and continuing problem'.[66] His Lordship continued:

> What Sachs LJ was saying, I think, is that if the court interferes with the way of life which the custodial parent is proposing to adopt so that he or she and the new spouse are compelled to adopt a manner of life which they do not want, and reasonably do not want, the likelihood is that the frustrations and bitterness which would result from such an interference with any adult whose career is at stake would be bound to overflow on to children. It would be bound to prejudice the relationship between the step-father . . . and the children, whom he must see as a drag on him (to put it no higher). It is that factor which is so important which has to be brought into account when the balancing exercise is done . . . Consequently, in ordinary sensible human terms the court should not do something which is, prima facie, unreasonable unless there is some compelling reason to the contrary.[67]

In a short concurring judgment, Griffiths LJ stressed the importance of the new family unit in which the child was living:

[62] ibid [16] (my paragraph numbering).

[63] ibid [11] (my paragraph numbering).

[64] *Moodey v Field*, 13 Feb 1981 (EWCA) [17] (my paragraph numbering); the case is available from the LexisNexis Official Transcripts 1980–1989. One should be wary of dissecting judgments as if they were Acts of Parliament, but note that 'beyond any doubt' is a standard of proof otherwise unknown to the law.

[65] *Chamberlain v de la Mare* (1983) 4 FLR 434 (EWCA).

[66] ibid 442.

[67] ibid 442–43.

> The welfare of young children is best served by bringing them up in a happy, secure family atmosphere. When, after divorce, the parent who has custody of the children remarries, those children then join and become members of a new family and it is the happiness and security of that family on which their welfare will depend. However painful it may be for the other parent that parent has got to grasp and appreciate that fact.[68]

The English courts therefore increasingly emphasised the importance to children's welfare of a stable and functional family unit, with contact between the child and the other parent seen as secondary.[69]

These developments were not explicitly discussed in New Zealand, where *Poel* continued to dominate; however, the first seeds of change began to emerge in the early 1980s. A particularly revealing case was *Wright v Wright* in the New Zealand Court of Appeal in 1984.[70] Cooke and Richardson JJ started by laying out the *prima facie* position: 'unless restricted by statutory provision or court order or agreement, the person entitled to custody must have reasonable freedom to select the child's place of residence'.[71] Thus far, this decision reflects *Poel*, but the judges continued:

> Restrictions, however, are common. By s 11(2) of the Guardianship Act[72] a custody order may be made subject to such conditions as the Court thinks fit. Consequently there can be conditions as to place of residence . . . Access rights ordered or agreed may be infringed by significant changes of the child's residence without consent or Court approval. For instance a term that the non-custodial parent is to have reasonable access could be broken by moving the child from one city to another.[73]

So, whereas the English courts were saying that international moves which were reasonable for the parent should not lightly be stopped, the New Zealand courts were suggesting that restrictions were common, even for moves within the country, and could be implied from a contact order (as it would now be called).

However, perhaps surprisingly, *Wright* appeared to have little effect in the New Zealand lower courts. There is little case law available, but it seems that *Poel* continued to be the main authority cited in the late 1980s and early 1990s.[74] As late as March 1995, courts in both jurisdictions were citing *Poel*,[75] seeing the applicant parent's well-being as the single most important factor in promoting the child's welfare.

[68] ibid 445; see similarly *Belton v Belton* [1987] 2 FLR 343 (EWCA); *Re B (Removal from Jurisdiction); Re S (Removal from Jurisdiction)* [2003] EWCA Civ 1149, [2003] 2 FLR 1043.

[69] See also *Lonslow v Hennig (Formerly Lonslow)* [1986] 2 FLR 378 (EWCA); *Re F (A Ward) (Leave to Remove Ward Out of Jurisdiction)* [1988] 2 FLR 116 (EWCA).

[70] *Wright v Wright* (1984) 2 NZFLR 335 (NZCA).

[71] ibid 341.

[72] The Guardianship Act 1968 (New Zealand), s 11(2) allowed custody orders to be made subject to such conditions as the court thought fit; the Act was repealed in 2005, but the equivalent power is now found in COCA 2004, s 48(5).

[73] ibid.

[74] See, eg, *Kennedy v Tyley* (1988) 4 NZFLR 708 (NZFC); *Reeves v Reeves* (FC Dunedin, FP190/92, 18 June 1993); *Bachelor v Parker* (FC Lower Hutt, FP432/92, Dec 1993).

[75] See, eg, *C v C* [1995] NZFLR 360 (NZFC); *MH v GP (Child: Emigration)* [1995] 2 FLR 106 (EWHC).

One notable event which did nothing to interrupt this steady development of relocation law was the introduction of the English Children Act 1989.[76] This outcome must be said to owe something to the vagaries of law reporting, since at least one Court of Appeal decision after the Act entered force took a different view, namely that earlier cases should be disregarded in the light of the new Act.[77] In *Re S (Minors)*, Waite LJ (with whom Beldam and Henry LJJ agreed) stated clearly that the Children Act meant that cases like *Poel* and *Chamberlain*

> need to be regarded with reservation . . . [T]hey were decided at a time when rights of parenthood were governed by the legalistic concept of custody . . . Custody is a concept which the Children Act has swept away. Notions of custody with its legalistic and proprietary overtones are now replaced with an approach which sees parents as sharing responsibility equally for the upbringing of their children.[78]

Beldam LJ specifically agreed that earlier cases were unlikely to provide 'either the "tests" or statements of principle in family cases after the passing of the Children Act 1989'.[79]

By contrast, the cases which were reported concluded that there was no significance in the changed terminology or the Children Act's focus on shared parental responsibility:

> The test remains the same as was laid down in *Poel v Poel,* although there is undoubtedly an emphasis by reason of the Children Act 1989 in relation to the wishes of the children where they are of sufficient age and understanding to be able to express any views.[80]

Any thought that the Children Act might change relocation law thus came to nothing. Indeed, at the end of 1994, a new level of certainty was reached in the English rhetoric. In an influential first instance decision, Thorpe J said that

> leave [to relocate] should not be withheld unless the interests of the children and those of the custodial parent [are] clearly shown to be incompatible. That statement of principle creates a presumption in favour of the reasonable application of the custodial parent.[81]

Although the New Zealand courts had never referred to a presumption, it can be seen that in the mid-1990s the approaches being taken by the two jurisdictions were similar, both underpinned by *Poel.* However, this similarity ended in May 1995 with the New Zealand Court of Appeal decision in *Stadniczenko v Stadniczenko*.[82] Because of the divergence in approaches at this point, the chapter now splits, looking first at England and then New Zealand.

[76] For an argument that the Act ought to have changed the approach, see C Barton, 'Emigration After Divorce: (Not) the Children Act 1989' (1990) 24 *The Law Teacher* 81.

[77] *Re S (Minors)*, 2 April 1996 (EWCA), available from the LexisNexis Official Transcripts 1990–1997.

[78] ibid [10] (my paragraph numbering).

[79] ibid [14] (my paragraph numbering).

[80] *M v A (Wardship: Removal from Jurisdiction)* [1993] 2 FLR 715 (EWHC) 720–21, approved in *H v H (Residence Order: Leave to Remove from Jurisdiction)* [1995] 1 FLR 529 (EWCA) 530; see also *Re W (Minors) (Removal from Jurisdiction)* [1994] 1 FCR 842 (EWHC).

[81] *MH v GP (Child: Emigration)* [1995] 2 FLR 106 (EWHC) 110.

[82] *Stadniczenko v Stadniczenko* [1995] NZFLR 493 (NZCA).

Building on *Poel*: England and Wales, 1995–2012

English law continued to build on the *Poel* approach. In terms of international relocation, the 'presumption in favour of the reasonable application' held sway in the English courts[83] until the Human Rights Act 1998 (HRA) entered force in October 2000. Following the HRA's introduction, relocation law was fully reconsidered in the now-leading case of *Payne v Payne*,[84] in which both Butler-Sloss P and Thorpe LJ gave full judgments.[85]

In *Payne*, the mother was a New Zealander who had lived in England for some years. She sought leave to relocate to New Zealand with their four-year-old child. After the mother's return to England following abduction proceedings in New Zealand, the child was spending about 40 per cent of her time with the father and the rest with the mother (though historically the mother had been the main carer). The trial judge granted leave to relocate, and the father appealed on the ground that a presumption in favour of the move was contrary to the welfare principle and the HRA.

Regarding the 'presumption' in favour of relocation, the Court of Appeal determined that this approach was unacceptable. The President said that a presumption 'over-emphasised one element of the approach',[86] while Thorpe LJ said that talk of presumptions was inappropriate:

> there is a danger that if the regard which the court pays to the reasonable proposals of the primary carer were elevated into a legal presumption then there would be an obvious risk of the breach of the respondent's rights not only under Art 8 [to respect for private and family life] but also his rights under Art 6 to a fair trial.[87]

As to the father's claim that existing case law was contrary to the Children Act, the Court of Appeal noted that all the authorities based themselves on the welfare principle,[88] and concluded that the welfare principle was itself compatible with the HRA.[89]

The Court of Appeal then turned to the substantive issues about relocation law. A review of the cases showed that the authorities 'have stood the test of time and give valuable guidance as to the approach the court should adopt in these most

[83] *MH v GP (Child: Emigration)* [1995] 2 FLR 106 (EWHC) 110; *Re K (Application to Remove from Jurisdiction)* [1998] 2 FLR 1006 (EWHC) 1015; *Re C (Leave to Remove from Jurisdiction)* [2000] 2 FLR 457 (EWCA) 464, 466 and 467.

[84] *Payne*; see A Bainham, 'Taking Children Abroad: Human Rights, Welfare and the Courts' [2001] *Cambridge Law Journal* 489; A Perry, 'Leave to Remove Children from the Jurisdiction: Payne v Payne' [2001] *Child and Family Law Quarterly* 455.

[85] Robert Walker LJ gave a short summary and agreed with both main judgments.

[86] *Payne* [83].

[87] *Payne* [40].

[88] *Payne* [16], [83].

[89] For criticism, see S Harris-Short, 'Family Law and the Human Rights Act 1998: Judicial Restraint or Revolution?' [2005] *Child and Family Law Quarterly* 329, 355; J Herring and R Taylor, 'Relocating Relocation' [2006] *Child and Family Law Quarterly* 517, 527–29.

difficult cases'.[90] From his discussion of the cases, Thorpe LJ reached the conclusion that

> relocation cases have been consistently decided upon the application of the following two propositions:
>
> (a) the welfare of the child is the paramount consideration; and
> (b) refusing the primary carer's reasonable proposals for the relocation of her family life is likely to impact detrimentally on the welfare of her dependent children. Therefore her application to relocate will be granted unless the court concludes that it is incompatible with the welfare of the children.[91]

The first point is unobjectionable, given section 1 of the Children Act 1989 and the equivalent legal provisions that came before it.[92] However, the second point requires analysis.

To paraphrase, children require psychological stability and security and, since those things come mainly from the primary carer, the primary carer herself needs psychological stability and security: '[t]he parent cannot give what she herself lacks'.[93] However, the link between the two clauses of point (b) is problematic. It is said that, because refusing leave 'is likely to' impact detrimentally on the mother and child, leave *will* be granted (unless incompatible with the child's welfare). This statement either creates a *de facto* presumption, or is a circuitous way of saying that the welfare principle applies.

Although *Payne* explicitly rejected presumptions, these words look like a presumption: relocation has to be shown to be 'incompatible' with the child's welfare for it to be vetoed by the court. There appears to be a burden on a respondent to show that relocation is not in the child's interests, which is different from ascertaining the solution which best meets the child's interests.

If, alternatively, point (b) is meant to be a formulation of the welfare principle, then the conclusion – that leave *will* be granted – is perhaps misplaced. Although refusing leave has been identified as detrimental to the child, it does not necessarily follow that that outcome is not in the child's best interests. If the other available options will impact on the child *more* negatively, refusal of leave might be in the child's best interests.[94] In other words, a negative effect caused by refusing leave to relocate does not automatically make relocation the best option, because there may be different (and possibly worse) negative effects from allowing the move.

The President and Thorpe LJ then laid out guidelines on how relocation should be approached. Butler-Sloss P prefaced her summary by saying that she was not excluding other factors that would arise in each case, but that the following should be taken into account:

[90] *Payne* [83]; similarly [27].
[91] *Payne* [26].
[92] Guardianship of Infants Act 1925 (England), s 1; Guardianship of Minors Act 1971 (England), s 1.
[93] *Payne* [31].
[94] See generally J Eekelaar, 'Beyond the Welfare Principle' [2002] *Child and Family Law Quarterly* 237, esp 244.

> (a) The welfare of the child is always paramount.
> (b) There is no presumption created by s 13(1)(b) [of the Children Act 1989] in favour of the applicant parent.
> (c) The reasonable proposals of the parent with a residence order wishing to live abroad carry great weight.
> (d) Consequently the proposals have to be scrutinised with care and the court needs to be satisfied that there is a genuine motivation for the move and not the intention to bring contact between the child and the other parent to an end.
> (e) The effect upon the applicant parent and the new family of the child of a refusal of leave is very important.
> (f) The effect upon the child of the denial of contact with the other parent and in some cases his family is very important.
> (g) The opportunity for continuing contact between the child and the parent left behind may be very significant.[95]

In his summary, Thorpe LJ said:

> To guard against the risk of too perfunctory an investigation resulting from too ready an assumption that the mother's proposals are necessarily compatible with the child's welfare I would suggest the following discipline as a prelude to conclusion:
>
> (a) Pose the question: is the mother's application genuine in the sense that it is not motivated by some selfish desire to exclude the father from the child's life? Then ask is the mother's application realistic, by which I mean founded on practical proposals both well researched and investigated? If the application fails either of these tests refusal will inevitably follow.
> (b) If however the application passes these tests then there must be a careful appraisal of the father's opposition: is it motivated by genuine concern for the future of the child's welfare or is it driven by some ulterior motive? What would be the extent of the detriment to him and his future relationship with the child were the application granted? To what extent would that be offset by extension of the child's relationships with the maternal family and homeland?
> (c) What would be the impact on the mother, either as the single parent or as a new wife, of a refusal of her realistic proposal? [Where the mother cares for the child or proposes to care for the child within a new family, the impact of refusal on the new family and on the stepfather or prospective stepfather must also be carefully calculated.[96]]
> (d) The outcome of the second and third appraisals must then be brought into an overriding review of the child's welfare as the paramount consideration, directed by the statutory checklist insofar as appropriate.
>
> In suggesting such a discipline I would not wish to be thought to have diminished the importance that this court has consistently attached to the emotional and psychological well-being of the primary carer. In any evaluation of the welfare of the child as the paramount consideration great weight must be given to this factor.[97]

[95] *Payne* [85]–[86].

[96] Thorpe LJ added this sentence in *Re B (Removal from Jurisdiction); Re S (Removal from Jurisdiction)* [2003] EWCA Civ 1149, [2003] 2 FLR 1043 [11].

[97] *Payne* [40]–[41].

While there have been recent judicial suggestions that the President's summary might be considered the main source of guidance in relocation cases,[98] in the decade after *Payne* it was Thorpe LJ's 'discipline' which dominated the English approach. The general approach set out by *Payne* has been affirmed many times, with the Court of Appeal rejecting calls to review the law,[99] and leave to appeal beyond the Court of Appeal being refused a number of times.[100] However, despite this apparent clarity of approach, the English law on relocation has seen some important changes of emphasis in the years since *Payne* was decided, together with some strong criticisms of that case and its later interpretation.

In the first few years after *Payne*, English law appeared to strengthen its pro-relocation approach. In particular, the Court of Appeal stressed the importance of the effect on the primary carer of refusing relocation,[101] together with the effect on that parent's new partner if she had one,[102] and consequently the effect on the child.[103] These factors, together with an impression from reported appeal cases that appellate judges were willing to overturn trial judges who gave inadequate attention to them, led to strong criticisms from academic and practitioner commentators alike. As Mary Hayes put it in 2006:

> The weight to be given to the wishes and feelings of the [applicant] mother has been elevated to a matter of principle . . . The Court of Appeal has ruled that a judge makes a serious error where he gives less weight to the impact on the mother of denial of leave than he does to other factors relevant to the welfare checklist . . . Treating the impact on the applicant of denial of leave as a consideration which the court must, as a matter of law, give very great weight, has enabled the Court of Appeal to respond in three ways where the mother's application has been denied. First, it may overrule the trial judge. Secondly, it may substitute its own discretion for that of the judge. Thirdly, it may grant the mother leave to remove the children from the jurisdiction of the courts of England and Wales.[104]

[98] *Re D (Leave to Remove: Appeal)* [2010] EWCA Civ 50, [2010] 2 FLR 1605 [18] (Wall LJ); see also, less strongly, the comments of Black LJ in *K v K (Relocation: Shared Care Arrangement)* [2011] EWCA Civ 793, [2012] 2 FLR 880 [143].

[99] *Re G (Leave to Remove)* [2007] EWCA Civ 1497, [2008] 1 FLR 1587; *Re W (Leave to Remove)* [2008] EWCA Civ 538, [2008] 2 FLR 1170 [18]; *Re H (Leave to Remove)* [2010] EWCA Civ 915, [2010] 2 FLR 1875; *Re W (Relocation: Removal Outside Jurisdiction)* [2011] EWCA Civ 345, [2011] 2 FLR 409.

[100] See, eg, *Re B (Removal from Jurisdiction); Re S (Removal from Jurisdiction)* [2003] EWCA Civ 1149, [2003] 2 FLR 1043 (leave refused 1 April 2004); *Re W (A Child) (Removal from Jurisdiction)* [2005] EWCA Civ 1614, [2006] 1 FCR 346 (leave refused 21 June 2006); *Re W (Leave to Remove)* [2008] EWCA Civ 538, [2008] 2 FLR 1170 (leave refused 9 June 2008); *Re F (Relocation)* [2012] EWCA Civ 1364, [2013] 1 FLR 645 (leave refused 4 February 2013).

[101] See, eg, *Re B (Leave to Remove: Impact of Refusal)* [2004] EWCA Civ 956, [2005] 2 FLR 239. It is clear from *Re E (Relocation: Removal from Jurisdiction)* [2012] EWCA Civ 1893, [2013] 2 FLR 290 [11] that judges must still consider the effect of refusing leave on the applicant parent, and may be justified in rejecting a CAFCASS proposal which fails to weigh this aspect in the balance.

[102] See, eg, *Re B (Removal from Jurisdiction); Re S (Removal from Jurisdiction)* [2003] EWCA Civ 1149, [2003] 2 FLR 1043.

[103] See, eg, *Re G (Removal from Jurisdiction)* [2005] EWCA Civ 170, [2005] 2 FLR 166.

[104] M Hayes, 'Relocation Cases: Is the Court of Appeal Applying the Correct Principles?' [2006] *Child and Family Law Quarterly* 351, 370–71.

Another line of attack on the English law claimed that *Payne*'s views on parenting and parent–child relationships after separation or divorce were 'outdated' and 'antiquated'. This argument was made to the Court of Appeal by Nicholas Mostyn QC in 2007. According to the summary of the argument given by Thorpe LJ, '[t]he essential complaint [is] that in modern times, when joint residence orders have become commonplace, judges [are] applying the principles in *Payne* . . . which were predicated upon a status of sole residence order and sole primary carer'.[105] As a newly appointed High Court Judge, Mostyn J reiterated this position in 2010. According to his Lordship's interesting but controversial discussion,[106] the *Payne* approach

> has not been uncritically accepted. Indeed, there is a strong view that the heavy emphasis on the emotional reaction of the thwarted primary carer represents an illegitimate gloss on the purity of the paramountcy principle. Moreover, some argue that it promotes selfishness and detracts from the importance of co-parenting. Some argue that on the birth of children parents are indentured to sacrifice throughout their minority, but that the one word missing from *Payne* is, in fact, sacrifice.[107]

In similar (if more moderate) vein, Wall LJ commented:

> There has been considerable criticism of *Payne v Payne* in certain quarters, and there is a perfectly respectable argument for the proposition that it places too great an emphasis on the wishes and feelings of the relocating parent, and ignores or relegates the harm done to children by a permanent breach of the relationship which the children have with the left behind parent.[108]

Perhaps in response to these criticisms, there has been something of a change of tone in some reported relocation cases in the last few years.[109] A number of recent decisions have emphasised that all relocation cases are fact-specific, and that no

[105] *Re G (Leave to Remove)* [2007] EWCA Civ 1497, [2008] 1 FLR 1587 [13], referring to Nicholas Mostyn QC's skeleton argument; see also C Geekie, 'Relocation and Shared Residence: One Route or Two?' [2008] *Family Law* 446, and points made by participants in M Freeman, *Relocation: The Reunite Research* (London, Reunite, 2009).

[106] See below, pp 148–49; see also R George, 'The International Relocation Debate' [2012] *Journal of Social Welfare and Family Law* 141; R George, *Ideas and Debates in Family Law* (Oxford, Hart Publishing, 2012), 115–17.

[107] *Re AR (A Child: Relocation)* [2010] EWHC 1346 (Fam), [2010] 2 FLR 1577 [8]; Mostyn J re-entered the debate in *Re TC and JC (Children: Relocation)* [2013] EWHC 292 (Fam), [2013] 2 FLR 484 [10]–[18], including a statement that he still held the views expressed in *Re AR*. For similar academic argument, see M Hayes, 'Relocation Cases: Is the Court of Appeal Applying the Correct Principles?' [2006] *Child and Family Law Quarterly* 351, 362–65.

[108] *Re D (Leave to Remove: Appeal)* [2010] EWCA Civ 50, [2010] 2 FLR 1605 [33]; but *cf* Wilson LJ in *Re H (Leave to Remove)* [2010] EWCA Civ 915, [2010] 2 FLR 1875 [23], suggesting that Wall LJ overstated the point. Wall P later accepted the criticism: *Re W (Relocation: Removal Outside Jurisdiction)* [2011] EWCA Civ 345, [2011] 2 FLR 409 [129].

[109] As will be seen below, p 109, this change was already under way when interviews for this research took place in 2008–09, since several participants talked in similar terms based on their experiences as trial judges or as lawyers. A similar suggestions can be seen in C Bridge, 'Comment: Re H (A Child) (Removal from Jurisdiction) [2007] EWCA Civ 222, [2007] 2 FLR 317' [2007] *Family Law* 707.

one factor can be said to have automatically great significance.[110] The Court of Appeal has emphasised that there is only one guiding principle in relocation cases, namely that the welfare of the child is the paramount consideration,[111] and that the guidance from *Payne* and other cases is just that – guidance.[112] Consequently, while the guidance itself has remained unchanged,[113] there has been some re-emphasis intended to clarify that judges are exercising their discretion in the pursuit of the child's welfare in each individual case, and there are no predetermined answers to that welfare question to be read between the lines of the Court of Appeal decisions.[114]

That is the position for the majority of relocation cases in England. However, before we examine the New Zealand position, there are two subsidiary lines of relocation law in England to discuss. Most English cases currently fit the broad fact pattern of *Payne* – that is, a clear primary carer seeking to relocate to another country. Outside this core area, however, we find authorities related to international relocation cases featuring genuinely shared care arrangements, and to proposed relocations within the UK.

Shared Care Relocation Applications

There are essentially two views about how shared care relocation applications should be approached.[115] One view is that it is inappropriate to apply different tests to relocation applications depending on whether the parents are sharing the child's primary care or not, and so *Payne* should apply regardless of care arrangements.[116]

[110] See, eg, *Re H (Leave to Remove)* [2010] EWCA Civ 915, [2010] 2 FLR 1875; *J v S (Leave to Remove)* [2010] EWHC 2098 (Fam), [2011] 1 FLR 1694; *Re W (Relocation: Removal Outside Jurisdiction)* [2011] EWCA Civ 345, [2011] 2 FLR 409; *K v K (Relocation: Shared Care Arrangement)* [2011] EWCA Civ 793, [2012] 2 FLR 880.

[111] Children Act 1989 (England), s 1(1).

[112] *K v K (Relocation: Shared Care Arrangement)* [2011] EWCA Civ 793, [2012] 2 FLR 880; see S Gilmore, 'The Payne Saga: Precedent and Family Law Cases' [2011] *Family Law* 970; R George, 'Reviewing Relocation?' [2012] *Child and Family Law Quarterly* 110, 115–20.

[113] In particular, *Payne* remains good law and, indeed, 'the leading case' on international relocation: see, eg, *Re W (Relocation: Removal Outside Jurisdiction)* [2011] EWCA Civ 345, [2011] 2 FLR 409; *Re S (Relocation: Interests of Siblings)* [2011] EWCA Civ 454, [2011] 2 FLR 678 [70]; *Re O (Residence)* [2012] EWCA Civ 1955, [2012] All ER (D) 39 (Dec).

[114] See, eg, *S v Z (Leave to Remove)* [2012] EWHC 846 (Fam), [2012] 2 FLR 581 [46]: Holman J explained that the fact that the effect on the mother of refusing her application, which would involve keeping her away from her new husband and the father of her second child, was a factor to consider in the overall balance, but that it 'did not create any primacy for the mother's application, still less any presumption in her favour'.

[115] Some of this discussion appeared previously in R George, 'Reviewing Relocation?' [2012] *Child and Family Law Quarterly* 110.

[116] See, eg, *Re G (Leave to Remove)* [2007] EWCA Civ 1497, [2008] 1 FLR 1587; *Re L (Internal Relocation: Shared Residence Order)* [2009] EWCA Civ 20, [2009] 1 FLR 1157 [36]; *Re TG (Relocation)* [2009] EWHC 3122 (Fam) [9].

The other view is that *Payne* should not be applied to a case of truly shared care because the reasoning in it is premised on there being a primary carer.[117]

Despite a 2011 Court of Appeal decision specifically addressing this issue,[118] to which we turn in a moment, it is still unclear which of these views has the better of the argument. However, the existence of any debate on this subject again owes much to the idiosyncrasies of law reporting, since the question was in fact authoritatively decided by the Court of Appeal in an unreported decision in 1999.[119] In *Re C and M (Children)*, there were two children aged eight and five. They had different fathers, but in both cases the parents had reached 'sensible and generous arrangements' whereby the children were with their respective fathers from Thursday afternoon until Sunday evening each week, and with their mother the rest of the time. The mother was from the Republic of Ireland, and wished to return home, being unhappy where she was. The trial judge directed himself according to the then-leading cases of *Poel v Poel*[120] and *Chamberlain v de la Mare*,[121] and granted the mother leave to relocate. Both fathers appealed.

The Court of Appeal (Thorpe LJ and Sir Oliver Popplewell) allowed the appeal and refused the mother leave to relocate. Thorpe LJ agreed with counsel that the judge had been 'lulled into' applying the wrong test by directing himself according to *Poel* and *Chamberlain*:

> the classic approach directed by the two authorities . . . is to be applied only in those cases where there is a relatively clear definition of roles between the parents into primary carer or custodial parent and secondary carer or contact parent. This was not such a case.[122]

The reason why this approach was not applicable to a case of truly shared care was that the factors relevant to the children's welfare were different:

> in a case in which the children are so reliant upon a division of their lives between two adjacent homes the child's sense of security is heavily dependent on the ready availability of each of those homes. In that situation it is very easy to see that however strong may be the mother's internal desire to return to her homeland, such a plan is almost certain to impact adversely on the child's sense of security and thereby on the child's welfare.[123]

However, with this case having disappeared into history, the debate over the right approach to shared care continued, coming to a head in *K v K (Relocation: Shared Care Arrangement)*.[124] Unsurprisingly, *Re C and M* was not brought to the

[117] *Re Y (Leave to Remove from Jurisdiction)* [2004] 2 FLR 330 (EWHC); *Re D (Leave to Remove: Shared Residence)* [2006] EWHC 1794 (Fam), [2006] *Family Law* 1006; *C v C (International Relocation: Shared Care Arrangement)* [2011] EWHC 335 (Fam), [2011] 2 FLR 701.

[118] *K v K (Relocation: Shared Care Arrangement)* [2011] EWCA Civ 793, [2012] 2 FLR 880.

[119] *Re C and M (Children)*, 30 July 1999 (EWCA), online at www.bailii.org/ew/cases/EWCA/Civ/1999/2039.html.

[120] *Poel v Poel* [1970] 1 WLR 1469 (EWCA).

[121] *Chamberlain v de la Mare* (1983) 4 FLR 434 (EWCA).

[122] *Re C and M (Children)*, 30 July 1999 (EWCA) [17] (my paragraph numbering).

[123] ibid [18] (my paragraph numbering).

[124] *K v K (Relocation: Shared Care Arrangement)* [2011] EWCA Civ 793, [2012] 2 FLR 880 [hereafter, *K v K*].

Court of Appeal's attention; the judges in *K v K* therefore assumed that the issue of shared care relocation was *res integra* and approached matters from first principles. On that basis, the two family law specialists sitting in that case – Thorpe and Black LJJ – reached different conclusions about the right approach to shared care relocation cases.[125]

Thorpe LJ's reasoning reflected his judgment in *Re C and M*: his Lordship thought that where there was a genuinely shared care arrangement such that neither parent could claim to be the child's sole primary carer, the *Payne* approach should not be applied. Rather, a judge should use the *welfare checklist* as the primary guidance. For Thorpe LJ, there was 'no doubt at all that the guidance in *Payne* is posited on the premise that the applicant is the primary carer':[126]

> [T]he survival of the authority of *Poel* into this century, in my judgment depends crucially upon the primacy of the applicant's care. As [counsel for the father] put it, if [the applicant] is supplying so much she must be supported in her task precisely because the children are so dependent on her stability and wellbeing. Once the care is shared there is not the same dependency and the role of each parent may be equally important. The judgments in *Poel* consider only the position of the primary carer and an earlier position where there is a pending contest as to who should be the primary carer. *Payne* does not anywhere consider what should be the court's approach to an application where there is no primary carer.[127]

By contrast, Black LJ's view was that she 'would not put *Payne* so completely to one side' in a shared care case.[128] Her Ladyship stressed that it was important to consider both main judgments in *Payne* and, looking at Butler-Sloss P's judgment, said this:

> Dame Elizabeth referred, of course, to the effect on the parent with residence (paragraphs 83 and 84) but she also stressed that the relationship with the other parent is highly relevant and that there are many other factors which may arise in an individual case (paragraph 84). I detect in her discussion of the factors and in her summary at paragraph 85 no weighting in favour of any particular factor. She said that the reasonable proposals of the parent with a residence order wishing to live abroad carry 'great weight' whereas the effect on the child of denying contact with the other parent is 'very important' but I do not infer from that phraseology any loading in favour of the reasonable proposals as opposed to the effect of the loss of contact.
>
> *Payne* therefore identifies a number of factors which will or may be relevant in a relocation case, explains their importance to the welfare of the child, and suggests helpful disciplines to ensure that the proper matters are considered in reaching a decision but it does not dictate the outcome of a case. I do not see Hedley J's decision in *Re Y* as representative of a different line of authority from *Payne*, applicable where the child's care is

[125] Moore-Bick LJ appears to give no answer to the question of whether *Payne* applies to a shared care case or not, though Munby LJ later suggested that his Lordship should be read as agreeing with Black LJ: see *Re F (Relocation)* [2012] EWCA Civ 1364, [2013] 1 FLR 645 [43]–[44]. For criticism of Munby LJ's ambitious reasoning on this point, see R George, 'International Relocation, Care Arrangements, and Case Taxonomy' [2012] *Family Law* 1478, 1482.

[126] *K v K* [41].

[127] *K v K* [46].

[128] *K v K* [96].

> shared between the parents as opposed to undertaken by one primary carer; I see it as a decision within the framework of which *Payne* is part. It exemplifies how the weight attached to the relevant factors alters depending upon the facts of the case.[129]

In other words, Black LJ suggested that, since all the guidance in *Payne* is fact-sensitive and does not involve presumptive assessments, there is no reason why the same guidance should not be used regardless of the particular care arrangements. The answers which will be reached to each sub-question might differ, but the questions themselves are equally applicable.

The advantage of Black LJ's approach is that it would keep international relocation disputes within a single analytical framework, and therefore avoid initial arguments between the parties about whether they are in a shared care arrangement or not.[130] It may also avoid possible knock-on effects on children's residence arrangements long before relocation becomes an issue. Two practitioners – a trial judge and a senior barrister – who were interviewed for this research reported experiences of parents seeking or opposing shared care arrangements principally to make possible future relocation applications more or less difficult.[131] On the other hand, relying on trial judges to modify the guidance every time creates a risk that they will neglect to do so, as arguably happened in *Re F (Relocation)*.[132]

Given the binding authority of *Re C and M*, which supports Thorpe LJ's approach in *K v K*, it may be that the technically better view is that shared care relocation applications should be approached differently from cases where there is a clear primary carer.[133] However, in practical terms, it can be argued that there is little difference between these two 'approaches'. Some of the factors mentioned in *Payne* – such as whether the application is brought in good faith, and whether the proposed move is adequately planned – will be relevant whether those questions are drawn directly from *Payne* or not. On the other hand, other factors – such as the relevance of the effect of refusing relocation, or the detriment to the child's relationship with the non-moving parent if relocation is allowed – will often be assessed differently in a shared care case, whether that is said to be a modification of the *Payne* guidance or to be a separate set of guidance entirely.

[129] *K v K* [143]–[144].

[130] *K v K* [145]. See also Munby LJ's discussion to the same effect in *Re F (Relocation)* [2012] EWCA Civ 1364, [2013] 1 FLR 645 [58]–[61], and Hedley J's application of this approach in *S v T (Permission to Relocate to Russia)* [2012] EWHC 4023 (Fam), [2013] 2 FLR 457 [5]–[6].

[131] Participant EB6 called these residence negotiations 'shadow-boxing' because they related mainly to relocation rather than residence, while participant EJ2 said that 'in anticipation of there being a relocation application further along the line, one of the parents – usually the father – will do his utmost to achieve a shared care arrangement, not just for its own sake but also in order to make the prospect of leave to remove more difficult'.

[132] *Re F (Relocation)* [2012] EWCA Civ 1364, [2013] 1 FLR 645; the argument is made more fully in R George, 'International Relocation, Care Arrangements and Case Taxonomy' [2012] *Family Law* 1478.

[133] Thorpe LJ noted that about 3.1% of families fitted this fact pattern, and so the exception is 'unlikely to affect many orders': *K v K* [59], citing J Ermish, M Iacovou and A Skew, 'Family Relationships' in S McFall and C Garrington (eds), *Understanding Society: Early Findings from the First Wave of the UK's Household Longitudinal Study* (Colchester, Institute for Social and Economic Research, 2011).

Relocation within the United Kingdom

As with relocation in shared care cases, relocation within the United Kingdom is outside the framework of *Payne.* Whereas international moves are prohibited by section 13(1)(b) of the Children Act in the absence of the written consent of all those with parental responsibility for the child, there is no statutory prohibition on moves within the UK, and so a different line of authority has developed in this area.[134] There is very little reported case law on internal relocation in England, for which two causes might be identified. One is that most internal relocation cases are tried by District Judges, and are consequently appealed to Circuit Judges (or High Court Judges if the District Judge was sitting in the Principal Registry), and consequently only reach the Court of Appeal (and therefore the public domain) in the exceptional case where a second appeal is pursued.

The second explanation for the lack of case law on internal relocation may be the court's approach to such disputes, stemming from *Re E (Residence: Imposition of Conditions).*[135] In *Re E,* the trial judge made a residence order in favour of the mother, but imposed a condition requiring her to live at a given address. On appeal, Butler-Sloss LJ concluded that, although the law provided a power to make restrictions on a child's place of residence,[136] Parliament could not have intended this power to be used broadly:

> [W]here the parent is entirely suitable and the court intends to make a residence order in favour of that parent, a condition of residence is in my view an unwarranted imposition upon the right of the parent to choose where he/she will live within the UK or with whom. There may be exceptional cases, for instance, where the court, in the private law context, has concerns about the ability of the parent to be granted a residence order to be a satisfactory carer but there is no better solution than to place the child with that parent.[137]

Later cases confirmed that restrictions on relocation within the United Kingdom were to be considered 'truly exceptional'.[138]

However, while *Re E* has been cited by the House of Lords with apparent approval,[139] it is not without its critics.[140] One difficulty is that the assumptions

[134] For an argument against having two lines of authority, see below, pp 138–43.

[135] *Re E (Residence: Imposition of Conditions)* [1997] 2 FLR 638 (EWCA).

[136] Children Act 1989 (England), s 11(7) makes clear that '[a] section 8 order may . . . impose conditions' and implies no legal limitations to the scope of those conditions.

[137] *Re E (Residence: Imposition of Conditions)* [1997] 2 FLR 638 (EWCA) 642.

[138] *Re B (Prohibited Steps Order)* [2007] EWCA Civ 1055, [2008] 1 FLR 613 [7]; see also *Re S (A Child) (Residence Order: Condition) (No 2)* [2002 EWCA Civ 1795, [2003] 1 FCR 138. For examples where restrictions were made, see *Re H (Children) (Residence Order: Condition)* [2001] EWCA Civ 1338, [2001] 2 FLR 1277; *B v B (Residence: Condition Limiting Geographic Area)* [2004] 2 FLR 979 (EWHC); *Re L (Internal Relocation: Shared Residence Order)* [2009] EWCA Civ 20, [2009] 1 FLR 1157.

[139] *Re G (Residence: Same-Sex Parents)* [2006] UKHL 43, [2006] 2 FLR 629 [15].

[140] Ward LJ has twice indicated that he is uncomfortable with the *Re E* approach: see *Re W (Children)* [2005] EWCA Civ 717 [12]; *Re G (Contact)* [2006] EWCA Civ 1507, [2007] 1 FLR 1663 [26].

which inform *Re E* may no longer hold true.[141] In 1997, when *Re E* was decided, residence orders were almost invariably made in favour of one parent only: a shared residence order required proof of 'positive benefit' and was 'not the conventional order'.[142] It may therefore be understandable that restrictions on relocation were considered to be appropriate only in rare circumstances. However, in child law cases 'statements of principle may not hold their value much beyond the times in which they were expressed'.[143] Since 1997, the English courts have increasingly favoured shared residence orders, though the relationship between such orders and the practical arrangements for children's day-to-day care is somewhat unclear.[144]

Alongside these background changes, three more recent Court of Appeal cases appear, between them, to have started to downplay the importance of the 'exceptionality' criterion that grew out of *Re E*, replacing it with a broader welfare test. Some practitioners interviews for this research in 2008–09 were certainly in favour of this kind of change,[145] and Court of Appeal cases in 2009, 2010 and 2012 might suggest that there has now been some shift in emphasis.

The first case to start this shift (though perhaps unintentionally) was *Re L (Internal Relocation: Shared Residence Order)*.[146] Having reviewed the previous authorities at length, including discussion of the exceptionality criterion, Wall LJ explained the proper approach to internal relocation cases in this way:

> In each case what the court has to do is to examine the underlying factual matrix, and to decide in all the circumstances of the case whether or not it is in the child's interest to relocate with the parent who wishes to move . . .
>
> For the reasons which I have given . . . the correct approach, in my view, is . . . to look at the underlying factual substratum in welfare terms, bearing in mind the tension which may well exist between the freedom to relocate which any parent must enjoy against the welfare of the child which may militate against relocation. In my judgment, it is this balance which is critical, and . . . the court [must not] lose sight of, or give insufficient weight to the former consideration.[147]

In other words, his Lordship emphasised that the core of the approach was the child's welfare, and made no reference to any exceptionality test.

[141] This argument is made more fully in R George, 'Re L (Internal Relocation: Shared Residence Order) [2009] EWCA Civ 20, [2009] 1 FLR 1157' (casenote) [2010] *Journal of Social Welfare and Family Law* 71, 74.

[142] *A v A (Minors) (Shared Residence)* [1994] 1 FLR 669 (EWCA) 678.

[143] *Re L, V, M and H (Contact: Domestic Violence)* [2000] 2 FLR 334 (EWCA) 365.

[144] See, eg, L McCallum, 'Shared Residence: Just a Label?' [2004] *Family Law* 528; P Harris and R George 'Parental Responsibility and Shared Residence Orders: Parliamentary Intentions and Judicial Interpretations' [2010] *Child and Family Law Quarterly* 151; S Harris-Short, 'Resisting the March Towards 50/50 Shared Residence: Rights, Welfare and Equality in Post-Separation Families' [2010] *Journal of Social Welfare and Family Law* 257.

[145] See below, pp 94–95.

[146] *Re L (Internal Relocation: Shared Residence Order)* [2009] EWCA Civ 20, [2009] 1 FLR 1157; for fuller discussion see R George, 'Re L (Internal Relocation: Shared Residence Order) [2009] EWCA Civ 20, [2009] 1 FLR 1157' (casenote) [2010] *Journal of Social Welfare and Family Law* 71.

[147] *Re L (Internal Relocation: Shared Residence Order)* [2009] EWCA Civ 20, [2009] 1 FLR 1157 [36] and [51].

The next case was *Re F (Children) (Internal Relocation)*,[148] where Wilson LJ said that he was 'puzzled' by three aspects of the authorities on internal relocation. One puzzle was precisely which section of the Children Act should be used to prohibit a relocation within the UK, with Wilson LJ cautiously opting for a *prohibited steps order* under section 8.[149] The second puzzle was about why domestic and international relocation law had developed so differently, and in particular why some factors were highlighted in one line of authority and completely sidelined in the other.[150] Wilson LJ's implication, that these two lines of authority ought to be reconsidered together and, if possible, harmonised, has much merit.[151]

Finally, Wilson LJ took issue with the requirement that only 'exceptional' facts would justify restrictions on internal relocation.[152] His Lordship expressed dissatisfaction with an exceptionality test in general, thinking that it constituted an unjustified gloss on the welfare principle. However, in contrast to earlier cases where similar 'glosses' have been removed by the Court of Appeal,[153] Wilson LJ thought that the Court of Appeal was bound by its own earlier decisions. Nonetheless, it is clear that the judges in *Re F* were uncomfortable, and the trial judge's creative approach of describing the case as 'truly exceptional' on the basis that it was 'as close . . . to a case of removal from the jurisdiction as one could possibly get',[154] was endorsed by Wilson LJ with the words '[s]ince that conclusion has to be expressed as a conclusion that the case was exceptional, so be it'.[155]

The final case in the trio was *Re S (A Child) (Residence Order: Internal Relocation)* in 2012.[156] Sir Mark Potter gave the leading judgment, Black LJ and Norris J agreeing. After discussing Wall LJ's judgment in *Re L*, Sir Mark summarised the correct approach to an internal relocation case as being 'to look at the factual matrix and determine what was in the child's best interests'.[157]

There is some discussion in *Re S* about whether the exceptionality test might continue to apply if the applicant is clearly the child's main carer, rather than the case involving truly shared care.[158] Although the judges reach no conclusion on that question, the better view is that it does not. As a matter of principle, Wall LJ

[148] *Re F (Children) (Internal Relocation)* [2010] EWCA Civ 1428, [2011] 1 FLR 1382; see R George, 'Re F (Children) (Internal Relocation) [2010] EWCA Civ 1428' (casenote) [2011] *Journal of Social Welfare and Family Law* 169.

[149] *Re F (Children) (Internal Relocation)* [2010] EWCA Civ 1428, [2011] 1 FLR 1382 [23]. The main alternative which his Lordship was considering was a condition on the residence order itself, as envisaged in Children Act 1989 (England), s 11(7). Another possibility is a *specific issue order* about the children's school or some other geographically fixed element of the child's upbringing.

[150] *Re F (Children) (Internal Relocation)* [2010] EWCA Civ 1428, [2011] 1 FLR 1382 [24].

[151] See further below, pp 138–43.

[152] *Re F (Children) (Internal Relocation)* [2010] EWCA Civ 1428, [2011] 1 FLR 1382 [25].

[153] See, eg, *D v D (Shared Residence Order)* [2001] 1 FLR 495 (EWCA), removing the earlier gloss which could be seen in cases like *A v A (Minors) (Shared Residence)* [1994] 1 FLR 669 (EWCA).

[154] Judgment of Mr Recorder Bullock, quoted by Wilson LJ in *Re F (Children) (Internal Relocation)* [2010] EWCA Civ 1428, [2011] 1 FLR 1382 [27].

[155] *Re F (Children) (Internal Relocation)* [2010] EWCA Civ 1428, [2011] 1 FLR 1382 [37].

[156] *Re S (Residence Order: Internal Relocation)* [2012] EWCA Civ 1031, [2012] 3 FCR 153.

[157] ibid [37].

[158] ibid [56]–[65] (Sir Mark Potter) and [79]–[82] (Black LJ).

thought that there should be no difference when he gave his judgment in *Re L (Internal Relocation: Shared Residence Order)*,[159] and in *Re S* itself the Court of Appeal made no criticism of the trial judge's decision to adopt a broad welfare analysis, despite that being a case where the applicant was clearly the primary carer.

Consequently, although the matter is not yet entirely clear, it seems reasonable to suggest that there has been a retreat from the exceptionality test in favour of a broad welfare analysis:

> The position now seems to be best expressed as being a pure welfare decision, albeit restrictions on a parent's movement within the United Kingdom will probably, as a matter of fact, be unusual because more often the welfare analysis will suggest that relocation, particularly over short or medium distances within the UK, should be allowed.[160]

Having thus established the English position, we can compare the approach in New Zealand. We saw earlier that, until the middle of 1995, New Zealand followed *Poel*. The next section addresses the shift which occurred thereafter.

Rejecting *Poel*: New Zealand, 1995–2012

The moment when New Zealand law departed from *Poel* can be identified clearly. In March 1995, the Family Court was following the English approach;[161] in May 1995, the New Zealand Court of Appeal set out a different approach in the case of *Stadniczenko v Stadniczenko*.[162] Since the key case involved internal relocation, it is worth noting that New Zealand takes the same approach regardless of whether the move is international or domestic. Indeed, there appears to be an increasing trend to litigate, and restrict, moves over very short distances,[163] though most cases continue to involve reasonably long distances.

In *Stadniczenko*, the mother wished to move from Wellington to Auckland. The Family Court allowed the move, but the High Court imposed conditions requiring the children to reside in Wellington. In dismissing the mother's appeal, the Court of Appeal set out general guidance on relocation.

The Court of Appeal began by echoing its earlier decision in *Wright v Wright*,[164] that '[w]here children should reside is normally a matter to be determined by the custodial parent',[165] albeit the court could impose conditions.[166] The Court of Appeal confirmed that the child's best interests should decide the matter; '[s]ubject to that consideration, the rights of the custodial parent to pursue his or

159 *Re L (Internal Relocation: Shared Residence Order)* [2009] EWCA Civ 20, [2009] 1 FLR 1157 [36].

160 R George, F Judd, D Garrido and A Worwood, *Relocation: A Practical Guide* (Bristol, Jordan Publishing, 2013) [2.51].

161 *C v C* [1995] NZFLR 360 (NZFC).

162 *Stadniczenko v Stadniczenko* [1995] NZFLR 493 (NZCA) (hereafter, *Stadniczenko*).

163 See, eg, *Brown v Argyll* [2006] NZFLR 705 (NZHC), restricting relocation of 21 miles (34 km).

164 *Wright v Wright* (1984) 2 NZFLR 335 (NZCA); see above, p 35.

165 *Stadniczenko*, 498.

166 Guardianship Act 1968 (New Zealand), s 11(2); see now COCA 2004, s 48(5).

her own life or career and the rights of the non-custodial parent to access can be taken into account' since these rights 'may also be important considerations in their impact on the welfare of the child'.[167] The Court of Appeal went on:

> The preferable approach is for the Court to weigh and balance the factors which are relevant in the particular circumstances of the case at hand, without any rigid preconceived notion as to what weight each factor should have. In most cases, an important factor in favour of the custodial parent is that the award of custody shows that from the day to day point of view the best interests of the child lie with its being with the custodial parent, and an incident of custody is the decision where to live. The wellbeing of the new family unit bears on the best interests of the child. The nature of the relationship between the child and the access parent will always be of importance, and the closer the relationship and the more dependent the child is on it for his or her emotional wellbeing and development the more likely an injury resulting from the proposed move will be. The reason for the move is important, and also the distance of the move. The child's views are relevant. The foregoing factors are far from representing a complete list of what may be relevant.[168]

The court therefore identified five 'important' factors bearing on the assessment of the child's welfare in a relocation case: the well-being of the new family unit; the relationship with the access parent; the reason for the move; the distance involved; and the child's views. This approach offers little guidance as to which of the relevant factors will be most important. In contrast to the English cases, the Court of Appeal evidently thought it would be not uncommon to refuse relocation.[169]

With this approach in place, there were few developments until the English Court of Appeal decision in *Payne*.[170] *Payne* received some attention in the New Zealand courts,[171] and led directly to the New Zealand Court of Appeal decision in *D v S*.[172] The mother was Irish, though she had lived with the New Zealander father in New Zealand for many years. After their relationship ended, she sought to return to Ireland with the three children, aged ten, eight and six. In her evidence, the mother said that she had decided to return to Ireland whether the children went or not. The mother was the main attachment figure in the children's lives, though they spent about 40 per cent of their time with their father. The Family Court refused leave, but the High Court, after discussing *Payne*, allowed the mother's appeal. No stay was obtained, and so by the time the father's further appeal was heard the mother and children had relocated.

[167] *Stadniczenko*, 500.

[168] ibid 500.

[169] Research showed that 48% of litigated relocation applications were successful in 1999–2000: see M Henaghan, B Klippel and D Matherson, 'Relocation Cases' (*New Zealand Law Society Seminar*, Wellington, 2000).

[170] For applications of *Stadniczenko* at first instance, see, eg, *Maaka v Field* [1996] NZFLR 172 (NZFC); *Shankar v Shankar* [1999] NZFLR 537 (NZFC); *S v C* [2000] NZFLR 103 (NZFC).

[171] For discussions in the Family Court, see *Gray v McGill* [2001] NZFLR 782 (NZFC); *Hemer v Eden* [2001] NZFLR 913 (NZFC).

[172] *D v S* [2002] NZFLR 116 (NZCA) (hereafter, *D v S*).

The Court of Appeal held that *Payne* was inconsistent with New Zealand law and should not be followed. In a full consideration of relocation law, the Court of Appeal made seven points of principle relevant to relocation, which can be summarised as follows:

1. Although the child's welfare was 'not the only consideration' (because, for example, 'freedom of movement is an important value in a mobile community'), it was paramount, meaning that it 'rules upon or determines the course to be followed'.[173]
2. '[T]he approach mandated by [the welfare principle] and the emphasis on the parents' responsibilities for the wellbeing of the child are wholly consistent with the relevant provisions of the United Nations Convention on the Rights of the Child'.[174]
3. The court needed to consider all aspects of welfare and 'weigh all relevant factors in the balance in determining what will be in the best interests of the child. It is necessarily a predictive assessment. It is a decision about the future. It is not a reward for past behaviour. There is no room for *a priori* assumptions'.[175]
4. There must be no presumptions about which parent will be best suited to being a child's primary carer based on gender.[176]
5. Decisions about relocation may be affected by 'the nature and duration of the existing custodial arrangements'.[177]
6. Decisions of foreign courts are of limited use, because even if those courts apply the welfare principle, 'the social landscape in which it is applied will not replicate our local circumstances.' Examples of differences include 'the growth and degree of involvement of both parents in family care, and a clear move in Family Court orders, away from . . . concepts of sole custody and access, to shared care'.[178]
7. Relocation cases were difficult and Family Court judges had given anxious thought as to how they should be resolved. It would not be appropriate to give further guidance, because that would interfere with the individualised assessment required in every case.[179]

The Court of Appeal also discussed *Payne*. The Court set out the two propositions which Thorpe LJ had extracted from the English authorities – namely (a) that the child's welfare is paramount, and (b) that refusing leave is very likely to be harmful for the child and so leave should be granted unless it is incompatible with the child's interests[180] – and said:

[173] *D v S* [30], quoting *J v C* [1970] AC 668 (UKHL) 710–11.

[174] *D v S* [31]; a similar conclusion was reached in *Payne* [39], [78], with regard to the Human Rights Act 1998 (England).

[175] *D v S* [32]–[33].

[176] *D v S* [34].

[177] *D v S* [35].

[178] *D v S* [36].

[179] *D v S* [37]–[38].

[180] *Payne* [26]; see above, p 38.

> so far as New Zealand law is concerned . . . proposition (a) is the governing requirement under New Zealand law and not simply a proposition to be weighed alongside [proposition] (b); and as to (b), there can be no justification for isolating one factor and according it presumptive effect.
>
> . . .
>
> *Payne v Payne* is thus marked by the emphasis on guidelines, by the prescribing of an approach to relocation cases where there is a primary carer who wishes to remove the child from the jurisdiction; and by the allocation of particular weight to the reasonable proposals and emotional and psychological wellbeing of the primary carer. It is not a long step to the assumption that the happiness of the relocating parent will meet the best interests of the child's welfare.
>
> For reasons apparent from the earlier analysis, presumptive or *a priori* weighing is inconsistent with the wider all-factor child-centred approach required under New Zealand law.[181]

The Court thereby affirmed *Stadniczenko*: all factors are to be weighed in determining best interests; no factor carries any a priori weight; it is for the trial judge to decide, on the facts, what is most important for this particular child.

In contrast with more recent developments in the New Zealand courts, attention may be drawn at this stage to one particular aspect, namely the effect on the applicant parent of allowing or refusing relocation. *D v S* held that New Zealand courts must not give this factor especial weight in advance of the hearing (which their Honours thought *Payne* required). However, this meant only that trial judges had to determine from the evidence before them what weight to give that factor (as with all other factors). Thus in *R v S*, Heath J said:

> It cannot be right to prevent a Family Court judge from taking into account, when dealing with . . . relocation, the fact that a parent who intends to [relocate] will improve his or her own wellbeing, and therefore his or her ability to provide parental guidance to a child. Those are the very sorts of considerations which ought to be taken into account.[182]

Priestley J later reiterated that '[t]he fact that the health and wellbeing of a primary carer will be enhanced if relocation occurs is a potent factor which should not lightly be ignored'.[183] We return to this point later.[184]

The next event of significance was the introduction of the Care of Children Act 2004 (COCA 2004).[185] The only explicit reference to relocation in COCA 2004 is the specification that relocation is a guardianship issue,[186] meaning that guardians

[181] *D v S* [41], [46] and [47].
[182] *R v S* [2004] NZFLR 207 (NZHC) [47].
[183] *MBS v EAC* [2005] NZFLR 1 (NZHC) [39].
[184] See below, pp 56–57.
[185] COCA 2004 entered force on 1 July 2005; see generally M Henaghan, 'Legally Rearranging Families: Parents and Children After Break-Up' in M Henaghan and W Atkin (eds), *Family Law Policy in New Zealand*, 3rd edn (Wellington, LexisNexis, 2007).
[186] COCA 2004, s 16(1) and (2)(b).

must cooperate to address relocation together (with the child as appropriate) and seek court assistance if they are unable to agree.[187] More generally, COCA 2004 confirmed the centrality of welfare,[188] which is guided by six 'principles relevant to the child's welfare and best interests',[189] and with considerable attention given to the views of the child involved.[190]

The introduction of COCA 2004 initiated a debate about whether the approach set out by *D v S* remained good law. One view was that the Act's provisions – particularly principles (b) and (d) of the section 5 *principles relevant to child's welfare and best interests*[191] – gave greater weight to the importance of shared care relationships and meaningful post-separation relationships between both parents and their children. On this view, one consequence would be an increased willingness to refuse a relocation application because of the detrimental impact that the move would have on the child's relationship with the non-moving parent. A key proponent of this view was New Zealand's Principal Family Court Judge, Peter Boshier, both extra-judicially before COCA 2004 entered force[192] and in subsequent judicial comments,[193] and some other judges took the same approach.[194]

Before being overtaken by a further appeal to the Supreme Court, the short-lived Court of Appeal decision in *Bashir v Kacem* in 2010 marked the high point for this approach.[195] Giving judgment and refusing the mother's proposed relocation to Australia, the Court of Appeal held that the wording of section 5 indicated 'some priority or weighting as between the various principles'.[196] In particular, the Court of Appeal thought that the entirety of principle (e) – relating to the child's safety – and the bracketed part of principle (b) – that '(in particular, the child should have continuing relationships with both of his or her parents)' – had priority over the other principles set out in COCA 2004. Accordingly, section 5 'provide[s] a structure or framework for consideration of what best serves a child's welfare and best interests, with a partial indication of weighting as between principles'.[197]

187 COCA 2004, ss 5(c) and 16.

188 COCA 2004, s 4.

189 COCA 2004, s 5, which is set out in full above, p 30.

190 COCA 2004, s 6; *C v S [Parenting Orders]* [2006] NZFLR 745 (NZHC).

191 See above, p 30.

192 P Boshier, 'Relocation Cases: An International View from the Bench' [2005] *New Zealand Family Law Journal* 77.

193 See, eg, *BDD v IBG [Relocation]* [2007] NZFLR 1 (NZFC).

194 See, eg, *MBF v SRF* (2007) 26 FRNZ 370 (NZFC) (Judge Callinicos).

195 *Bashir v Kacem* [2010] NZCA 96, [2010] NZFLR 865.

196 ibid [51].

197 ibid [52]. Judges hearing relocation cases after the Court of Appeal decision but before the Supreme Court appeal clearly thought that these dicta had 'imposed a presumption that relocation will not be allowed unless it can be proven to preserve and strengthen children's relationships with their parents primarily, but also their wider family': *DJP v KDF [Relocation]* [2011] NZFLR 386 (NZFC) [16(d)] (Judge Coyle); see similarly *AMO'H v AMO'H [Relocation]* [2011] NZFLR 298 (NZFC) [73] (Judge von Dadelszen); *Figgs v Figgs* [2011] NZFLR 86 (NZFC) [22] (Judge Murfitt).

However, on further appeal to the New Zealand Supreme Court,[198] a different view was adopted. For Blanchard, Tipping and McGrath JJ in the majority,[199] there was no priority between the principles set out in section 5 of COCA 2004.[200] When there were safety concerns, the child's safety would, as a matter of fact, be the most important factor, but that was not a legal prioritisation.[201] As to the importance of parent–child relationships, the Supreme Court held that the effect of the bracketed part of principle (b) was to create 'internal emphasis within principle (b)'; crucially, that approach meant that the bracketed sub-principle did not have 'presumptive emphasis or priority as against the other lettered principles in s 5'.[202]

Turning away from general principles and towards relocation law in particular, the Supreme Court adopted the view that COCA 2004 should not make relocation applications more difficult.[203] With particular reference to Principal Family Court Judge Boshier's extra-judicial views, the Supreme Court said this:

> the view expressed by the Principal Family Court Judge Peter Boshier in his article entitled 'Relocation Cases: An International View from the Bench' (2005) 5 NZFLJ 77 cannot be supported. The Judge considered that the terms of principle (b) indicated 'parents should not relocate if to do so would have a detrimental impact on the [child's] relationship with the other parent' (at 79). With respect, most relocations are likely to involve some detrimental impact on the relationship with the other parent. The suggested approach would constitute a strong presumption against relocation. This is not the right reading of principle (b).[204]

The full effect of this decision on the practice of the Family Court is still to be seen. The handful of reported decisions since the Supreme Court decisions suggest that, in general, the message from *Kacem* has been accepted in the lower courts.[205] A typical remark came from Judge A Wills, that 'the principles in s 5 of

[198] *Kacem v Bashir* [2010] NZSC 112, [2010] NZFLR 884 [hereafter, *Kacem*]; for commentary, see R George, 'Principles Relevant to Child's Welfare and Best Interests' [2011] *New Zealand Family Law Journal* 26.

[199] Elias CJ and William Young J agreed with the majority about what the law was, but disagreed with the majority's interpretation of the Court of Appeal's judgment. However, it is hard to square the minority's interpretation of what the Court of Appeal meant with what the Court of Appeal actually said.

[200] *Kacem* [21].

[201] *Kacem* [22]; for criticism of this reading of principle (e), see R George, 'Principles Relevant to Child's Welfare and Best Interests' [2011] *New Zealand Family Law Journal* 26, 28.

[202] *Kacem* [28].

[203] For earlier High Court decisions to the same effect, see, eg, *Brown v Argyll* [2006] NZFLR 705 (NZHC) [58], [59] and [63] (Priestley J); *ACCS v AVMB [Parenting Orders]* [2006] NZFLR 986 (NZHC) [52]–[53] (Panckhurst J); *Downing v Stamford* [2008] NZFLR 678 (NZHC) (Priestley J).

[204] *Kacem* [28].

[205] Judge Grace's decision in *SNO v MLT [Relocation]* [2011] NZFLR 881 (NZFC) is less true to the Supreme Court's message. His Honour discussed the Court of Appeal decision in *Bashir v Kacem* [2010] NZCA 96, [2010] NZFLR 865, describing it (at [24]) as 'the leading authority', and seemingly approving of the Court of Appeal's view that COCA 2004 contains 'some indication of the weighing to be given to the various [s 5] principles'. Judge Grace did go on to concede (at [25]) that the Court of Appeal's view on the meaning of s 5(b) had been overturned by the Supreme Court, but his Honour appeared to accord no broader significance to this fact in terms of whether the Court of Appeal judgment constituted good law.

COCA apply but no one of those principles should be given any more weight than another'.[206]

Indeed, in the first relocation appeal reported since *Kacem*, Kós J reiterated the Supreme Court's focus on the highly fact-specific nature of a section 5 analysis.[207] His Honour also commented specifically on principle (b), explaining why (as the Supreme Court had also said) it cannot be seen automatically to militate against a relocation application, while also acknowledging that, as a matter of fact, that consideration might pull against relocation in some cases:

> [Principle 5(b)] cannot be thumb-nailed as preservation of the 'status quo'. It is a more sophisticated inquiry. It is focused more on people than place, for a start. Particular consideration must be given to continuity of children's relations with both parents. In many (perhaps most) cases, relocation of children involves such a degree of dislocation that s 5(b) and (d) tend toward what might be called the 'status quo'.[208]

Elsewhere in his judgment, Kós J addressed the issue of how to approach a relocation application which was made after a parent had already relocated within New Zealand. Some earlier Family Court cases had indicated that moving without permission in this way would usually count against the relocation application,[209] and many participants in this research reported that that was their experience as well.[210] However, in keeping with the Supreme Court's focus on the facts of each case and the relevance of those facts to the welfare enquiry, Kós J observed that the applicant's changed location 'is simply one of the circumstances we must deal with under ss 4 to 5. It is a fact, as it is a fact that the [respondent] remains in [the original location]'.[211] Counsel had been concerned that failure to admonish the mother for her approach would encourage parents seeking to relocate to do so without permission and then present the move to the court afterwards as a fait accompli. For the judge, that consideration was not crucial:

> It may be that this approach encourages relocation, or the presentation of a fait accompli transfer on the part of one parent. If so (and I express no view), it is a policy judgment that Parliament has made. The relocating parent will still usually face something of a minefield in traversing the s 5 principles. In my view it is better to focus on s 5, the welfare of the children, and not allow ourselves to be distracted by inquiring into the adequacy or otherwise of the mother's rationale for her relocation.[212]

[206] *CAA v AAM [Parenting Order]* [2012] NZFLR 109 (NZFC) [23]; *AJB v MJM; TJR v TBM [Relocation]* [2012] NZFLR 993 (NZFC) [9] (Judge Walsh).

[207] *Millett v Clyde* [2012] NZFLR 351 (NZHC) [11].

[208] ibid [56].

[209] See, eg, *BDD v IBG [Relocation]* [2007] NZFLR 1 (NZFC); *JA v LAD*, FAM:2007-070-1478, 28 November 2007 (NZFC).

[210] See below, pp 120–21.

[211] *Millett v Clyde* [2012] NZFLR 351 (NZHC) [50].

[212] ibid.

Thus these factors suggest a slight relaxation of the view expressed before *Kacem* whereby it was thought that courts were unlikely to see relocation as being in the child's best interests in most cases.[213]

However, one key factor which was not addressed specifically by the Supreme Court or subsequent cases is the weight given to the applicant parent's health and well-being in assessing the child's welfare. The 2001 Court of Appeal decision in *D v S* took the view that English law gave especial weight to the emotional and psychological well-being of the applicant parent.[214] The Court of Appeal rejected this approach, saying that there must be no a priori weighing of any factor in the welfare assessment.[215] Within this analysis, though, it was clear that the applicant's psychological health might still be important in a particular case if the evidence supported that conclusion.[216]

However, later cases appeared increasingly to take a different view.[217] In one case, Duffy J criticised the trial judge for assuming that relocation would enhance the mother's psychological well-being without obtaining expert evidence, and said that:

> Relocation will only be in the child's best interests if his mother is so harmed by having to remain in New Zealand that her emotional and psychological health will deteriorate to a point where it will impact detrimentally on the child.[218]

With respect, this decision comes close to giving a priori weight to one factor – that is to say, the primary carer's emotional and psychological well-being is being given presumptively little weight.[219] *D v S* requires that judges assess the weight of this, and every, factor based on the facts of the case before them. It is not yet clear whether there has been any shift in approach to this factor following *Kacem*.

The current position in New Zealand is therefore not entirely clear. Mark Henaghan's research showed a drop in the success rate of litigated relocation cases between 2005 and 2008;[220] and although that rate has since risen,[221] it is likely that relocation is nonetheless harder, since lawyers will be 'gatekeeping' cases based on

[213] See F Mackenzie, *Uneasy Trends in Relocation Law* (unpublished LLM Thesis, Victoria University of Wellington: 2009); *CTAI v KMB [Relocation]* [2009] NZFLR 877 (NZFC) [17]; and see the views of participants in this research in 2009, discussed below, pp 128–131.

[214] Recent cases in the English courts have attempted to downplay this interpretation: see above, pp 41–42.

[215] Above, pp 51–52.

[216] See *R v S* [2004] NZFLR 207 (NZHC) [47]; *S v L [Relocation]* [2008] NZFLR 237 (NZHC) [35]–[36], discussed above, p 52.

[217] See, eg, *Bartlett v Bartlett* [2003] NZFLR 49 (NZFC) [51]; *LH v PH [Relocation]* [2007] NZFLR 737 (NZHC), [37]; *CPS v PKD [Relocation]* [2010] NZFLR 601 (NZFC) [58].

[218] *B v B [Relocation]* [2008] NZFLR 1083 (NZHC) [62].

[219] R George, 'The Shifting Law: Relocation Disputes in New Zealand and England' [2009] *Otago Law Review* 107, 125.

[220] M Henaghan, 'Going, Going . . . Gone – To Relocate Or Not To Relocate, That Is The Question' (*New Zealand Family Law Conference*, Auckland, 2009).

[221] ibid.

their understanding that the law opposes relocation.[222] We will see in chapter five that New Zealand practitioners interviewed for this research were clear that relocation had become more difficult in the years leading up to 2009 when interviews took place, which suggests that New Zealand was then rightly seen as 'anti-relocation'; the current position after *Kacem* is less easy to characterise until further cases from the Family Court and High Court are available.

Discussion

This chapter has mapped the development of the legal principle applied to relocation cases as apparent from the available case law in England and New Zealand. However, while those cases can tell us a lot, it is far from being a complete picture. In particular, reported cases cannot tell us what difference the two approaches might make to individual cases. While in New Zealand we know that the success rate of litigated cases dropped after 2005 before rising again,[223] in England there were no equivalent data on success rates,[224] making it impossible to compare the two jurisdictions. Such a comparison might, in any case, tell us little, because cases in each jurisdiction are decided against different background factors, and lawyers filter the cases that reach the courts based on their understanding of how the law is likely to be applied.[225]

It is therefore difficult to tell from the case law discussed in this chapter whether the legal approach itself is likely to make a difference to relocation case outcomes. In the chapters that follow, we investigate these issues further. In chapter three, we examine the likely effects of the law on individual cases by asking practitioners who are experienced in the day-to-day working of relocation law to analyse three hypothetical relocation disputes. In chapters four and five we analyse what those practitioners think about the law in their respective countries.

[222] F Mackenzie, *Uneasy Trends in Relocation Law* (unpublished LLM thesis, Victoria University of Wellington: 2009); in the Australian context, see J Behrens, B Smyth and R Kaspiew, 'Outcomes in Relocation Decisions: Some New Data' [2010] *Australian Journal of Family Law* 97, 100. See generally R Mnookin and L Kornhauser, 'Bargaining in the Shadow of the Law: The Case of Divorce' (1979) 88 *Yale Law Journal* 950.

[223] M Henaghan, 'Care of Children Act Cases: Where Are We, Where Are We Going?' (*LexisNexis Annual Child Law Conference*, Auckland, 2008); M Henaghan, 'Going, Going . . . Gone – To Relocate Or Not To Relocate, That Is The Question' (*New Zealand Family Law Conference*, Auckland, 2009).

[224] Data for 2012 are now available: R George, 'Relocation Disputes in England and Wales: First Findings from the 2012 Study' (Oxford Legal Studies Research Paper, 2013), online at http://ssrn.com/abstract=2306097.

[225] J Behrens, B Smyth and R Kaspiew, 'Outcomes in Relocation Decisions: Some New Data' [2010] *Australian Journal of Family Law* 97, 100.

3

Applying the Law to Hypothetical Facts: Practitioners' Views on Three Case Studies†

English and New Zealand approaches to relocation disputes have developed in different ways since 1995, as we saw in chapter two. However, it is difficult to assess from these separate developments whether different outcomes would be reached in the two jurisdictions were identical cases to come before their courts. Does the English approach guided by *Payne v Payne* make relocation easier to achieve?[1] Does the New Zealand all-factor approach with subsequent statutory guidance make relocation less likely?[2] This chapter offers one way to address these questions. In the first of three chapters drawing on qualitative interviews with legal practitioners, this chapter looks at three hypothetical cases in the form of 350-word vignettes, or short stories, which participants were asked to assess. The vignettes were designed to explore practitioners' views on different aspects of relocation disputes.

In this study,[3] 44 legal practitioners (22 in England and Wales, 22 in New Zealand) were interviewed about their experiences of relocation law.[4] In each country, participants included trial judges, barristers, solicitors and court welfare advisers.[5] Table 3.1 lists these participants, showing their nationality, professional group, sex,[6] the length of time they had been in practice,[7] and the approximate

† Some of the material reported in this chapter, including the graphic illustrations of the predicted outcomes of the case studies, was previously published in R George, 'Practitioners' Views on Children's Welfare in Relocation Disputes: Comparing Approaches in England and New Zealand' [2011] *Child and Family Law Quarterly* 178. I am grateful to Jordan Publishing for permission to reproduce that work here.

[1] *Payne v Payne* [2001] EWCA Civ 166, [2001] 1 FLR 1052 (hereafter, *Payne*).

[2] *D v S* [2002] NZFLR 116 (NZCA) (hereafter, *D v S*); Care of Children Act 2004 (New Zealand) (hereafter, COCA 2004).

[3] See Methodological Appendix for detail on the research methodology.

[4] One English barrister (EB2) and one New Zealand barrister (NB3) did not discuss the vignettes during their interviews, and therefore did not contribute to the data being analysed in this chapter.

[5] New Zealand has less strictly separate legal professions than England. New Zealand lawyers who identified themselves as specialist barristers are referred to as barristers, while those who work as both solicitors and barristers are referred to as solicitors.

[6] To preserve anonymity, the sex of the judges who participated is not indicated on the table. There were five men and two women amongst the English judges, and three men and three women amongst the New Zealand judges.

[7] To preserve anonymity, the time that judges who participated had been on the bench is not indicated on the table. Five of the English judges were Circuit Judges and two sat in the Family Division of the High Court; the average time sitting full time was 9.5 years. All six New Zealand judges sat in the Family Court, and the average time sitting full time was 8.5 years.

Table 3.1 – List of participants showing identifying tag, nationality, professional group, sex, time in practice, and approximate number of relocation trials per year

English participants					New Zealand participants				
Identifying tag	Professional group	Sex	Time in practice (years)	Approximate number of relocation trials per year	Identifying tag	Professional group	Sex	Time in practice (years)	Approximate number of relocation trials per year
EJ1	Judge			4	NJ1	Judge			9–14
EJ2				1	NJ2				5–6
EJ3				2	NJ3				3–4
EJ4				3	NJ4				5–6
EJ5				2/3	NJ5				5–6
EJ6				3–4	NJ6				10–12
EJ7				2–3	NB1	Barrister	F	23	2–3
EB1	Barrister	M	7	1	NB2		M	25	1–2
EB2		M	18	2–3	NB3		F	15	1–2
EB3		M	19	2–3	NB4		M	40	3–4
EB4		F	8	1	NB5		F	35	3–4
EB5	Barrister, QC	M	30	2–3	NB6		F	21	3
EB6		F	24	5–6	NB7		M	25	1–2
EB7		F	24	1–2	NS1	Solicitor/Barrister	M	23	2–3
ES1	Solicitor	M	28	1	NS2		F	30	1–2
ES2		F	9	1–2	NS3		F	22	3
ES3		M	15	2	NS4		F	18	2–3
ES4		F	18	1–2	NS5		F	19	2–3
ES5		M	12	6–8	NS6		F	31	1
EC1	Court Welfare Officer	F	20	1–2	NC1	Psychologist	M	25	7–8
EC2		M	25	3–4	NC2		F	25	12
EC3		F	33	1–2	NC3		M	13	6

number of relocation cases they dealt with each year, and shows the identifying tags by which they are referred to in the text. For ease of reference, identifying tags indicate nationality and professional group. Participants in England and Wales start with an *E*,[8] while those in New Zealand have an *N*. Judges then have a *J*, barristers a *B*, solicitors an *S*, and court welfare advisers a *C*. So, for example, EJ1 is an English judge, NB5 a New Zealand barrister, ES2 an English solicitor, and so on.

Tom's Case

The first vignette is Tom's case.[9] Tom has a primary carer mother and frequent contact with his father; his mother has re-partnered, and her partner's desire to return to his home country has prompted the application to relocate. The full vignette as given to participants is reproduced in Figure 3.1.

> Tom's parents separated when he was two years old. Now aged six, Tom lives with his mother. He has always had good contact with his father, which has been increasing since the parents separated and now includes overnight stays once or twice a fortnight. Although the parents' relationship has been reasonably amicable, Tom's father thinks the mother is indifferent about contact, and she has sometimes resisted increases in the amount of contact between Tom and the father. About a year ago, the mother married an American and is four months pregnant with their first child. The mother's husband is very keen to return to California to be nearer his family, to make a home there, and because he thinks it will provide better opportunities for his growing family. Tom's mother lived in California for a year when she was a student and strongly supports her husband's desire to move home. The father opposes the move because of the great difficulties of contact and otherwise maintaining his relationship with Tom. He is unconvinced by the mother's plans for webcam chat, thinking it more likely he will be sidelined, given Tom's age and the mother's history of indifference to contact generally. The father points out that the mother and Tom are both happy living in [the United Kingdom/New Zealand], and all of the mother's wider family and support networks are here. He is also worried that the mother was unable to tell him what she would do if Tom did not settle well in the USA. The mother counters that her husband's family will all be nearby if they move, and is worried that her husband would be very resentful if he were stopped from returning home because Tom could not be taken too. She also stresses her role as primary carer and the fact that Tom's father works long hours and is not well placed to care for Tom if she went to America anyway.

Figure 3.1: Tom's case, as given to participants

[8] One participant self-identified as being Welsh, though participants were not asked about their nationality.

[9] Tom's case was based loosely on *Re B (Leave to Remove: Impact of Refusal)* [2004] EWCA Civ 956, [2005] 2 FLR 239.

Of the three vignettes, Tom's case most sharply drew out the significance of the differences in legal approach between England and New Zealand, both in terms of participants' discussions of the case and their predictions of the likely outcome. The presence of a primary carer and an international move put the case within *Payne*'s guidance for English participants, while New Zealanders were governed by *D v S* and COCA 2004 (as with all relocation cases).[10] From the discussion of the law in chapter two, it is not surprising that English and New Zealand participants saw Tom's case differently.

As chapter two demonstrated, English law requires relocation cases to focus on the applicant's motivation for relocating and the details of the plan as the first considerations,[11] and the guidance generally assumes a primary carer.[12] In New Zealand, the law stresses that 'the child's relationships with his or her family . . . should be stable and ongoing (in particular, the child should have continuing relationships with both of his or her parents)',[13] and such relationships 'should be preserved and strengthened'.[14]

Looking at participants' reasoning in Tom's case, four key themes emerged, highlighting clearly the differences in the application of relocation law to particular facts. The four themes, which overlap and interrelate, are:

- the reasons for the relocation, together with the impact of refusal of leave on the mother, the stepfather and their family unit;
- Tom's age and relationship with his father, and the likely effect of relocation on that relationship;
- the mother's attitude to contact between Tom and the father; and
- the role of the wider family in Tom's life.

These themes will be addressed in turn.

Starting, then, with the reasons for relocation and the effect of refusal of leave to relocate, although this factor was frequently mentioned by both English and New Zealand participants, its relevance differed. English participants generally thought that the motivations for moving to California ('to be nearer [the stepfather's] family, to make a home there, and because [the stepfather] thinks it will provide better opportunities for his growing family') indicated 'that the mother was wanting to relocate for sound reasons' (EJ3). One English barrister said that 'the absolute point, to me, is the belief that the move to California will provide better opportunities for the growing family' (EB6). This barrister went on, like most English participants, to say that she wanted to know more about these

[10] Interviews took place before either the Court of Appeal or Supreme Court decisions in 2010: see *Bashir v Kacem* [2010] NZCA 96, [2010] NZFLR 865, partly rev'd by *Kacem v Bashir* [2010] NZSC 112, [2010] NZFLR 884; see above, pp 53–55. Since the effect of the Supreme Court decision is largely to reinforce the *D v S* approach, participants' views from 2009 are likely to remain valid.

[11] *Payne* [40(a)].

[12] *Payne* [86]; *K v K (Relocation: Shared Care Arrangement)* [2011] EWCA Civ 793, [2012] 2 FLR 880.

[13] COCA 2004, s 5(b).

[14] COCA 2004, s 5(d).

'better opportunities', but most agreed that 'the mother is going to be able to be convincing about it . . . and she sounds like she has got it all sussed' (ES1). Although some participants said that specific plans such as a job offer would help the application, little difficulty was expected about the details of the plans: 'you can make an assumption that if he is going back to America to be near his family, the plans are likely to be reasonable and realistic' (ES3). In other words, the mother would easily meet *Payne*'s requirement that her application be 'founded on practical proposals both well researched and investigated'.[15]

English participants linked these reasons for relocating to the likely effect of refusal of permission. As the barrister quoted above went on to say, 'then I would be looking at the Sedley judgment in *B and S*' (EB6). In the conjoined appeals of *Re B* and *Re S*, Sedley LJ's supporting judgment puts 'emphasis on the importance to the children's welfare of a stable and viable family unit in which to grow up'.[16] Participants frequently picked this point up:

> **EB1:** Authorities are quite clear on this: if you have a new family unit, and you want to move abroad, and you are going to find it very difficult to maintain that new family unit if you are split over different continents, [you] will probably be allowed to go.
>
> **EJ3:** It seemed likely that, if relocation was refused, not only would that cause [the mother] considerable distress, but would also put pressure on her new marriage.

Most English participants therefore thought that refusing permission would impact negatively on the stepfather and put a strain on the marriage,[17] which would be bad for Tom.

In contrast, New Zealand participants were generally unimpressed with the reasons for wanting to relocate, and were sanguine about the possible effects of refusing permission. While some said that the reasons for moving were 'not frivolous' (NJ1), more thought that it was 'not the best reason in the world to go' (NJ2). Some suggested that the outcome 'will be very much dependent on how *essential* [the relocation] is' (NB2, emphasis added), but most did not think it a strong reason. As one New Zealand lawyer said, 'it is just that he wants to go back to make a home there – it is not as if his job has been transferred – so that questions the genuineness of the move' (NS4).

As to the impact of a refusal of leave, some New Zealand participants thought that this factor could be relevant (NS2, NS5). One barrister, when 'playing devil's advocate', wondered whether 'one of the repercussions [of refusing relocation] is potentially that her new husband is going to hate the father . . . [and] is going to be so bloody annoyed about this that he is going to create every problem he can' (NB5). Most, however, thought these considerations – especially the effect on the stepfather – to be 'not particularly significant at all' (NC3), as these two exchanges show:

[15] *Payne* [40(a)].

[16] *Re B (Removal from Jurisdiction); Re S (Removal from Jurisdiction)* [2003] EWCA Civ 1149, [2003] 2 FLR 1043 [31].

[17] Some participants queried this impact, with two judges (EJ2, EJ5) and a barrister (EB7) suggesting that it would need to be proved in the evidence.

Q: What about the suggestion that the mother's husband will be resentful?
NS3: Well, he'll get over it. He should have thought of that before he decided to marry a Kiwi woman.

Q: The mother says her husband will be resentful if he is stopped from going.
NJ4: Yes, well, he will definitely be giving evidence, just to hear what he has to say about that, but of course that's nothing really. I mean, too bad. I think really he is the least of the issues.

Others doubted whether there would, in fact, be much detriment to the stepfather:

NS1: There isn't a lot of information [to show] that . . . having to stay here . . . is actually a bad result for them. It may not be that bad. . . . Yes, [the stepfather] may be grumpy,[18] but he might not be in two weeks' time. This may not be the beginning of life-long domestic violence, disharmony and separation.

The dismissal of this factor by New Zealanders is particularly remarkable in contrast to the dominant treatment which it received in English discussions. The views of two judges highlight the difference particularly well:

EJ5: It looks as though one would let her [relocate] because otherwise it looks as though it is going to have a very negative impact on her new family unit.

NJ2: Her husband may be unhappy, and that may spill over onto the mother, but when you keep your eye on Tom, on Tom's needs, I think that is not a good enough reason.

However, these differences between the English and New Zealand participants fit with the legal approaches of each country.[19] Similarly, when looking at participants' discussions of Tom's relationship with his father, the two national groups again tell sharply different stories. With one exception,[20] the English saw the father as having 'a contact role, and that is always going to be his role' (EB3). English participants thought that Tom 'obviously has a good relationship with the father, but it is not what you might call an unusually close one' (EJ6). Overall, most English practitioners thought that Tom was 'very young to be going that far away from his father, . . . but I don't think that would tip [the outcome] in the father's favour' (EB5). Indeed, as will be seen,[21] most English participants thought relocation so likely in Tom's case that their advice to the father was that 'we would be better trying to get some concessions about the amount of time the child can spend online . . . [and for] financial support . . . for the father to make trips to the

[18] New Zealand participants frequently described the effect on the stepfather with words like 'grumpy', which was notably different from English descriptions of 'resentment' and 'distress'.

[19] For England, see *Payne* [40(c)], [41] and [85(e)] and *Re B (Removal from Jurisdiction); Re S (Removal from Jurisdiction)* [2003] EWCA Civ 1149, [2003] 2 FLR 1043; for New Zealand, see COCA 2004, s 5(b) and (d), *D v S* [46] and *B v B [Relocation]* [2008] NZFLR 1083 (NZHC) [46].

[20] ES2 was concerned that, 'at the age that Tom is, which is relatively young, a move away would have a significant effect on [his] increasing contact [with his father] at a stage where presumably their relationship is really developing'.

[21] See below, p 67.

States, that sort of thing' (EB4).

The focus for the English was therefore on ensuring 'that we get very good contact arrangements' (EB7). Many spoke in detail about the arrangements they would seek ('telephone contact once a week, webcam . . . four visits a year . . . and I am talking four or five weeks in the summer': EB7), which they saw as crucial.[22] The English, therefore, saw Tom's relationship with his father as 'a pretty standard contact arrangement which, in terms of days and nights spent between father and son, can almost be made up [with a different arrangement after relocation]' (EJ6). The contrast, when looking at New Zealanders, could not be more stark.

While New Zealand participants accepted that Tom 'has good contact with his dad' (NJ5), they were 'very concerned at a boy of this age only seeing his dad once or twice a fortnight – why is that?' (NJ5). New Zealanders were 'surprised that he only has overnight stays once or twice a fortnight' (NC2), and there was considerable emphasis on the fact that Tom has 'an evolving relationship' with his father (NB4). Participants thought that Tom's case fitted a broad pattern whereby 'in the normal course of events, [contact] would be expected to increase' (NS2). Indeed, whereas the English thought that Tom's father was always going to be a contact parent, several New Zealand practitioners thought that 'you could envisage it moving into a shared care type of arrangement' (NC3), with 'the possibility for Tom to come, maybe in a year or thereabouts, to live with his father' part of the time (NJ2).

Given that New Zealanders thought that Tom's 'overall interest is to increase [contact]' (NJ5), it is not surprising that they were concerned about the loss of that relationship if he relocated. The fact that Tom was only six years old, coupled with 'increasing . . . albeit still not extensive' contact (NB7), raised a concern that Tom 'is actually quite vulnerable at this stage to the loss of the relationship with the left-behind parent' (NJ1). Participants thought the relationship would be 'very adversely affected' (NJ6) and 'seriously disrupted' (NB4); several remarked that there was 'a developing relationship, so you would be concerned at this age of killing it' (NB2).[23] These findings again fit with what one would expect given the statutory provisions and case law in the two countries.

The third theme of Tom's case – the mother's attitude to contact between Tom and the father – links strongly to the second. For the English, the mother's apparent indifference to contact raised two difficulties: whether her attitude suggested 'some selfish desire to exclude the father from the child's life',[24] and whether the detailed contact plans, which they thought so important, were likely to be complied with. A noticeable feature of English comments on the mother's attitude was the lack of surprise. A typical remark was that 'a certain amount of indifference is to be expected in a situation like this' (EB3). For most participants, the mother's attitude was less significant than her actions, because 'there is a difference between

[22] A common theme was that the mother would need to fund a large part of the cost of contact.

[23] *cf* NJ2 ('it would be something like an end to his relationship with his father'), NB5 ('it is going to end that [relationship], almost certainly') and NS3 ('this will be one of those cases where Tom goes off to America and that will be [the end of] that').

[24] *Payne* [40(a)].

indifference and positive obstruction' (EJ2): '[the father] says she has been indifferent to contact, [but] he's still having regular contact' (EB1). Participants thought that the problems over contact were minor – described by one judge as 'the odd niggle' (EJ6) – and 'if contact is going well now, that is probably what the court is going to draw a line under' (EB4).

English participants also thought that, although the mother's attitude could be significant,[25] it would be difficult to build the point up enough for it to have much effect:

> **EJ5:** she may be somewhat indifferent and see [relocation] as a good excuse not to support the father's position, but it is going to be very hard to winkle that out because she, if she is represented ably, is going to present you with a nice little package of how she is going to achieve it all.

> **EJ7:** I would have to be convinced that [the mother's] indifference would spill over into actually stopping [contact] or . . . allowing it to wither on the vine . . . But I suspect, having heard her, she would probably say all the right things, even if she didn't mean them.

The English therefore saw the mother's attitude as relatively unimportant, because they saw 'no convincing evidence that the mother would not . . . facilitate contact' (EJ6). In any case, the English thought they would obtain a mirror order with the American courts. Lawyers thought that a mirror order would 'show the court that they can really trust her to promote contact' (ES2), while one judge referred to 'another decision of Lord Justice Thorpe's . . . where he says, "she may be indifferent about contact, but if you have got an enforceable contact order then you have got to assume that the foreign court will enforce it"' (EJ2).[26]

New Zealand participants took a different approach to both of these aspects. As to the enforcement of contact orders, many New Zealanders said that they would have 'no confidence whatsoever that the Americans would uphold the legal arrangements we put in place' (NB4). This was particularly an issue in America, participants thought, because of 'the ability to be transient within the USA . . . you go to a different State, and all of a sudden you have got enforcement issues' (NJ5).

As to the mother's attitude, a number of New Zealand participants said that it would need exploring, but many took the view that 'if it emerged at trial that she is [indifferent], I think that is definitely the last nail in the coffin' (NB5). Another lawyer made a similar comment as the first thing she said about Tom's case:

> **NS3:** The mother's history of indifference – well, she's sunk before she starts . . . Sorry mum, you can't head off and be indifferent. That's not what it's about. You have got to promote, improve, maintain, and indifference is not enough . . . She's not even trying.

[25] ES5 thought that the point had potential to be decisive in the father's favour, though this was by no means certain.

[26] Possibly *Re B (Children) (Removal from Jurisdiction)* [2001] 1 FCR 108 (EWCA) [14], or *Re B (Leave to Remove)* [2008] EWCA Civ 1034, [2008] 2 FLR 2059, though the latter would seem suggest that a desire to terminate contact may justify refusing relocation despite an enforceable contact order in the destination country.

New Zealanders placed great weight on Tom's relationship with his father, and were concerned about the mother's attitude to contact, which made them 'wonder whether the mother has . . . an agenda not to genuinely support the relationship' (NJ1). They doubted whether an enforceable contact order would overcome the mother's lack of support.

The final theme in Tom's case related to the importance of wider family for Tom's welfare. New Zealanders described these relationships as being 'important for this child' (NB6) because 'they seem to feature prominently here too' (NS3). Several New Zealand participants linked the wider family specifically to statutory provisions about the continuity of family relationships,[27] which was of particular concern to participants who questioned the stability of the mother's relationship with her husband: '[The fact that the mother's family would be left behind] doesn't bode well, to start with: statistically, we know that second marriages have got quite a high risk of collapsing' (NC2).

The English analysis of this point had a very different feel. While some English participants mentioned the mother's new husband's family in California – which New Zealanders dismissed as 'far less important (NB6) – only three made specific reference to the extended family who would be left behind in the UK, and none gave significant weight to this consideration in its own right. For two participants, the importance of Tom's left-behind family related to opportunities for contact between Tom and the father:

> **ES2:** [The mother] would be leaving her own support network behind . . . so hopefully she may be visiting here quite regularly, and that will hopefully give an opportunity for there to be good contact [between Tom and his father].

> **EJ5:** Enforcement of contact orders can become rather problematic, but she has got quite a family here, so she is going to be coming back now and again, so I am sure something could be held over her.

The only other reference amongst English practitioners picked up *Payne*'s question about the extent to which the loss of relationships in one country can be 'offset' by the development of relationships in another:[28] 'the stepfather's ties with [California] . . . would go to ameliorate the loss of the paternal family in this country' (EB6).

The analysis of Tom's case shows that English and New Zealand practitioners focused on different aspects in assessing the relocation application. The English were concerned to protect the mother as primary carer and her relationship with the stepfather, which they saw as likely to be affected detrimentally by refusal of leave. They saw the father as a secondary figure in Tom's life whose role could be adequately preserved with post-relocation contact. New Zealanders, by contrast, focused on Tom's relationship with his father, which they saw as developing towards shared care and likely to be all but destroyed by relocation. The effect of refusal of leave on the mother and the stepfather was not significant for most New Zealanders.

[27] NJ1, NJ5 and NB6 specifically mentioned COCA 2004, s 5(b) ('the child's relationships with his or her family . . . should be stable and on-going') regarding Tom's extended family.

[28] *Payne* [40(b)].

These differences are consistent with the differences in legal approach seen in chapter two, thus highlighting the potential effect of those legal differences in practice.

From these conclusions, it is not surprising to find that the two national groups also disagreed about the likely outcome of Tom's case, as set out in Table 3.2 and illustrated in Figure 3.2. Many participants in both countries saw Tom's case as the most clear-cut, the one about which they were most sure, of the three at which they looked. The opening remarks of two participants illustrate the certainty felt by many, and highlight the differences between the two countries: an English judge's opening words were, '[w]ell, she's going isn't she' (EJ2),[29] while a New Zealand lawyer said that the mother was 'sunk before she starts' (NS3).[30]

Table 3.2 – Table showing numerical representation of participants' views on the likely outcome of Tom's case, on a scale from 0 to 10 where 10 is most likely to allow relocation, arranged by nationality and professional group

	ENGLISH PARTICIPANTS				NEW ZEALAND PARTICIPANTS			
	EJ	EB	ES	EC	NJ	NB	NS	NC
1	8	9	8	8	2	4	2	–
2	9	–	7	7	3	4	4	2
3	9	9	9	8	1	–	1	2
4	9	9	8		2	3	2	
5	9	8	9		2	3	3	
6	9	8			5	3	2	
7	8	9				4		
Mean	8.43				2.70			

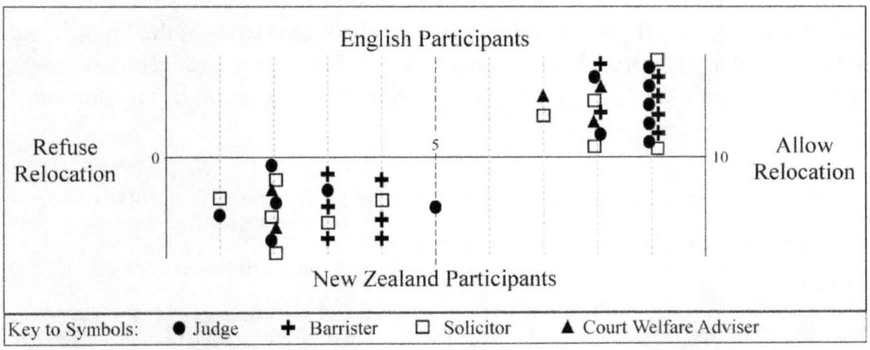

Figure 3.2 – Illustration of participants' views on the likely outcome of Tom's case, on a scale from 0 to 10 where 10 is most likely to allow relocation, arranged by nationality and professional group

[29] As another English judge concluded, 'I can't really envisage any other decision being made' (EJ6).

[30] A New Zealand judge said that 'unless . . . this father was a bit of a prick, I wouldn't think [the mother had] much chance of success' (NJ3).

As Figure 3.2 shows, participants in the two countries had strongly divergent views on Tom's case. English participants unanimously thought the mother's application very likely to succeed, with almost all predictions being eight or nine out of ten.[31] By contrast, with the exception of one judge who said Tom's case 'could go either way' (NJ6), New Zealand participants thought that the mother's application would probably fail. This divergence of both analysis and outcome in Tom's case highlights the key differences arising from the legal approaches of England and New Zealand. The differences between *Payne* and *D v S* when applied to Tom's case meant that practitioners in the two countries applied different processes to their evaluations of the facts, which in turn led to highly divergent outcomes. Might the same variation occur if *Payne* is removed from the English analysis?

Jane's Case

The second vignette, Jane's case,[32] was designed to look at a relocation dispute in circumstances when *Payne*'s influence is lessened because of a shared care arrangement.[33] The care arrangements here were more unusual from an English perspective,[34] but fitted a fairly standard pattern for New Zealanders. Jane, who is 12 years old, spends four nights per week with her mother and three with her father. Jane has a mixed cultural heritage and is bilingual; her father is either Welsh or Māori,[35] and her mother is South African.[36] Her mother, feeling unhappy where she is, wishes to return to South Africa. The full vignette as given to participants is reproduced in Figure 3.3.

Compared to Tom's case, the facts relating to Jane produced similar analyses from the two national groups, which may reflect the similarity of the English and New Zealand legal approaches to cases involving shared care arrangements. Jane's maturity meant that her age and views were the dominant factors for most

[31] It will be unsurprising, following the discussion above, that one English participant who rated the mother's chances at 'only' seven out of ten was ES2, the solicitor whose discussion was seen in many ways to fit more neatly with New Zealanders' analysis: see above, n 20.

[32] Jane's case was based loosely on *Re Y (Leave to Remove from Jurisdiction)* [2004] 2 FLR 330 (EWHC).

[33] Interviews were conducted before *K v K (Relocation: Shared Care Arrangement)* [2011] EWCA Civ 793, [2012] 2 FLR 880, but since that case does not seem to advance the position from that reached in the High Court before already, it does not substantially affect the validity of participants' discussions; see further above, pp 43–45.

[34] As a reminder, the term 'English' is used here as a shorthand for 'the legal jurisdiction of England and Wales', and participants were recruited from around the jurisdiction.

[35] NB6 thought the combination of a Māori father and South African mother unlikely, but no other participants commented on it.

[36] Only one participant (NB6) thought to ask whether this also meant that Jane had a mixed racial heritage; race was an issue conspicuous by its absence in almost all discussions.

Jane is 12 years old, the only child of a [Welsh/Māori] father and a South African mother, currently living [in Pembrokeshire/near Taupo]. Before her parents separated three years ago, Jane's parents were both very involved in her day-to-day care. Although they have had some difficulties in their post-separation relationship, the parents have managed to co-operate well over issues to do with Jane. They live close to one another and, by flexible and informal agreement, Jane normally spends three nights a week with her father and the rest with her mother. The father views his cultural background as particularly important and, with the mother's support, has ensured that Jane is fully aware of her bi-cultural heritage. Both the father and Jane are fluent in [Welsh/Māori], and the mother has what she calls a workable use of the language. Jane's mother has begun to feel increasingly isolated in [Wales/New Zealand], and has several times mentioned that she would prefer to live in Cape Town with her family. The mother has kept close ties with her family, and South Africa generally, and she and Jane have returned many times for visits. The mother has now decided that she wants to return permanently to Cape Town, and take Jane with her. She says she would facilitate generous contact, both in [the UK/New Zealand] and South Africa, and continue to promote Jane's [Welsh/Māori] heritage. The mother has suggested that she might go even if leave to take Jane is refused because she feels so trapped and unhappy, but says that she would be torn and hopes not to have to make that choice. The father opposes the move because of the impact it would have on his relationship with Jane, and on her exposure to the [Welsh/Māori] culture and language. He says he is happy to have full-time care of Jane if the mother decides to move, and would facilitate generous contact both in [the UK/New Zealand] and South Africa. Jane says she wants the present arrangement of shared care to continue, but also that she wants her parents to be happy.

Figure 3.3 – Jane's case, as given to participants

participants,[37] along with the shared care. The two points which showed divergence between the groups were the importance of Jane's mixed heritage, and the psychological and emotional well-being of her mother.

While Jane's views were probably the single most significant factor in participants' discussions, the current shared care arrangement is discussed first since, to some extent, it underpins Jane's views. Participants were told in the vignette that Jane's parents had an amicable relationship and, 'by flexible and informal arrangement, Jane normally spends three nights a week with her father and the rest with her mother'.

English participants saw this split of Jane's care as 'most unusual' (EJ1), reflecting 'an unusually close father-child relationship' (EJ6). Because the English courts allow an arrangement to be called 'shared residence' where the child splits their time substantially unequally between two homes,[38] English participants needed to

[37] While the analysis which follows will show that Jane's age and views are separate, albeit connected, factors, in the first section it is necessary to treat them as one 'factor', since most participants linked them together. A typical start to Jane's case was that 'she is 12, so her views are going to carry probably significant weight' (NJ1).

[38] See, eg, *Re F (Shared Residence Order)* [2003] EWCA Civ 592, [2003] 2 FLR 397; *Re A (Joint Residence: Parental Responsibility)* [2008] EWCA Civ 867, [2008] 2 FLR 1593.

specify that this was 'shared care *stricto sensu*' (EJ1) or 'a real shared care arrangement' (EB6). The effect of shared residence arrangements on relocation is not entirely clear, but the predominant view of cases available at the time was that 'many of the factors to which the court drew attention in *Payne*... whilst relevant may carry less weight' in such cases.[39]

Some English participants thought that the law required them 'to ask, almost as a preliminary question, "who is the residential parent?"' (EJ1). These participants may have been particularly concerned to answer this question because of the mother's indication that she might move even if Jane could not go with her. This meant that shared care was likely to end either way, and so Jane would need to have one main carer to a greater extent than at present. In other words, the question was, 'which parent could she more easily lose?' (EJ2). However, given that 'both parents ... are perfectly capable of looking after the child' (EB3), most English participants agreed that, other things being equal, 'the balance would fall in favour of the child going to live with her father and her mother leaving the country, rather than going to live with her mother and leaving the country' (EB5).

In many ways, New Zealanders agreed about the effect of the shared care. There were, however, two differences. The first related to Jane's split care itself. New Zealand relocation law places little weight on a parent's role as primary carer, and does not adopt different approaches to sole and shared care cases. However, in practice, most New Zealanders agreed that 'the closer to shared care you are, the harder it is to move, because the child is losing more' (NS4). That was not to say that Jane's mother had no chance of success. Indeed, 'the fact that [the mother has] actually promoted this relationship is going to assist [her] in some ways' (NB6) because she was not open to a charge of trying to terminate Jane's relationship with the father.[40] While the English saw Jane's care as unusual, New Zealanders made no particular comment on it, other than to say, for example, that 'they have both been responsible parents who have been actively parenting the child' (NB4). Indeed, participants thought the care arrangement in Jane's case fitted the New Zealand trend towards shared parenting.[41]

The second difference, consequent in part on the normality of shared care in New Zealand, was that the English desire to nominate a primary carer was not mirrored by New Zealanders. New Zealanders said that 'the father is as able to look after Jane as the mother' (NJ2), and that 'dad is in a position to assume full-time care' (NB1). Although two participants asked about '[Jane's] relationship with her mother and the implications of her mother leaving' (NJ1 and similarly NB6), most thought that 'the longevity of arrangements [and] the equality of ability of both

[39] *Re Y (Leave to Remove from Jurisdiction)* [2004] 2 FLR 330 (EWHC) [14].

[40] *cf* Tom's mother, whose 'history of indifference' to contact meant that she was 'sunk before she starts' in seeking to relocate (NS3): see above, p 65.

[41] See generally M Henaghan, 'Legally Rearranging Families: Parents and Children After Break-Up' in M Henaghan and W Atkin (eds), *Family Law Policy in New Zealand*, 3rd edn (Wellington, LexisNexis, 2007), 325–33.

parents [mean] there is not the need for Jane to go . . . with her mother, and it is less critical . . . whether she goes with mum or stays with dad' (NJ2).

So, English and New Zealand participants agreed that shared care was 'not necessarily a bar to removal, because it depends on the circumstances' (EB6), but both thought that the split of care in Jane's case made the mother's application more difficult. This was especially so given Jane's own views, which were given particular attention by participants because of her age (12 years old).

Participants in both countries thought that Jane's views were a powerful factor, with some going so far as to say that her views were 'pretty much going to carry the day' (ES4). Precisely what Jane's views were, though, was unclear. According to the vignette, 'Jane says she wants the present arrangement of shared care to continue, but also that she wants her parents to be happy', with this second point relating to the mother's unhappiness, which was the cause of her desire to relocate. Participants had various interpretations of Jane's views.

One perspective was that Jane probably did not want to make the decision. As one English solicitor said, 'she does what all children do: she wants everyone to be happy, and really she wants her parents to get back together and live happily ever after' (ES3). A second view, which often overlapped with the first, was that 'Jane is going to be pinned down somewhat more' (ES4) and required to give more of a preference. A number of participants said that they 'would be surprised if a 12-year-old didn't have some view about such a move' (EJ3). The third perspective, which was most commonly held, was that, although Jane had expressed separate and somewhat inconsistent views, her desire for the shared care to continue was her main view. Many participants indicated adherence to this perspective tacitly, summarising Jane's position as 'want[ing] . . . things to go on being as they are' (NS5). However, some participants explained why they focused on this aspect:

> **EB3:** the girl's wishes are that . . . she just wants the current arrangements to continue. She says she also wants the parents to be happy, but . . . that is an add-on, and she is saying it second. It is 'and also', and that is a less firmly expressed wish than 'I want the current arrangements to continue'.

For most New Zealanders, Jane's views were one of many factors pointing against relocation, and they were connected to those other considerations by many participants. One judge, for example, saw Jane's views as 'based on continuity of relationships' (NJ1), and so connected to broader concepts of children's welfare in New Zealand law.[42]

Many English practitioners saw Jane's case as relatively borderline, and Jane's views were taken to be a way of deciding what was otherwise a finely balanced case. Two English judges explicitly took this approach:

> **EJ6:** If [Jane] is saying anything, it is that she doesn't want any change. . . . [I]f one were looking for a [deciding] factor – because this is a very nicely balanced case – . . . her apparent wish might be it, against the application.

[42] COCA 2004, s 5(b).

> **EJ7:** Jane's views are important because of her age, and she wants the present arrangement [to continue]. . . . Well, that would give me ground for refusing [relocation], wouldn't it?

While these participants recognised that the mother might move without Jane, and so disrupt the shared care anyway, most were far from convinced that she would actually leave. They thought it likely that the mother would stay, thus allowing the shared care to continue, but also saw the father as capable of taking over the main care if the mother did move and so end the shared care.

Aside from the strength that it lent to her views, Jane's age raised three considerations. One, seen more in English responses, was that, by the age of 12, Jane would be 'very embedded in her community, and so she is not at an age where it is so easy for her to make the move' (EJ2).[43] Most participants who raised this point (nine English, six New Zealanders) saw Jane's age as a reason to oppose relocation because of her established school and social life. However, there was some recognition that this was not the only view. When thinking about how a judge would see the issue, an English barrister highlighted two positions:

> **EB4:** One [judge] could say, 'well, a child of 12, children move schools, still quite adaptable', but [another judge] could also say, 'by that time you are quite settled with friends and it is quite hard to move'. There are two sides of the coin.

Only one participant, a New Zealand judge (NJ1), took the view that Jane was at an age when she could readily move, but a more common concern was about disrupting Jane's schooling and friendships.

Another aspect of Jane's age was that it was not long until she would be grown up. This fact led some participants to have less sympathy for the mother, because it was 'not that many years [for her] to hang on' (EB6). As a New Zealand solicitor said, 'the mum only has to spend three or four more years being here and then she will be free to do as she wishes . . . so that is not too much to ask, I think' (NS5).

The final aspect of Jane's age was noted by only three participants, all of whom came to this point in contrast to what they had said about Tom, namely that 'at 12, a child could hold onto a relationship with the other parent at a distance' (NB2). While this fact in itself neither favours nor disfavours relocation, those participants who mentioned it saw it as a reason for taking the risk that the mother would relocate without Jane. As one English barrister put it, 'I wouldn't expect the mother to find it so impossible to go back [to South Africa] and yet maintain a good relationship with her daughter' (EB7).

This brings us to the mother's suggestion that she will relocate whether the court allows Jane to go or not. According to the vignette, Jane's mother 'has suggested that she might go [to South Africa] even if leave to take Jane is refused because she feels so trapped and unhappy'. This issue was raised by around half of participants (12 English, 11 New Zealanders), though some questioned whether the mother really meant it (EB4, NS4).

[43] On the value of community in a welfare analysis, see now *Re G (Education: Religious Upbringing)* [2012] EWCA Civ 1233, [2013] 1 FLR 677 [27]–[30].

Many English participants connected the mother's intentions to the fact that shared care was unlikely to continue in any event. One solicitor thought that the mother's best strategy for winning the case was to say that she was going anyway, since 'if she just says, "no, I'll just carry on living here", I don't think she is going to go' (ES2). New Zealand practitioners, on the other hand, criticised the mother's suggestion of moving anyway, seeing it as a form of 'blackmail' (NS1). One New Zealand barrister referred to a case 'where the Court of Appeal basically said, "don't you threaten us like that", so I tend to say to clients, "don't issue that threat"' (NB5).[44] Most New Zealanders were unimpressed with the mother's attitude, describing her as 'bloody-minded' (NC1) and as 'thinking more of herself than of the child' (NJ6). As one lawyer put it, 'if the mum will go anyway, well, then she is not worth it' (NS5).

Only one New Zealander specifically linked the mother's willingness to leave Jane behind to her psychological state (NB5), and even this barrister was unconvinced that it would matter, because 'I can just hear a judge saying . . . "well, where is your psychological evidence?", so you would really have to call [expert] evidence' (NB5). Many New Zealand participants thought that they would require medical evidence of the mother's claimed unhappiness, which reflected recent authority on the point.[45] One judge said that 'if [the mother] has got medical reports and is able to back [her claims] up, I would have a look at that' (NJ4), while other participants noted that there was no indication that the mother had such evidence. This dismissive approach fitted the concerns of one lawyer, who was critical of the New Zealand law's attitude to parental well-being, and who said that '[t]he real factor is [the mother's] health and happiness, and the court is simply going to give it no traction' (NS2).[46]

While some English participants similarly questioned 'the extent to which [the mother] really is as isolated as is suggested' (EJ4) – with one barrister reflecting New Zealanders' desire for 'some kind of medical evidence' (EB4) – most tended to accept the mother's claim at face value. Participants said they 'would imagine that she is very isolated in Wales' (EC3), and 'she doesn't need to prove that she is psychiatrically ill' (EJ6). The English approach – seeing 'the big factor in the mother's favour [as being] the unhappiness that she would feel at being here' (EJ7) – fits with *Payne*'s instruction to attach 'great weight' to the emotional and psychological well-being of a primary carer (though of course the mother here would probably not be classified as Jane's primary carer).[47]

It can be seen, therefore, that the English were generally more willing to accept the mother's claim to be feeling trapped and unhappy, and also more willing to ascribe weight to this factor. Given the contrast seen in chapter two between the two countries on this issue, such a difference is not surprising.

[44] Possibly *D v S*, where the mother had decided to return to Ireland regardless of the outcome, though the point in question is not apparent from the judgments.

[45] *B v B [Relocation]* [2008] NZFLR 1083 (NZHC).

[46] See below, pp 125–28.

[47] *Payne* [41].

The significance accorded to Jane's mixed heritage by New Zealanders is also unsurprising, given the role of Māori culture in New Zealand legal policy-making in the last 25 years or so,[48] reflected in the statutory instruction that 'the child's identity (including . . . culture [and] language) should be preserved and strengthened'.[49] Indeed, only one New Zealand participant did not mention culture at all. English and Welsh participants tended to see Jane's culture as less significant (though one barrister suggested that, 'as the case would be tried in Wales, that might actually play more part in it': EB5).

For participants in England and Wales,[50] Jane's Welsh heritage provoked mixed responses. Some thought it to be an 'important heritage' (ES2) which would probably be lost if she moved to South Africa, despite her mother's best efforts to preserve it. Other participants said that they 'wouldn't get too steamed up about the Welsh cultural aspect of it' (EB5): it was 'something to weigh in the balance', but 'not a determinative factor' (EJ3; EJ7 used almost identical words).

Two participants linked their dismissal of the Welsh heritage issue to the fact that 'one has to assume that [Jane] has a South African heritage as well' (ES3); at the moment, 'the child is not experiencing her South African cultural roots' (EB5). The fact that 'the cultural thing . . . works both ways' (NS1), and that Jane 'has two competing cultures' (NJ1), was also picked up by New Zealand participants. However, most New Zealanders preferred, nonetheless, to focus on Jane's Māori heritage.

Three reasons were advanced for this preference, two related directly to New Zealand legal provisions. First, 'the principle of continuity of arrangements in section 5 might tend to weigh more heavily in favour of her Māori identity being maintained' (NJ1).[51] Second, 'we have principles in the Care of Children Act about children having access to their culture and having that preserved' (NS4).[52] While this statement reveals a focus on preserving Jane's Māori culture rather than on giving her greater access to her South African culture, when read alongside the point about continuity of arrangements there may be some justification for such an approach. Finally, several participants referred to Jane's wider family, known in Māori culture (and New Zealand generally) as *whānau*:[53] 'being part of the whānau is very important . . . In Māori culture, the child is very much part of the wider family' (NJ6).

A small number of New Zealand participants wondered whether the cultural issue would turn out to be that significant. As one senior barrister put it, the cul-

[48] See, eg, J Ruru, 'Indigenous Peoples and Family Law: Issues in Aotearoa / New Zealand' [2005] *International Journal of Law, Policy and the Family* 327; J Metge and J Ruru, 'Kua Tut Te Puehu, Kia Mau: Māori Aspirations and Family Law Policy' in M Henaghan and W Atkin (eds), *Family Law Policy in New Zealand*, 3rd edn (Wellington, LexisNexis, 2007).

[49] COCA 2004, s 5(f).

[50] One participant self-identified as being Welsh, though participants were not asked about this.

[51] COCA 2004, s 5(b).

[52] COCA 2004, s 5(f).

[53] The word is pronounced 'fɑːnaʊ. See generally C Cunningham, B Stevenson and N Tassell, *Analysis of the Characteristics of whānau in Aotearoa* (Palmerston North, Massey University, 2005).

tural concerns 'might have more headline impact than substantive impact' (NB7). One judge wanted a cultural report,[54] because 'it may just not be an issue . . . or it may be that it is a real issue' (NJ4). Another judge was also 'not particularly convinced about the Māori heritage . . . It is important to her dad, but . . . what is important to Jane? . . . [H]er interest in Māoritanga [that is, Māori culture] may come much later in life, or it may already be important to her' (NJ5).

In general, though, culture was far more dominant in New Zealanders' analyses of Jane's case than it was in English discussions. Moreover, like most aspects of the case, New Zealanders saw this element as being more strongly opposed to Jane's relocation than did their English colleagues. As we come to predictions of the likely outcome of Jane's case, therefore, it will not be surprising that New Zealanders generally saw the case against relocation as being stronger than the English.

Participants' predictions of the likelihood of relocation are contained in Table 3.3, and are illustrated in Figure 3.4. There is far more similarity between the two national groups in Jane's case than was seen in Tom's case: the main group in both countries thought the mother's application likely to fail, with only three participants (two English and one New Zealander) giving her a more than a five out of ten chance of success. Five participants (two English and three New Zealanders) thought the case 'too close to call' (NB6), or dependent entirely on Jane's evidence.

However, although most participants in both countries thought the mother's application likely to fail, New Zealanders seemed more certain of this prediction. More New Zealand participants put the mother's chances between zero and two

Table 3.3 – Table showing numerical representation of participants' views on the likely outcome of Jane's case, on a scale from 0 to 10 where 10 is most likely to allow relocation, arranged by nationality and professional group

	ENGLISH PARTICIPANTS				NEW ZEALAND PARTICIPANTS			
	EJ	EB	ES	EC	NJ	NB	NS	NC
1	3	6	4	3	3	3	5	–
2	5	–	3	3	2	2	0	3
3	2	3	6	4	4	–	2	3
4	3	3	5		6	0	3	
5	2	2	4		5	1	2	
6	4	3			2	5	2	
7	4	4				2		
Mean	3.60				2.75			

[54] COCA 2004, s 133.

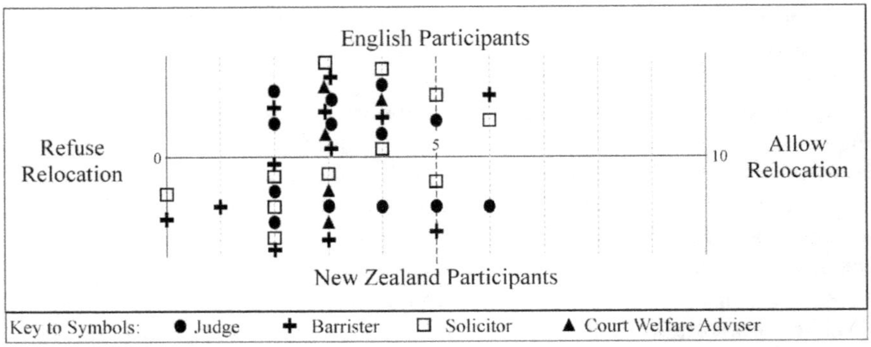

Figure 3.4 – Illustration of participants' views on the likely outcome of Jane's case, on a scale from 0 to 10 where 10 is most likely to allow relocation, arranged by nationality and professional group

out of ten (ten New Zealanders, three English), and more English put the mother's chances at three or four out of ten (14 English, six New Zealanders). The average for New Zealanders was 2.75, whereas for English participants it was 3.60.[55]

While the difference between the two countries is much less than in Tom's case, the significance of Jane's case is that the two jurisdictions are applying a similar legal test and yet still producing divergent results. The English are unable to apply *Payne* to Jane's case, and so are left to assess welfare without any 'gloss on the welfare principle'[56] – which is what *D v S* demands of New Zealanders in every case. Yet even with *Payne*'s 'discipline' removed, English practitioners continue to look more favourably on relocation than do New Zealanders.[57]

Mark and Hannah's Case

The final vignette, Mark and Hannah's case,[58] was described by a number of participants as 'a very different case altogether' (NJ5). Unlike the previous two vignettes, the proposed relocation in Mark and Hannah's case was not international, but was within the country. The children live with their father and have

[55] These numbers are indicative only due to the small sample size and the qualitative nature of the data.

[56] M Hayes, 'Relocation Cases: Is the Court of Appeal Applying the Correct Principles?' [2006] *Child and Family Law Quarterly* 351, 362.

[57] As an English judge who was strongly critical of *Payne* said, 'we are all so conditioned by the current law that it will take time to move out of that mode' (EJ1); for English participants' views on *Payne*, see ch 4.

[58] Mark and Hannah's case was based loosely on *Re H (Children) (Residence Order: Condition)* [2001] EWCA Civ 1338, [2001] 2 FLR 1277.

fortnightly contact with their mother, who works long hours in a City job and has an alcohol problem. The father wants to move from a big city (London or Auckland) to a rural, coastal area about four to five hours' drive away (Cornwall or Whakatane).[59] Figure 3.5 contains the full vignette in Mark and Hannah's case, as given to participants, and Figure 3.6 shows the relevant locations on maps of New Zealand and the United Kingdom.

Both sets of participants focused on the existing care arrangements for Mark and Hannah, along with the reasons for moving, and the prospects for contining contact after relocation. However, there were key differences: English participants were unsure about whether their law permitted restrictions on geographic movement within the country, while New Zealanders expressed stronger interest in the children's ages and views. These two key points of divergence are taken first, followed by the issues on which there was greater consistency.

> Mark and Hannah, aged 10 and 7, have been living near [London/Auckland] with their father for four years since their mother left the family to pursue a City career. The father has dedicated himself to being Mark and Hannah's primary carer, giving up his own career to care for them. The mother has maintained regular contact with the children, seeing them at least fortnightly and often more frequently. However, she finds her job very stressful, works long hours, and drinks heavily. At an earlier hearing, a judge suggested that the mother would be generally more suited to being the children's primary carer because of her warmer character, but concluded that her alcohol use and long hours precluded her from having the day-to-day care of Mark and Hannah. The father has announced his intention of moving from [London/Auckland] to [Cornwall/Whakatane]. The father has close friends in [Cornwall/Whakatane], and has visited many times. He says that the children would have a better quality of life and that living costs would be lower in that region. The mother opposes the move and seeks a court order imposing conditions on Mark and Hannah's place of residence. A report from a [welfare officer/psychologist] suggests that the father is 'strong minded, determined, and possibly obstinate in character', while the mother, although warm, shows no signs of being able to control her alcohol use. It is suggested that the absence of the children from the mother's normal routine may cause her to lose what control she has over her drinking, and put at risk her ability to support the children financially. The father has been offered part-time work by his friends if the move goes ahead, and he says that contact with the mother could be maintained on a reasonably regular basis. The [welfare officer/psychologist] is concerned that the children may react badly to losing regular contact with the mother, but makes no specific recommendation.

Figure 3.5 – Mark and Hannah's case, as given to participants

[59] Whakatane (pronounced 'fa:ka:.ta:neɪ) is about 190 miles (300 km) south-east of Auckland, and takes just over four hours to drive in good traffic conditions. There is an airport in Whakatane, with three or four flights to and from Auckland per day. Cornwall is about 220 miles (360 km) south-west of London, but, because the roads are better, also takes just over four hours to drive in good traffic conditions. There are airports in Plymouth and Newquay, with several flights each day to and from London airports.

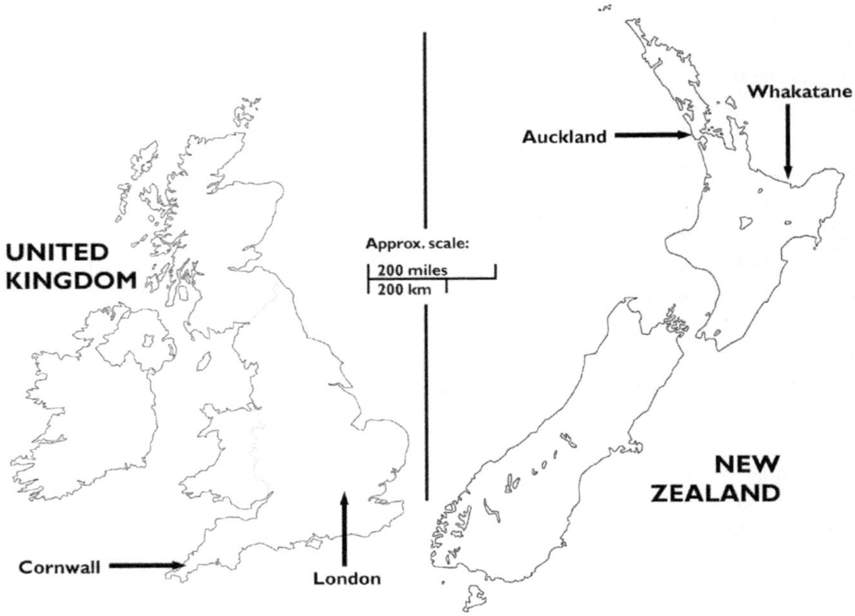

Figure 3.6 – Maps of the United Kingdom and New Zealand, approximately to scale, showing the locations of London, Cornwall, Auckland and Whakatane.

New Zealand participants made no comment about the legal provisions relevant to Mark and Hannah's case. Since New Zealand law does not distinguish between internal and international moves, this is unsurprising. By contrast, when interviews took place in 2008–09, 11 English participants raised concerns about the law itself, five of them as the first thing they said. English authorities at the time suggested that making a restriction on that parent's geographic place of residence is 'a truly exceptional order',[60] and 'an unwarranted imposition upon the right of the parent to choose where he/she will live within the UK'.[61] (More recent cases may have relaxed the approach slightly, though the exceptionality test has not been formally abandoned.[62])

The English participants who raised this point knew these cases: '[o]n the basis of the authorities, I can't see that this is a case where the court would have the power to impose a geographic condition . . . I think the law stands in the way of doing that' (EJ3). Two barristers explained that, as a result, the court was not going to *allow* the father to relocate, but rather it had little power to *stop* him:

[60] *Re B (Prohibited Steps Order)* [2007] EWCA Civ 1055, [2008] 1 FLR 613 [7].

[61] *Re E (Residence: Imposition of Conditions)* [1997] 2 FLR 638 (EWCA) 642.

[62] See now *Re L (Internal Relocation: Shared Residence Order)* [2009] EWCA Civ 20, [2009] 1 FLR 1157, *Re F (Children) (Internal Relocation)* [2010] EWCA Civ 1428, [2011] 1 FLR 1382 and *Re S (Residence Order: Internal Relocation)* [2012] EWCA Civ 1031, [2012] 3 FCR 153, discussed above, pp 47–49.

> **EB4:** I'm not sure how [the father] could be stopped from going . . . It is not that anyone would say, 'yes, you can [relocate]' . . . but [rather], 'we can't really prevent you'.

> **EB5:** The decision was that the father would be the primary carer, and . . . once that has happened . . . the exceptionality test would apply, and there are plainly no exceptional features whatever in this case, and so the mother's claim . . . would be bound to fail.

While English participants who raised the legal point continued to consider the factors they thought relevant, they had a different purpose from other English participants (and from New Zealand participants). Whereas the latter group examined the facts to decide, overall, whether relocation should be allowed or not,[63] the former were assessing whether the case was 'exceptional' (as the quotation from EB5 above shows). Once the legal test of exceptionality was identified, even participants who admitted to being 'lacking in sympathy for father' thought that only 'a brave judge who wasn't overly concerned about his track record on appeals might say . . . dad should stay' (EJ3).

English participants' knowledge of particular cases was therefore significant to the way in which they assessed Mark and Hannah's case.[64] For those who explicitly incorporated the legal test into their reasoning, the 'truly exceptional' nature of restrictions on internal relocation was the dominant factor. This fact should be borne in mind as the remainder of the analysis unfolds since, as stated above, it affected the basis on which other factors were discussed.

Turning to the second point of divergence between the two national groups – Mark and Hannah's ages and views – it is the New Zealanders this time who raised the issues and the English who largely ignored them. The mandatory obligation in the Care of Children Act 2004 to give a child 'reasonable opportunities to express views' which then 'must be taken into account',[65] coupled with the High Court's criticism of judges and lawyers who fall short in meeting these requirements,[66] make it unsurprising that New Zealand participants frequently discussed Mark and Hannah's views. That said, English law also includes reference to children's 'ascertainable wishes and feelings',[67] and in other contexts children of ages similar to Mark and Hannah have had their views given significant weight.[68]

No English participant expressly referred to Mark and Hannah's views, though one welfare officer suggested that 'the ten-year-old may have some idea of the implications' of the move (EC1). There were only two other references to the children's ages or views from English participants. This same welfare officer suggested that, since Mark was probably shortly to start secondary school, it 'might be a

[63] This approach may be akin to the broader approach which later cases appear to endorse: see above, pp 46–49.

[64] For discussion of English participants' views on the law related to internal relocation in general, see below, pp 94–95.

[65] COCA 2004, s 6.

[66] See, eg, *C v S [Parenting Orders]* [2006] NZFLR 745 (NZHC).

[67] Children Act 1989, s 1(3)(a).

[68] See, eg, *Re D (Abduction: Rights of Custody)* [2006] UKHL 51, [2007] 1 FLR 961: in a Hague Convention case, a seven-year-old should have had his views considered.

good time, if they are going to move' (EC1). Similarly, an English judge pointed out that the children were nearly old enough to 'be able to make the journey to London by themselves' (EJ4), thus making post-relocation contact easier.

By contrast, many New Zealanders were concerned to know the children's views, because 'a lot would depend on what the kids want' (NS2). As one psychologist said, there were many unanswered questions about Mark and Hannah's views:

> **NC1:** What do the kids want here? . . . Do they find it easy to make friends? Do they feel part of the Auckland community? Do they feel like fish out of water in Whakatane? . . . What do the kids feel about their quality of life?

Indeed, so crucial were the children's views that some participants found the vignette 'a difficult one [to analyse] because that is such a glaring absence from the case' (NB7).

A brief issue to touch on relates to the genders of the parties, with a primary carer father and an employed mother. While New Zealanders seemed to find this point unremarkable, several English participants commented on the arrangement. Some stated explicitly that they would cross-check their conclusions 'by reversing the roles: you have always got to think about what you would do if the mother had been in the same position' (EB5).

Despite this attempt to disregard gender, many thought that, in practice, it might make a difference. One English solicitor, for example, had earlier said that she 'fear[ed] that the loss of contact with a mother may be seen to be more significant than the loss of contact with a father', and thought that this bias might affect Mark and Hannah's case: 'I think that the fact that [the mother] is an alcoholic is not really the end of the story in this case, whereas it might have been if it was the other way around' (ES2). An English barrister agreed: 'if it was the mother who was going [to Cornwall] and the alcoholic father, I don't think we would be having the same debate that we are. . . . [T]here is an unspoken sexism' (EB1). Most participants who raised this point therefore thought that the father was likely to face more difficulty than a mother in his position would.[69]

Having noted these points on which the English and New Zealanders diverged to some extent, the uniformity of the remainder of the analysis is noteworthy. As we turn to look at various aspects of the children's relationships with their parents, and at the father's plans for relocation, it will be seen that participants were not in total agreement with one another, but that the variation was seen equally between the national groups.[70]

[69] *cf* NS2, who thought that an alcoholic father who was having contact would have better chances of stopping the relocation, because Mark and Hannah's contact mother would be perceived to be 'a bad mother'; see generally S Kielty, 'Mothers Are Non-Resident Parents Too: A Consideration of Mother's Perspectives on Non-Residential Parenthood' [2005] *Journal of Social Welfare and Family Law* 1; J Wallbank, 'Getting Tough on Mothers: Regulating Residence and Contact' (2007) 15 *Feminist Legal Studies* 189.

[70] Indeed, there is no pattern to the variance at all, whether of nationality, profession, age/experience or gender.

The first point is the children's current care arrangements. Participants were told that the father had been the primary carer for four years, from which several people calculated that the children had been with the father from ages three and six – in other words, 'for a very large chunk of their middle childhood' (NS5). There were two views taken of the father. A small group of participants (three New Zealanders and one English) thought that 'he is not the greatest father' (NB2) and 'is not a nice guy' (NJ2). These participants relied on the expert report which said that the father was 'strong minded, determined and possibly obstinate in character', and the judgment in earlier proceedings that 'the mother would be generally more suited to being the children's primary carer because of her warmer character'. However, even these participants conceded that, although they were 'probably not going to like him', the father 'is actually the most functional parent' (NJ2). An English barrister who took this view thought that 'you have got to derive the best of each of the parents, because each of them has some limitation on their capacity as parents' (NB6).

A larger group of participants tended to disregard those pieces of evidence, saying that they were 'not that interested in [what] the judge suggested' (NJ1), because it had little practical bearing on the situation now. As an English judge explained, 'what an earlier judge said I would interpret as what we all try to do when we are making a decision against one party, which is to let them down lightly' (EJ6).[71] These participants thought that the parents' characters were 'by the by – parents have all sorts of characters' (NB6):

> **EC1:** most of us, at times, can be described as 'strong minded, determined and obstinate' and also . . . as having 'a warmer character'. How either of those makes either parent more capable of meeting the needs of their children is a matter for discussion and debate.

Moreover, many participants not only dismissed the criticisms of the father, but were positive in their remarks about him. These comments ranged from acknowledging that 'the care he is providing is good-enough care' (ES3) to more effusive praise:

> **NC2:** The father has been child-focused . . . The fact is, this father is very steady. They have been with him four years . . . so he can demonstrably deliver the parenting.

> **EC3:** He is the one who has provided them with consistency and stability. He has already shown his commitment to them.

By contrast, most participants criticised the mother, who 'clearly is not able to be the primary carer – the problem with alcohol stands in the way' (EJ3). One or two participants diplomatically said that 'the mother, while in her way a good parent, has not proved herself so capable' (EJ6),[72] but a more common reaction was to worry about 'a safety risk to the children with her alcohol use' (NJ5). One

[71] Other participants were less sympathetic to the earlier judge: 'Where are you coming from? Bloody anti-father judge!' (NC1); 'First thought: have the judge shot' (EC2).

[72] This was the judge who commented that parties should be 'let down gently' when decisions go against them.

English judge spoke for almost all participants in saying that 'I don't think that anyone could possibly take the risk of the children living with her' (EJ2).[73]

Overall, participants were content that 'the dad's dedication and the fact that the children have been with him four years' were the key aspects (NS5), while the mother 'doesn't seem to be seeking more involvement – she is pretty occupied with the drinking and her career' (NB6). Having thus concluded that the mother could not take over the children's care even if she wanted to, the question was whether her existing relationship with the children could be maintained if the father relocated.

Again, participants in each country were split on this issue, but a clear group in both countries took the same view. That view looked at the existing relationship between the mother and the children, and at the distance involved in the relocation, and concluded that '[s]he has at least fortnightly contact . . . but she would still be able to have that at that distance' (NB1). New Zealanders were slightly more optimistic in their estimates of the frequency of contact that could be arranged after relocation to Whakatane. The journey to Whakatane 'can be a bit tricky' (NJ1) and 'is getting to the point where it is uncomfortable for regular travel' (NS2), but was thought by most to be 'not so far from Auckland that it would impede on regular contact' (NB4).[74]

English participants similarly commented that although 'Cornwall is a long drive' (EJ6), contact could be fairly regular. However, many thought that 'it is probably going to be once a month, rather than once a fortnight' (EJ2). However, they thought this reduced frequency of contact could be compensated by longer visits during holidays.

The participants in each country who took the dissenting view had two concerns. One stemmed from scepticism about the realities of post-relocation contact, as one New Zealand barrister explained:

> **NB7:** [There is currently] a system that works. The kids . . . are able to have a relationship with a hard-working, hard-drinking mother, [and that] might be put in jeopardy even though [the move] is only five hours. It really precludes weekend contact . . . [and anyway] at ten and seven the kids aren't going to want to have their weekends disrupted. . . . Five hours is a bit further than [would be comfortable], or the kids at the end of a long school week are going to be bunged on a plane and then whisked back on the Sunday. It's all hopeless.

Other participants were similarly concerned about the relationship between the children and the mother being 'reduced to snatched weekends every four, five or

[73] One New Zealand lawyer, while supporting the relocation, wanted to 'build [the mother] into the children's lives on an increasing basis' (NS2), while a New Zealand judge, who opposed the relocation, was 'looking to improve the mother's relationship with the children . . . moving more to a shared care arrangement' (NJ3). One English barrister wanted to call the arrangement 'shared residence' so as 'to emphasise the importance of the children's time in London' (EB5), but he was not envisaging shared care in practice.

[74] Two New Zealanders suggested that the mother 'should look at a shift [to Whakatane] herself' (NS2 and similarly NB6).

six weeks' (EJ1), which ran the risk of 'distance just finish[ing] the relationship' (NB2).

The second concern related to the impact of the loss of contact on the mother, and so consequently on the children. Most participants who addressed this point either thought it immaterial to their child-based decision,[75] or thought that, since they hoped to sort out contact which was just as good as at present, 'that would take care of that' (NS2). For some participants, however, this aspect was significant, because 'if the family finances are grinding to a halt because this is the straw that broke the mother's back, that is something you have got to look at' (EB6). This potential problem over finances combined with the fact that 'not only would [Mark and Hannah] lose regular contact . . . but if the mother then reacts adversely as well then they have lost more than that' (EB6).[76] These participants therefore began to see relocation as increasingly problematic.

The same participants tended also to be unimpressed by the father's reasons for wanting to relocate. Again, both national groups were split in their view of this factor, though many of the English who looked unfavourably on the father's reasons also pointed out that, for internal moves, the law did not require them to ask about motivation, so long as the move was not designed to end contact with the mother.[77]

For some participants, the father's motivation 'doesn't really amount to much more than a lifestyle choice' (EB6). In other words, 'dad's wish to move doesn't have massive imperatives in it at all – he kind of fancies the move' (NB7). However, a few of those who took this view nonetheless thought that relocation might be in the children's interests:

> **EJ6:** He doesn't have to go, but it is a reasonable aspiration which seems practical and . . . [gives] the children the prospect of living in a much more agreeable place, which will be in their interests.

> **EB4:** Dad's plan may not be the best, and you may think, 'why is he doing it?', [but] mum's plan isn't any better and could be worse.

Other participants thought that the father had 'good reasons for wanting to move – that is, both for personal support and for work' (NJ1). As an English barrister put it, 'it is a very, very plausible, reasonable plan' (EB3).

These three issues – the father's motivation, the existing care arrangements, and the prospects for maintaining contact after relocation – tended to line up in participants' accounts. Those who queried the father's parenting ability also

[75] For example, one New Zealand barrister said that he 'wouldn't regard that as of great significance at all: that is an adult issue, not a child issue' (NB7).

[76] In *Re H (Children) (Residence Order: Condition)* [2001] EWCA Civ 1338, [2001] 2 FLR 1277 (on which Mark and Hannah's case was based), the effect of loss of contact on the mother was highly significant. Thorpe LJ, upholding the trial judge's decision to prevent internal relocation, said (at [26]) that, if relocation occurred, 'the effect upon the mother would be devastating. The [trial] judge noted that to devastate the mother would be to indirectly devastate the children'.

[77] See, eg, *Re L (Internal Relocation: Shared Residence Order)* [2009] EWCA Civ 20, [2009] 1 FLR 1157.

doubted whether contact with the mother could be maintained if the children relocated, and found the father's motivation unconvincing.[78] Conversely, participants who praised the father's care of the children tended also to think that the mother's role in the children's lives could be preserved via contact after relocation, and thought the father's motivations either laudable or irrelevant.[79]

Turning to the outcome of Mark and Hannah's case, Table 3.4 contains the numerical representations of participants' predictions of the likely result. These predictions are illustrated in Figure 3.7, which shows that a main group of participants in both countries thought the relocation likely to be permitted. Three

Table 3.4 – Table showing numerical representation of participants' views on the likely outcome of Mark and Hannah's case, on a scale from 0 to 10 where 10 is most likely to allow relocation, arranged by nationality and professional group, together with averages for each national group

	ENGLISH PARTICIPANTS				NEW ZEALAND PARTICIPANTS			
	EJ	EB	ES	EC	NJ	NB	NS	NC
1	4	7	9	10	8	9	2	–
2	9	–	3	10	6	6	7	8
3	10	9	9	9	2	–	7	8
4	10	10	10		4	8	8	
5	10	10	9		6	8	7	
6	10	4			7	7	4	
7	9	10				3		
Mean	8.62				6.25			

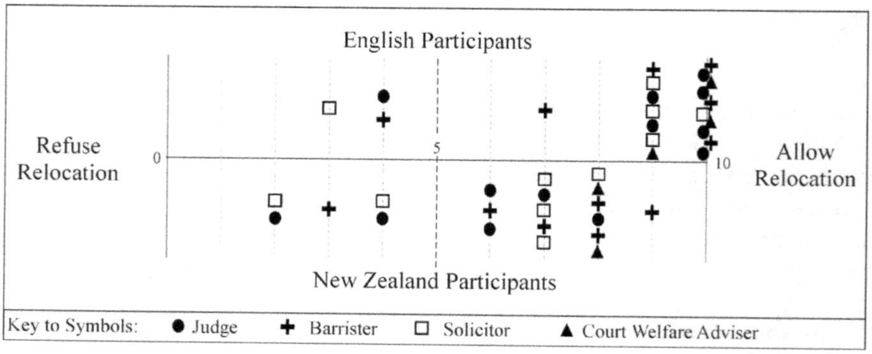

Figure 3.7 – Illustration of participants' views on the likely outcome of Mark and Hannah's case, on a scale from 0 to 10 where 10 is most likely to allow relocation, arranged by nationality and professional group

[78] EB6 and NB2 are the best examples, along with EJ1, ES2, NJ3 and NB7.
[79] EJ6 and NB1 may be the best examples, though most participants fell into this category.

English participants and five New Zealanders thought relocation would be refused, though some said only 'by a narrow margin' (EJ1). However, although the general view of participants in both countries was that the relocation would be allowed, Figure 3.7 shows that New Zealanders saw the case as being more borderline than did the English. Looking at Table 3.4, which contains the data which inform Figure 3.7, it can be seen that the mean for all New Zealand participants was 6.25, whereas for the English it was 8.62. If participants who would refuse the relocation are excluded, the mean for the remaining New Zealanders was 7.33, and 9.44 for the English.

It is tempting to think that part of the reason for this disparity was identified at the start of this section, namely, that many English participants based their analysis on an understanding that the law makes restrictions on relocation within the United Kingdom 'truly exceptional'.[80] However, looking at the 18 English participants who would have allowed the relocation,[81] there is no noticeable difference between those who focused on the exceptionality test and those who did not: those who did averaged 9.36,[82] while those who did not averaged 9.57.[83]

It may be, therefore, that Mark and Hannah's father fared better in England regardless of any advantage given to him by the law, rather than because of it. Although the headline result of the case is the same in both countries – the father being allowed to relocate – his case was stronger in England than in New Zealand.

Overall, Mark and Hannah's case supports the findings of the earlier vignettes. While the English law favours internal relocation, not all English practitioners were aware of this approach. However, those who did not know the detail of the case law applied a quasi-*Payne* approach, leading to much the same result. Whichever test was being applied, English participants were more likely to allow the relocation.

Discussion

This chapter has sought to look at whether there might be differences in the analysis of relocation cases caused by the different legal approaches of England and New Zealand. The analysis of these three vignettes suggests a number of conclusions. The

[80] *Re B (Prohibited Steps Order)* [2007] EWCA Civ 1055, [2008] 1 FLR 613 [7].

[81] The three participants who would have refused the relocation did not specifically refer to the legal test when discussing Mark and Hannah's case, though all three had said earlier in their interviews that *Payne* did not apply to internal relocation, and that internal relocation was easier to achieve than international relocation. See generally below, pp 94–95.

[82] Removing EB1 who, at 7 out of 10, is an outlier in this group, the average becomes 9.60, which is almost identical to those who did not mention the 'exceptionality test' at all.

[83] This apparent lack of difference may raise questions about whether any 'retreat' from the exceptionality test that may have happened in recent years (see above, pp 46–49) will have much practical effect on case outcomes, though there in insufficient information available here to draw any clear conclusions.

first point is that in two of the three cases, participants in the two countries agreed about the likely outcomes – that Jane would not relocate and that Mark and Hannah would. Only in Tom's case were the two national groups in disagreement.

However, this headline finding belies two significant points. One is that, even in the two cases where English and New Zealand practitioners agreed, the English were more pro-relocation than the New Zealanders. Mark and Hannah's relocation was all but certain for the English, but more borderline for New Zealanders; and the refusal in Jane's case was very likely for New Zealanders, but less clear for the English.

The second point is that both Jane's case and Mark and Hannah's case were unusual for English practitioners. Tom's case, which so divided the two national groups, reflects the core facts of the majority of English relocation disputes. The shared care arrangement in Jane's case required English participants to assess the issues without *Payne*, while the internal relocation in Mark and Hannah's case introduced a different line of cases (though the effect may be similar to *Payne*). For New Zealanders, all three cases were reasonably typical.

The analysis of these three vignettes therefore suggests, consistently with the conclusions of chapter two, that English practitioners are more inclined to think that relocation applications will be allowed than are their New Zealand counterparts. Participants in the two countries tended to deploy different reasoning and to focus on different aspects of the vignettes, which resulted in a different prioritisation of factors when making the final decision about relocation. In one case, that process led to variation in the outcomes between the two countries; in the other two, the outcomes were the same but the English nonetheless looked more favourably on relocation.

With these conclusions in mind, the next two chapters examine English and New Zealand participants' understandings and critiques of the detail of relocation law. This analysis starts in Chapter 4 with English participants and the leading case of *Payne v Payne* which, it will be seen, provoked mixed reactions from English participants. The analysis then turns, in chapter five, to New Zealand law, looking at New Zealand practitioners' experiences of a legal system that rejected *Payne*.

4

Evaluating Relocation Law in England and Wales

Most relocation applications in England and Wales are governed by the Court of Appeal guidance from *Payne v Payne*,[1] which applies to all international relocation cases where it is reasonable to identify one parent as the primary carer of the child involved. *Payne* sits alongside two subsidiary lines of authority which apply, respectively, to international moves in shared residence cases,[2] and to applications for relocation within the United Kingdom.[3] Despite the Court of Appeal's firm defence of *Payne*,[4] the English approach to relocation has been subjected to significant criticism.[5] To give one example, Mary Hayes suggests that the English approach is 'focused on too narrow a range of questions', with judges 'disempowered in the proper exercise of their statute-based discretion'.[6] Perhaps in part because of this criticism, recent cases have emphasised that *Payne* contains no legal principles but merely guidance which judges should use to help them reach a conclusion that promotes the child's welfare, bearing in mind that every case turns on its own facts.[7]

This chapter considers English practitioners' views on relocation law in practice. Drawing on qualitative interviews with 22 practitioners,[8] it examines participants' discussions of what the law is and how it is applied 'on the ground' (that is, in day-to-day cases, rather than those of special difficulty or interest which reach the law reports). The chapter then asks how practitioners evaluate and critique

[1] *Payne v Payne* [2001] EWCA Civ 166, [2001] 1 FLR 1052 [hereafter, *Payne*].

[2] *Re Y (Leave to Remove from Jurisdiction)* [2004] 2 FLR 330 (EWHC); *K v K (Relocation: Shared Care Arrangement)* [2011] EWCA Civ 793, [2012] 2 FLR 880.

[3] *Re E (Residence: Imposition of Conditions)* [1997] 2 FLR 638 (EWCA); *Re L (Internal Relocation: Shared Residence Order)* [2009] EWCA Civ 20, [2009] 1 FLR 1157.

[4] See, eg, *Re G (Leave to Remove)* [2007] EWCA Civ 1497, [2008] 1 FLR 1587 [13]–[18]; *Re W (Relocation: Removal Outside Jurisdiction)* [2011] EWCA Civ 345, [2011] 2 FLR 409.

[5] See above, pp 40–42.

[6] M Hayes, 'Relocation Cases: Is the Court of Appeal Applying the Correct Principles?' [2006] *Child and Family Law Quarterly* 351, 351–52.

[7] See, eg, *J v S (Leave to Remove)* [2010] EWHC 2098 (Fam), [2011] 1 FLR 1694; *K v K (Relocation: Shared Care Arrangement)* [2011] EWCA Civ 793, [2012] 2 FLR 880.

[8] For a note about participants, see above, pp 58–60; on methodology, see Methodological Appendix. It is worth remembering that 'England' is used in this book as a shorthand meaning 'the legal jurisdiction of England and Wales'; one participant self-identified as Welsh, though participants were not asked about their nationality.

the law. The story which practitioners tell suggests that the law itself is coherent and well-understood but, when evaluating that approach, opinions were divided, with many participants expressing discomfort at the English approach to relocation disputes.

Practitioners' Experiences of Relocation Law in Practice

Consistent with the analysis of reported cases in chapter two, and with the themes explored through the three *vignettes* in chapter three, practitioners' discussions suggest that relocation law in England has three strands. The main strand is represented by *Payne*, covering international relocation disputes in most cases. The second covers those international moves to which *Payne* does not – or, at least, might not – apply, namely cases involving children whose parents share their care to a significant extent. The third involves moves which are within the United Kingdom, generally known as 'internal relocation' cases. However, the story told by practitioners shows the dominance of *Payne*, the influence of which extends across all three strands of relocation law.

Given that there are these strands to the law, a key point for practitioners was to decide under which strand a case fell. As between international and internal moves, the straightforward issue was whether the proposed destination is within the UK or not.[9] As between the two lines of authority on international moves, the question was whether the child could be said to have a clear primary carer or not, because 'the *Payne* analysis . . . places a great deal of weight on who is and is not the primary carer' (EB5). Consequently, it was necessary 'to ask, almost as a preliminary question, "who is the residential parent?"' (EJ1), and practitioners suggested that only in cases where there is no clear answer will the secondary line of cases on shared care relocation apply.[10] Although these interviews took place before the Court of Appeal's decision in *K v K (Relocation: Shared Care Arrangement)*,[11] participants pre-empted the debate between Thorpe LJ and Black LJ in that case based on earlier High Court decisions,[12] and it is suggested that the views discussed in this chapter remain valid after *K v K*.[13]

Given that *Payne* is the leading case, we start with that line of authority. The centrality of *Payne* was apparent from the detailed way in which practitioners

[9] Some participants expressed uncertainty about whether moves to Scotland and Northern Ireland were properly treated as domestic or international moves.

[10] See similarly F Judd and R George, 'International Relocation: Do We Stand Alone?' [2010] *Family Law* 63, 67: *Payne* applies unless 'the child can live equally happily with either parent, and . . . either parent could act as "primary carer"'.

[11] *K v K (Relocation: Shared Care Arrangement)* [2011] EWCA Civ 793, [2012] 2 FLR 880; see above, pp 43–45.

[12] In particular, *Re Y (Leave to Remove from Jurisdiction)* [2004] 2 FLR 330 (EWHC).

[13] Informal follow-up discussions with some participants in 2012 support this view.

discussed its requirements, especially Thorpe LJ's 'discipline'.[14] However, while recognising the importance of Thorpe LJ's judgment, several participants expressed a preference for Butler-Sloss P's summary – a view reiterated judicially a number of times since these interviews were conducted.[15] These participants thought that key aspects were 'sometimes lost within *Payne* because of Lord Justice Thorpe's guidelines . . . [The approach is] more easily expressed in the judgment of the President' (EJ2). As one barrister put it, 'what has happened with *Payne* is that everyone goes to paragraphs 40 to 43 and says, "there it is, that's the test", but they need to read on from that and . . . read the decision of Butler-Sloss . . . She does it completely differently from Thorpe' (EB6).

Despite this criticism, Thorpe LJ's 'discipline' was central to participants' discussions. Near the start of each interview, participants were asked how they would summarise relocation law to a client (or, for judges, to a litigant in person). The link between the 'discipline' and those summaries is striking, as this example shows:

> **EB3:** I would say that, firstly, the principle that guides the court is that the welfare of the child is the paramount consideration – that is section 1 of the Children Act. Secondly, it is incumbent on any applicant seeking to take a child abroad to put forward as detailed a set of proposals as possible, and the court will scrutinise them very carefully. Thirdly, the court will scrutinise very carefully the relationship between the parent who is staying behind and the child. And fourthly, I would say that, normally, if a child is being cared for by a parent, and that parent comes up with a reasonable plan to go abroad, there is almost a presumption that that will happen. It is difficult to resist these applications if the caring parent has got a carefully thought out plan for relocation.

In other words, practitioners knew *Payne* well and were able to summarise its key aspects.

Taking the steps of Thorpe LJ's discipline in turn, participants first picked out the necessity of asking 'whether the application is genuine, whether it is realistic' (ES2), and they were clear that the court would scrutinise the plan with care. As to the requirement that the application be genuine, participants stressed that they were 'on the *qui vive* for applicants who are wanting . . . simply . . . to get the child away . . . from the respondent, and the basic motivation is to pick those cases out and refuse them' (EJ1). In terms of showing their plans to be realistic, applicants 'prepare an entire lever arch file that will deal with health, education, travel, other family members, socialisation in that country, friends and . . . contact with the absent parent' (EB2).

Secondly, participants thought that the child's relationship with the respondent was important, but that once the applicant had shown her proposals to be genuine

[14] *Payne* [40]–[41], as amended by Thorpe LJ in *Re B (Removal from Jurisdiction); Re S (Removal from Jurisdiction)* [2003] EWCA Civ 1149, [2003] 2 FLR 1043 [11]. The discipline is set out above, p 39.

[15] See, eg, *Re D (Leave to Remove: Appeal)* [2010] EWCA Civ 50, [2010] 2 FLR 1605 [18] (Wall LJ) or, in less strong language, *K v K (Relocation: Shared Care Arrangement)* [2011] EWCA Civ 793, [2012] 2 FLR 880 [143] (Black LJ).

and realistic, the respondent would need to explain why he opposed the relocation. Moreover, given the importance attached to the effect on the applicant of refusing relocation,[16] the child's relationship with the respondent was unlikely to stop the relocation 'unless the result [of relocation] is going to be a very deleterious effect on what has become a very important relationship with the respondent' (EJ1).

Finally, participants addressed plans for contact after relocation,[17] which they thought to be 'crucial' (EB2). The applicant would need to be putting forward 'a package of contact, direct and indirect, and possibly some deal about the funding of transport' (ES1).

It is notable that most practitioner overviews either started or concluded with a remark about it being 'hard to argue' against relocation (ES3), about there being 'almost a presumption' in favour of the applicant (EB3). One solicitor, asked how she would summarise the law to a client, said with a wry laugh, 'I would put it to them that there is a tendency in this country for applications which are made by primary carers . . . to be successful' (ES2). Similar summaries, such as that 'sensible, determined proposals to relocate which are sincerely meant and well researched tend to get through' (EB5), were typical, though as will be seen some participants were clearly uncomfortable that the law had reached this position.[18]

By contrast with this detailed knowledge of *Payne*, practitioners were less certain of the other two strands of relocation law, which is unsurprising given their comparative rarity. One solicitor spoke for many when he said that 'there are a couple of cases, but I'd need to look them up to be sure what they said' (ES1).

Turning first to shared care international relocation disputes, the cases available when interviews took place in 2008–09 were divided about whether *Payne* applied to shared care applications or not,[19] and participants' responses reflected this split view. (Indeed, since the same disagreement was later seen between Thorpe and Black LJJ in *K v K (Relocation: Shared Care Arrangement)*,[20] participants' views probably remain relevant despite later judicial developments.[21]) Some participants thought that shared care simply added a step at the beginning

[16] See below, pp 107–08.

[17] The point is more apparent from Butler-Sloss P's judgment: *Payne* [85(g)]. Thorpe LJ's only comment on the matter is part of [40(b)], asking about 'the extent of the detriment to [the respondent] and his future relationship with the child were the application granted'.

[18] See below, pp 104–12.

[19] *cf Re Y (Leave to Remove from Jurisdiction)* [2004] 2 FLR 330 (EWHC), saying that the factors identified as relevant in *Payne* did not carry the same weight where there was shared care, and *Re G (Leave to Remove)* [2007] EWCA Civ 1497, [2008] 1 FLR 1587. The latter, reported despite technically being a decision refusing permission to appeal, was interpreted as showing *Payne* to apply to shared care in *Re TG (Relocation)* [2009] EWHC 3122 (Fam), decided shortly after the final interviews for this research.

[20] *K v K (Relocation: Shared Care Arrangement)* [2011] EWCA Civ 793, [2012] 2 FLR 880. It is likely that most practitioners are more aware of shared care relocation after *K v K*, though whether that case will have helped anyone to know what the law on shared care relocation is or not is a matter of debate: see above, pp 42–45; R George, 'Reviewing Relocation?' [2012] *Child and Family Law Quarterly* 110.

[21] On the other hand, Munby LJ subsequently expressed preference for Black LJ's approach (see *Re F (Relocation)* [2012] EWCA Civ 1364, [2013] 1 FLR 645 [43]–[44]) and Thorpe LJ has since retired, thus suggesting that Black LJ's approach is likely to win out.

of the welfare enquiry in relocation disputes, determining which parent was better placed to become primary carer. Two participants explained this approach particularly clearly:

> **EJ2:** There is a series of cases which says [shared care] doesn't make any difference, and if one of the parents needs to [relocate] then you need to make a decision as to who is going to be the primary carer, and those are very difficult cases.
>
> **ES2:** If you don't have a primary carer . . . then *Payne* isn't the starting point. You're really going back to strict welfare principles . . . and establishing who is the best person to be the primary carer, in a way, before you even get to the relocation.

For these participants, the aim was to make findings about the child's relationship with each parent so as to identify a primary carer – though, as several participants pointed out, 'sometimes it is quite hard to tell' (EB5). Nonetheless, assuming the applicant was the person identified as the primary carer, these participants would then proceed to apply *Payne* as usual.

Other participants thought *Payne* 'not quite so adequate' (EB4) in shared care cases, because the approach in that case would be 'much harder to apply in that situation' (ES3). These participants tended to be more tentative in their explanations (not yet having the benefit of Thorpe LJ's judgment in *K v K* in support of their approach), but one solicitor put it like this:

> **ES4:** [When there is shared care], you are then looking at it all in the round. So, when considering, 'what are the alternatives [to relocation]?', there is actually a realistic alternative . . . Where you have got shared residence . . . you've actually got a perfectly feasible option.

This approach fits well with *Re Y (Leave to Remove from Jurisdiction)*,[22] which was subsequently adopted by Thorpe LJ in *K v K*.[23] As discussed in chapter two,[24] the previous binding authority of *Re C and M (Children)* means that technically this approach may be preferred,[25] though absent authority there are good reasons why having a single analytical approach to all relocation cases would be preferable.[26] However, it is arguable that, in practice, there may be little difference between the two approaches.

The final strand of relocation law covers internal relocation cases – that is, moves within the United Kingdom. Most participants reported never or rarely having seen a case where internal relocation was contested, though two barristers said that applications were increasing (EB2, EB4). Participants thought that the question which parents brought to them as lawyers or as judges in relation to internal relocation was most often about revising contact arrangements after a move had taken place, rather than contesting the move itself. The infrequency of

[22] *Re Y (Leave to Remove from Jurisdiction)* [2004] 2 FLR 330 (EWHC).

[23] *K v K (Relocation: Shared Care Arrangement)* [2011] EWCA Civ 793, [2012] 2 FLR 880 [35].

[24] See above, p 45.

[25] *Re C and M (Children)*, 30 July 1999 (EWCA), online at www.bailii.org/ew/cases/EWCA/Civ/1999/2039.html.

[26] See below, pp 138–43.

cases requiring knowledge of internal relocation law specifically meant, again, that practitioners expressed some uncertainty about the legal approach. While most knew that *Payne* did not apply directly, some thought that its guidance might be relevant, if perhaps with less vigour given that the move was within the country.[27] These participants pointed out that 'one is still looking at similar considerations' (EJ5) for moves within the UK, and therefore that many of the points raised in *Payne* were still relevant: as one barrister put it, '*Payne* is a guidance, not a governance, of internal relocation' (EB2).

The more dominant view, though, was that *Payne* was inapplicable to internal relocation. This view was expressed clearly by one judge, who said that 'although . . . *Payne* . . . was later interpreted as applying with full vigour to [internal relocation], it doesn't really, or not in normal circumstances' (EJ6). These participants were aware of other cases which meant that 'you don't stop people moving [within the UK] unless there are exceptional grounds for doing so' (EB5).[28] In other words, 'removal of children within the UK . . . is something that a residential parent . . . is quite free to do' (EB3).

That said, three participants described 'a back door way of approaching internal relocation' (EB6). Since direct restrictions were difficult to obtain, these participants suggested applying for a *specific issue order* to prevent any change of the child's school (assuming the child to be of school age).[29] As one barrister put it, 'the battle isn't about where you live, it's about the school change. You can't stop someone moving within the UK – what you can do is stop them changing the school the child goes to' (EB1). A judge expressed the point similarly: 'save in exceptional circumstances, you can't prevent people moving inside the jurisdiction. . . . Of course, you can prevent the children's school being changed, so if you have got school-aged children, that is a way of preventing children being removed' (EJ2). In other words, 'it tends to turn on a specific issue [application] in relation to education, which is artificial and is a code for, "should this parent be allowed to move?"' (EB6).

Practitioners' Evaluations of Relocation Law in Practice

Having established that practitioners in this study had a clear understanding of the core features of relocation law, the next step is to ask how they evaluate that legal

[27] This view may have been caused by Wall LJ's comment in *E v E (Shared Residence: Financial Relief: Yardstick of Equality)* [2006] EWCA Civ 843, [2006] 2 FLR 1228 [32], that applications to relocate internally should be 'tested by taking an analogy with . . . *Payne*'. Relying on this dictum, a practitioner text said that 'the *Payne* approach should be adopted in cases of relocation within England and Wales although a less stringent test than . . . external relocations': D Hodson, *A Practical Guide to International Family Law* (Bristol, Jordan Publishing, 2008) 320.

[28] See, eg, *Re E (Residence: Imposition of Conditions)* [1997] 2 FLR 638 (EWCA); *Re B (Prohibited Steps Order)* [2007] EWCA Civ 1055, [2008] 1 FLR 613.

[29] Children Act 1989 (England), s 8.

approach. Participants were asked about their views on the advantages and disadvantages of the English approach to relocation law; about the ways in which it was helpful to them and about the problems it created in practice; and about whether there were aspects of the law which they thought could be improved. Some participants had relatively little to say on these aspects: as one judge explained, 'I have never thought about it much in a principled way' (EJ5). Other participants had evidently given considerable thought to the law: EB7 knew that not everyone shared her views because the barristers in her chambers 'chat and banter about it', and one judge said, after making a detailed point that had clearly been prepared for the interview, 'I wanted to get that off my chest' (EJ1). Before focusing on *Payne*, we start with a brief discussion of the other aspects of relocation law.

Cases not Decided under *Payne*

Starting with international relocation cases where the child has an equal or near-equal shared care arrangement, participants made only a few comments, perhaps because there was little authority on this point at the time. Crucially, because of the frequency with which the courts make orders called 'shared residence' in cases where the division of care is substantially unequal,[30] participants thought that it was necessary to ask 'whether you're using shared residence as a label in order to pacify everyone . . . or whether it really is a true shared care arrangement' (EB6).

Relocation law divides depending on whether the child has a primary carer who is bringing the application or not.[31] However, participants were uncomfortable with this binary division, pointing out that there was a spectrum of arrangements between equally split shared care and what one participant described as 'a usual-ish, normal-ish [arrangement with staying contact] one night in the week and every other weekend' (ES2). In many of these cases, trying to identify a main carer would be a difficult exercise:

> **EB5:** An arrangement whereby a fortnight in term is divided 9:5 is very common; an arrangement whereby the holidays are divided equally . . . is almost standard. . . . [O]n those sorts of facts, it would be very hard from the child's point of view to say whom they regarded as being their primary carer.

A similar point was made by one judge, who thought that looking at the care arrangements in their own right, without applying such labels, would be more helpful:

[30] See, eg, *Re A (Temporary Removal from Jurisdiction)* [2004] EWCA Civ 1587, [2005] 1 FLR 639 (residence in South Africa, staying with the father in England 'whenever that can be arranged'); *Re W (Shared Residence Order)* [2009] EWCA Civ 370, [2009] 2 FLR 436 (75:25 time split shared residence order); for commentary, see L McCallum, 'Shared Residence: Just a Label?' [2004] *Family Law* 528; P Harris and R George, 'Parental Responsibility and Shared Residence Orders: Parliamentary Intentions and Judicial Interpretations' [2010] *Child and Family Law Quarterly* 151.

[31] *K v K (Relocation: Shared Care Arrangement)* [2011] EWCA Civ 793, [2012] 2 FLR 880 (Thorpe LJ); see also *Re Y (Leave to Remove from Jurisdiction)* [2004] 2 FLR 330 (EWHC); F Judd and R George, 'International Relocation: Do We Stand Alone?' [2010] *Family Law* 63, 67.

> **EJ1:** One of . . . the features of the present law is to ask, almost as a preliminary question, 'who is the residential parent?' I am not sure that in my ideal jurisprudential world I would want necessarily to ask that question, as it were, in advance. I am not saying that the present [care] arrangements are not relevant – they clearly are.

Many participants therefore thought that differentiating between sole and shared care was 'an artificial distinction' (EJ2), and would have preferred to apply the same legal principles regardless of the child's care arrangements. Some thought that a better approach would be to ask, in every case, 'what are the alternatives [to relocation]?', taking into account that in a real shared care case 'there is actually a realistic alternative' (ES4). The similarity between these comments and Black LJ's subsequent judgment in *K v K (Relocation: Shared Care Arrangement)* is notable:[32] both aim to keep all international relocation disputes within a single analytical framework and accommodate the shared care with a different factual assessment rather than a different legal approach.

In terms of applications to relocate within the United Kingdom, participants were more divided in their views. Some saw the law, which makes restrictions on internal relocation 'truly exceptional',[33] as both correct in principle and as the only approach that would work in practice. These participants described restrictions on relocation within the country as 'a major invasion of somebody's liberty' (EB3). They thought that the (relative) practical ease of on-going contact after an internal move, coupled with certainty that court orders could be enforced, reduced the concerns which applied to international moves. Some participants were also worried about the wisdom of making orders stopping internal relocation. As one judge explained, 'I've got reservations about [stopping internal relocations] because there is no point imposing a condition which . . . is simply something for one party to beat the other's head with' (EJ6). In other words, allowing restrictions to be made more frequently might incentivise litigation and give former partners another way to try to interfere in each other's lives.

Other participants doubted whether the law had adopted the right approach. Several thought that internal relocation disputes should be considered with a full welfare analysis, rather than saying that moves could only be stopped in exceptional cases.[34] As one judge said, 'I do wonder sometimes if we are quite as careful as we should be about these' (EJ4). The reason for this concern was that 'the effect of moving a child [within the country] can be very striking' (EB5); in such cases, 'you may be talking about only a one-hour or two-hour journey, but they are still equally destructive' of the relationship between the child and the other parent (ES5).

[32] *K v K (Relocation: Shared Care Arrangement)* [2011] EWCA Civ 793, [2012] 2 FLR 880. For the avoidance of doubt, Black J (as she then was) was not a participant in this research.

[33] *Re B (Prohibited Steps Order)* [2007] EWCA Civ 1055, [2008] 1 FLR 613 [7].

[34] As discussed in ch 2 (see above, pp 47–49), this view may now have started to be reflected in the law following *Re L (Internal Relocation: Shared Residence Order)* [2009] EWCA Civ 20, [2009] 1 FLR 1157, *Re F (Children) (Internal Relocation)* [2010] EWCA Civ 1428, [2011] 1 FLR 1382, and *Re S (A Child) (Residence Order: Internal Relocation)* [2012] EWCA Civ 1031, [2012] 3 FCR 153.

Echoing these concerns, and explaining that it was difficult to fight an internal relocation proposal because of the way the law required judges to think about the issues, one barrister explained how he would try to make the court see the case differently:

> **EB2:** You have to make these judges alive to the seriousness of the decision they are about to make. You need to elevate the judge's mind from [thinking], 'this is a Children Act case and these are disputing parents who can't co-parent and I need to determine, on balance, who is probably putting the interests of the children before their own and therefore . . .' – well no, you need to go much further than that, judge. You need to actually look at this much more carefully and say, 'if I make this decision to [allow the applicant to] relocate internally, miles away from the birth father, what is the medium- to long-term effect of that? Is it going to be reasonable for the dad to have fortnightly contact?' Often not, if the distance is vast and it involves huge amounts of driving.

In terms of internal relocation, therefore, participants were divided. Some thought that it was impractical and, in any case, inappropriate to stop parents from moving within the United Kingdom, while others thought that such cases needed to be investigated in more depth and that the court should be free to conclude that a child's welfare would be better served by preventing relocation, whether the facts were 'exceptional' or not. As we turn, in the remainder of this section, to look at the core of relocation law – that is, cases following *Payne* – a similar variation in views will be seen.

Cases Decided under *Payne*

In assessing their understandings of the guidance from *Payne*, practitioners tended to take one of three positions. Some practitioners defended *Payne*, both in principle and in practice; some took no particular view on the principle, but found the current approach to work reasonably well in practice; and others rejected what they saw as the principle underpinning *Payne*, regardless of their views on its practical application. In addition, regardless of their overall evaluations, all participants identified particular aspects of the practice of the law which worked well, along with aspects which they found problematic.

Before starting this analysis, however, it is worth pausing to note two points. The first is an apparent gender split amongst participants in their views on the law.[35] (To ensure the anonymity of judicial participants, the identifying tags of judges are omitted in certain parts of the following text; 'EJ*x*' is used to identify female judges and 'EJ*y*' to identify male judges.) The participants who defended *Payne* most strongly – a judge, two barristers and a solicitor – were all women,

[35] Note that this split in participants' critiques of the law was not mirrored in their views on case outcomes in the previous chapter, which fits with the 'persistent lack of empirical evidence to support any consistent gender differences in judging': R Hunter, C McGlynn and E Rackley, 'Feminist Judgments: An Introduction', in R Hunter, C McGlynn and E Rackley (eds) *Feminist Judgments: From Theory to Practice* (Oxford, Hart Publishing, 2010) 6.

while those who were most critical of it – two judges, four barristers and three solicitors – were all men, apart from one of the solicitors. Two important caveats need to be stated here. First, as a qualitative study of 22 practitioners, this research can suggest lines of enquiry based on observations from the data, but cannot draw any conclusions about the relationship between gender and views on relocation law. Second, the sizes of the groups (four supporters, nine opponents) are not indicative of anything: this was a qualitative study which did not have a representative sample of participants, in particular with regards to gender (13 men, nine women).

Bearing these points in mind, it may nonetheless be interesting to wonder whether the *Payne* approach to relocation law is more appealing to women than to men. One reason for this might be that whilst women (unconsciously) place more importance on the well-being of primary carers – usually mothers – and on their freedom of movement, men (unconsciously) prioritise children's relationships with non-resident parents – usually fathers. It might also be possible that a gendered division reflects different normative conceptions, exemplified by Carol Gilligan's work on the ethic of justice (typically favoured by men) and the ethic of care (typically favoured by women).[36] Perhaps men's greater focus on 'justice' causes them to object to what is seen as one-sided reasoning in *Payne*,[37] whereas women's greater focus on 'care' makes them more inclined to prioritise caring relationships and case outcomes. It could be that, in this respect, relocation law typifies family law as a whole. Carol Smart has suggested, for example, that 'in recent decades, English family law has been more concerned with the welfare of children, and also the importance of caring relationships, than it has been about justice or equality between spouses or adults'.[38] On the other hand, whether such developments appeal more to women than to men is difficult to assess.

The second point to note relates to the group who took no strong view on the principle of the English law. The interesting aspect of this group is not gender (there were five men and four women), but rather the professional groups: four of the nine participants were judges and three were welfare officers.[39] This group, taking no strong view on whether *Payne* was right or not, focused on the fact that they thought it worked well in practice. It might be that, given their jobs, trial judges and welfare officers are most likely to 'look at the law and follow it rather uncritically' (EJ5). The benefits of having 'a fairly clear template to follow' (EJ3) may be more important for practitioners whose job it is to apply the law than it is

[36] See C Gilligan, *In A Different Voice* (London, Harvard University Press, 1982). This work attracts a degree of controversy in its link between gender and the ethics of justice and care. Citing work by O Hankivsky, *Social Policy and the Ethic of Care* (Vancouver, University of British Columbia Press, 2005), it has been said that 'the "second generation" of care ethicists have tended to downplay the argument that the ethic of care is a female way of thought': S Choudhry and J Herring, *European Human Rights and Family Law* (Oxford, Hart Publishing, 2010) 125.

[37] See below, pp 103–12.

[38] C Smart, 'The Ethic of Justice Strikes Back: Changing Narratives of Fatherhood' in A Diduck and K O'Donovan (eds), *Feminist Perspectives on Family Law* (Abingdon, Routledge-Cavendish, 2007) 123.

[39] A barrister and a solicitor were also in this group.

for advocates. The Court of Appeal has not been slow to criticise trial judges[40] and welfare officers[41] who misunderstand or misapply the law; giving judges 'quite an easy case to apply' (EJ7), and helping welfare officers 'to focus on what the court is going to be focused on' (EC2), may therefore be particularly important for these professional groups.

Supporters of the *Payne* Approach

Four participants put up a strong defence of the English approach to relocation. Looking at these defences of *Payne*, one judge explained clearly why she supported the Court of Appeal's approach. These were difficult cases, she said, but the crucial assessment was the effect on the child's main carer:

> **EJ*x*:** I think you have to have a starting point, and I think that the starting point of *Payne* is a good discipline, providing that you don't just say, 'oh, [the applicant] is crying a bit, she ought to go'. You have really got to see what the true impact on mother is going to be if she is not permitted to go . . . I do think it has to be recognised that the impact on the children of removal, and removal from the other parent, can be very profound, and you shouldn't just rubber-stamp these decisions – but I don't accept that the position in the Court of Appeal is one of not examining the facts and not examining the realities of the people who are before them. The question which has to be asked . . . is the impact on the primary carer, if there is one, of a refusal of her plans to relocate, and I think if you regard that as something that needs to be examined rigorously rather than just . . . taken at face value, then I do not see anything wrong with the test. . . . I don't think that there is a problem with having a starting point in relation to leave to remove, providing that you treat these applications seriously.

In other words, so long as the questions asked by *Payne* were pursued seriously, the basic approach was appropriate. A barrister took much the same view, saying that 'the courts have been repeatedly reminding us that the checklist in *Payne* has to be looked at very carefully and applied very rigorously, and the [trial] courts have got that' (EB6). Moreover, this barrister's experience was that the courts were scrutinising applications carefully and not making assumptions about issues which were really questions of fact. A female solicitor agreed, and rejected the suggestion that the English courts place presumptive weight on the applicant's well-being:

> **ES4:** I don't think the English courts think that factor is more significant than others. I think it has had to be pointed out as a significant factor because it gets ignored, so that, for some reason, the English courts have had to remind themselves that, actually, that is one of the factors.

[40] See, eg, *Re S (Children: Application for Removal from Jurisdiction)* [2004] EWCA Civ 1724, [2005] 1 FCR 471; *Re M-K (A Child) (Relocation Outside the Jurisdiction)* [2006] EWCA Civ 1013, [2007] 1 FLR 432; *Re W (Relocation: Removal Outside Jurisdiction)* [2011] EWCA Civ 345, [2011] 2 FLR 409; *K v K (Relocation: Shared Care Arrangement)* [2011] EWCA Civ 793, [2012] 2 FLR 880.

[41] See, eg, *Re W (Leave to Remove)* [2008] EWCA Civ 538, [2008] 2 FLR 1170.

These views find support from judicial statements made by various judges in the time since interviews for this research took place. For example, Eleanor King J has pointed out that the effect of refusing leave to relocate is a factual assessment and should not be presumed,[42] and the Court of Appeal has not only approved this remark,[43] but also made a number of similar comments.[44] However, despite this ex post facto support, this defence of *Payne* was not the dominant narrative found in interviews for this research.

Particular Benefits of *Payne*

Turning away from this general support of the English law, many participants praised individual aspects of *Payne* and the supplementary guidance,[45] whether they generally agreed with *Payne* or not. Three aspects were noted as being particularly important.

The first was that *Payne* highlighted the need to look at the medium- and long-term consequences of allowing or refusing relocation, as well as the short-term ones. One senior barrister, who criticised *Payne* generally, identified this as one of its benefits:

> **EB5:** presumably out of worry . . . about short-termism, *Payne* has thought it necessary to emphasise that one should take the medium to long-term view of the situation. . . . I can understand why the Court of Appeal would want to make those points. . . . *Payne* does have the effect of stopping short-termism.

This argument links to the reason that some participants supported *Payne*, recognising the importance of the primary carer's well-being in promoting the child's welfare.

The second benefit of *Payne* was in providing a degree of certainty. As one barrister explained, 'compared to a lot of areas of . . . family law, at least you know what is going to happen . . . I think there is a big thing to be said for that' (EB1). In other words, *Payne* performed an important function by 'set[ting] out a fairly clear template to follow' (EJ4), with practitioners able to offer clear advice and help their clients to prepare their cases.

One particular example which came through from several participants was that the Court of Appeal had made it clear that 'quite a significant level of planning and detail [needs] to be there' when putting together a relocation application (EB3). On the other hand, other participants criticised the requirement for applicants to

[42] *J v S (Leave to Remove)* [2010] EWHC 2098 (Fam), [2011] 1 FLR 1694 [81]. The similarity between these comments and the views of some study participants is coincidental since, for the avoidance of doubt, Eleanor King J was not a participant in this research.

[43] *K v K (Relocation: Shared Care Arrangement)* [2011] EWCA Civ 793, [2012] 2 FLR 880 [84].

[44] See, eg, *Re H (Leave to Remove)* [2010] EWCA Civ 915, [2010] 2 FLR 1875.

[45] *Re C (Permission to Remove from Jurisdiction)* [2003] EWHC 596 (Fam), [2003] 1 FLR 1066 and *Re B (Removal from Jurisdiction); Re S (Removal from Jurisdiction)* [2003] EWCA Civ 1149, [2003] 2 FLR 1043 were mentioned frequently.

produce this level of detail. For example, when asked if there was anything that would improve the law, one judge suggested reducing the number of documents:

> **EJ2:** You could generate them from a computer: they are all exactly the same! All those vast bundles of documents proving what there is available in the country to which the children are going to be moved, which is almost like going through some ritual, and nobody ever looks at the documents once they have been filed – but of course [you need them because] people do lose sometimes on the 'insufficiently formulated plan/lack of information' ground.

The importance of this information, therefore, related mainly to the risk of being refused leave because of inadequately researched plans.[46]

A final aspect of *Payne* which was praised compared it to internal relocation. Given that the law did not usually impose restrictions on relocation within the UK, and given that many parts of the UK take longer to travel between than some international destinations, some practitioners thought it sensible to look reasonably favourably on international relocation: 'it reduces the differences between somebody who wants to move to Newcastle and somebody who wants to move to Brussels' (EB5). This similarity was particularly significant for European Union countries, because 'we can't go back to a stage where people are imprisoned within one EU country as opposed to another EU country – that's clearly not the drift of history' (EB5).[47] However, given that some of these participants (including EB5, quoted above) were critical of the approach to internal relocation,[48] this comparison was perhaps not entirely positive.

The benefits of *Payne* which participants identified were, therefore, that it prevented a focus on short-term consequences, and made clear that applications must be thoroughly researched. Some practitioners also thought, as we saw in the previous section, that the law had adopted the correct general approach. As this chapter moves to look at criticisms, both specific and general, of the English law, this broad support of *Payne* by some participants should not be forgotten.

Criticisms of Details within the *Payne* Approach

As we look at detailed criticisms of *Payne*, it is worth noting that many of the points made here came from participants who supported the Court of Appeal's approach. In other words, these criticisms are not necessarily inconsistent with *Payne* (though many who criticised details of *Payne* also disagreed with it in principle as well). To structure participants' comments, it is helpful to return to Thorpe LJ's 'discipline' and address each element in turn.

The first of Thorpe LJ's points asks whether the application is 'genuine in the sense that it is not motivated by some selfish desire to exclude the father from the

[46] See, eg, *H v F (Refusal of Leave to Remove a Child from the Jurisdiction)* [2005] EWHC 2705 (Fam), [2006] 1 FLR 776.

[47] On the possible relevance of EU law for relocation law, see below, pp 141–42.

[48] See above, pp 94–95.

child's life', and 'realistic', meaning 'founded on practical proposals both well researched and investigated'.[49] One barrister described these as the 'two hurdles under *Payne* that if you fall, you do not get back up from' (EB2). However, several participants (including this barrister) doubted whether failing these tests was necessarily fatal to an applicant. Several participants reported cases relating to both aspects.

As to 'genuineness', a series of cases that one judge had done while at the Bar gave an interesting insight:

> **EJ2:** I won one [for the father] where the mother was so poisonous about the father that the judge thought that it wasn't right to let the children go at that stage . . . but she got to go three years later. [Then] I did one where the mother made false accusations of sex abuse against the father, but she got to go three years later.

In other words, a finding that the applicant was 'motivated by some selfish desire to exclude the father from the child's life' might serve only to delay relocation, not to prevent it altogether.

Participants had similar experiences of the 'realisticness' criterion:

> **EB1:** you might succeed [in opposing an application] if you can show that they haven't thought about the consequences [of the move], but then the problem with that is that someone can apply again . . . [T]hey can come back in a year's time.

> **EB2:** Once you have attacked the plan, you have attacked the plan, but usually the plan can be repaired.
> **Q:** So, if that is the ground that you win on, it may only be a matter of time?
> **EB2:** Of time, yes, you're absolutely right.

Practitioners therefore thought that challenging an application on the first stage of *Payne*'s discipline might be a short-lived victory, even if the respondent succeeded.[50]

Participants were also aware that 'the bar as to practicalities that must be jumped by the relocation applicant is set at a wide variety of heights depending on the facts and circumstances of the case'.[51] Several had experience of relocation applications succeeding despite the plan being 'so vague, so non-specific, so full of holes that [the respondent argued] that [the application] didn't even get into the first criterion of the guidelines in *Payne*' (EB3).

Thorpe LJ's discipline then asks whether the respondent is 'motivated by genuine concern for the future of the child's welfare or is . . . driven by some ulterior motive'.[52] One judge thought it unfortunate that this formulation appeared to leave fathers with a choice between, on the one hand, concern about the child's

[49] *Payne* [40(a)].
[50] For explicit judicial acknowledgement (and perhaps even encouragement) of the failed applicant's ability to reapply later, see *Re W (Relocation: Contact)* [2009] EWCA Civ 160, [2009] All ER (D) 120 (May) [26].
[51] *Re F and H (Children: Relocation)* [2007] EWCA Civ 692, [2008] 2 FLR 1667 [9]; see also *S v T (Permission to Relocate to Russia)* [2012] EWHC 4023 (Fam), [2013] 2 FLR 457 [6(1)].
[52] *Payne* [40(b)].

safety or the mother's parenting ability,[53] or, on the other, an ulterior motivation, meaning '[g]eneral hostility towards the mother and obstructiveness' (EJ2). These alternatives failed to give weight to 'most fathers' objections . . . that the severance between father and child is going to cause detriment to the child's welfare' (EJ2). However, as other participants noted, this limb might be designed primarily to ensure that the opposition to a relocation application was not being made purely to spite the applicant, with the detail of the respondent's opposition reserved to the next stage of the 'discipline'.

The next question asks about 'the extent of the detriment to [the respondent] and his future relationship with the child were the application granted'.[54] Many participants thought this point better expressed in Butler-Sloss P's judgment: '[t]he effect upon the child of the denial of contact . . . is very important', and '[t]he opportunity for continuing contact . . . may be very significant'.[55] However, although participants were clear that contact was 'incredibly important' and thought that 'the courts really do take that seriously' (EB7), the focus was on contact *after* relocation. As one barrister explained, in terms of *stopping* a relocation, 'general [arguments] about . . . not . . . hav[ing] as much contact don't carry much sway' (EB1).[56]

The third stage of the discipline addresses the effect on the applicant (and her new partner, if she has one) of refusing leave,[57] guided by Thorpe LJ's instruction that 'the emotional and psychological well-being of the primary carer [is a] consideration [to which] great weight must be given'.[58] The points raised in relation to this aspect reflect broader concerns about English relocation law; put briefly, the concern that many participants expressed was that this point appeared to be 'saying that all [applicants] will be equally distressed' by a refusal of leave (ES5). Most elements of this discussion are held until the following section,[59] but here we consider participants' comments on the approach to so-called 'lifestyle cases'.

Lifestyle cases are applications to move to a country with which the applicant has no pre-existing connection, as opposed to cases where the applicant wishes to return to her home country or go to her partner's home country, or where there is a new connection, such as a job transfer.[60] Participants were aware that the Court of Appeal has said there are no 'sub-classes of case to which some different

[53] EJ2 gave the example of a case tried by another judge who refused leave 'because he thought the risk of [the mother] going back to cocaine use [if she moved] was too high'.

[54] *Payne* [40(b)].

[55] *Payne* [85(f)–(g)].

[56] See similarly *Re C (Permission to Remove from Jurisdiction)* [2003] EWHC 596 (Fam), [2003] 1 FLR 1066 [24(10)].

[57] *Payne* [40(c)]; see also *Re B (Removal from Jurisdiction); Re S (Removal from Jurisdiction)* [2003] EWCA Civ 1149, [2003] 2 FLR 1043.

[58] *Payne* [41].

[59] See below, pp 103–12.

[60] The categorisation of cases can 'sometimes [be] in the eye of the beholder' (EJ2), as was demonstrated by the fact that EB7 *contrasted* lifestyle cases with moves for job opportunities, whereas ES1 thought that most moves for job opportunities *were* lifestyle cases.

approach or principle would be applied',[61] and so *Payne* applies regardless of the applicant's motivation for seeking to relocate.[62] However, some participants were unconvinced. Not only did practitioners think that, as a matter of fact, 'lifestyle choice cases are the hardest to get home' (EB6), but many also thought that there ought to be a formal distinction. The reason that participants thought that lifestyle cases should be treated less favourably was that the impact of refusing leave is likely to be less pronounced: one barrister contrasted the likely 'devastation' of an applicant being unable to return home with the 'disappointment' of an applicant unable to move in search of a better climate (EB1). As a judge explained:

> **EJ2:** Although [the Court of Appeal has] said, 'it is not appropriate to characterise them as "lifestyle" as though it were just a whim',[63] you have actually got to look at what the impact is of saying they can't go. There are cases where someone does wish to go just on a whim, and it is really not going to make much real difference to them if they are forced to stay behind, [and] then I think judges are justified in subjecting the reasons for going to a very high degree of scrutiny.

In other words, most participants thought that they should be more sceptical of claims that the applicant's well-being was at stake in lifestyle cases, and that 'you need to scrutinise [the application] in more detail, and I think you need to get away from the emotional side of it' (ES3).

In the final part of Thorpe LJ's discipline, the previous considerations come together in 'an overriding review of the child's welfare as the paramount consideration, directed by the statutory checklist insofar as appropriate'.[64] Again, many participants' comments regarding this 'overriding review' of welfare raised broad concerns about the approach of the English law, addressed below.[65] First, however, we look at two connected points which participants thought could have been accommodated within the discipline.

One related to the fact that, despite *Payne*'s explicit reference to the *welfare checklist* in section 1(3) of the Children Act 1989,[66] the Court of Appeal had said that 'technically' applications brought under section 13 of the Act to remove a child from the jurisdiction were 'not subject to the welfare checklist'.[67] In an article published just before participant interviews started, I argued that this view was based on a mis-reading of the statute.[68] It is true that the Act does not make 'section 13 applications' subject to the welfare checklist, but the article suggested that the reason is that section 13 is merely injunctive in nature: it prohibits international relocation without the consent of those with parental responsibility or,

[61] *Re B (Leave to Remove: Impact of Refusal)* [2004] EWCA Civ 956, [2005] 2 FLR 239 [16].
[62] *Re S (Children: Application for Removal from Jurisdiction)* [2004] EWCA Civ 1724, [2005] 1 FCR 471 [17].
[63] Probably *Re B (Leave to Remove: Impact of Refusal)* [2004] EWCA Civ 956, [2005] 2 FLR 239.
[64] *Payne* [40(d)].
[65] See below, pp 103–12
[66] Children Act 1989 (England), s 1(3).
[67] *Payne* [33].
[68] R George, 'Changing Names, Changing Places: Reconsidering Section 13 of the Children Act 1989' [2008] *Family Law* 1121.

failing that, the leave of the court. However, there is no apparent power contained in section 13 itself, and so the application to relocate ought to be brought under section 8, to which the checklist does apply. Several participants expressed agreement with this argument. As one senior barrister said, 'I am sure . . . that you are right and that section 1(3) applies to relocation cases, and any thought that it doesn't seems to me, with all respect to whatever the decision was that said otherwise, ridiculous' (EB5). In practice, however, participants thought that the factors on the checklist were given little attention. As one barrister said, disputes about children's upbringing are supposed to be decided 'using the welfare checklist, but I don't think that's applied [to relocation], basically' (EB1).

The second point was that, according to participants, inadequate attention is given to children's views in relocation cases.[69] It is not that children's wishes and feelings are entirely ignored,[70] but that they are given insufficient weight.[71] It was accepted that 'younger children will have very little idea what [relocation] really means' (EB5), so the court should address 'wishes and feelings using the caveats that the Children Act uses, which is, "considered in the light of the child's age and understanding"' (EC1). However, the dominant view was that more attention needed to be given to this element. The most common suggestion was for the automatic appointment of a *guardian ad litem* to represent the child:

> **EB2:** [The law] doesn't appropriately balance the child's wishes and feelings . . . It's still not regular that one has a 9(5) guardian in [relocation] cases, but . . . can there be any more important decision in a child's life than the determination of where it is going to spend its childhood, vis-à-vis its relationship with its parents? How can it be right that there shouldn't be an independent view voiced [about] the effect on the child . . .?

In other words, participants thought that the decision was so important, with potential for the child's perspective to be significantly different from either parent's, that separate representation was likely to be appropriate (even given the resource implications of that decision).

To summarise, participants offered a detailed critique of almost all aspects of *Payne*, and even participants who supported *Payne*'s basic approach identified parts which they wanted reconsidered. However, in addition to these criticisms, a significant dissatisfaction was expressed by many practitioners about the entire approach being taken.

Criticisms of the *Payne* Approach Itself

Amongst the participants who were unhappy with *Payne*, there was one clear concern, namely that 'the welfare principle is being compromised in these cases'

[69] Children Act 1989 (England), s 1(3)(a): 'the ascertainable wishes and feelings of the child involved'.

[70] Several participants thought that CAFCASS's most important function in relocation disputes was 'as a conduit through which the child's views are passed' (EJ7).

[71] On the conspicuous absence of any reference to the child's views in *Payne*, see A Perry, 'Leave to Remove Children from the Jurisdiction: Payne v Payne' [2001] *Child and Family Law Quarterly* 455.

(EB3). These participants – eight men and a woman[72] – agreed with Mary Hayes that *Payne* amounts to 'a gloss on the welfare principle' which is 'weighted towards one party'.[73] There were three connected aspects to these views.

The first was that the current reasoning was 'old-fashioned' (EB3), relying inappropriately on principles which were formulated 40 years ago. The second was that this focus inappropriately prioritised factors in the welfare analysis, over-emphasising the applicant parent's well-being and under-emphasising the importance of the child's relationship with the other parent. Thirdly, this prioritisation led the law, in effect, towards a presumption in favour of relocation; moreover, this was a presumption which the Court of Appeal was 'very willing to step in and . . . defend' (EB1). This impression of a presumptive and interventionist approach, which these participants thought was driven especially by Thorpe LJ, caused participants to be concerned about whether trial judges' discretion was being over-ridden too readily. Several participants compared the approach in relocation appeals with that in international child abduction. As one senior barrister explained:

> **EB7:** the House of Lords hasn't taken on *Payne v Payne*, whereas on the non-Hague Convention [abduction] cases you can see that Baroness Hale . . . said, very tellingly I think, . . . 'if people think that appeals will always be determined one way rather than another, it gives an impression of bias'.

In the case cited by EB7, *Re J (A Child) (Return to Foreign Jurisdiction: Convention Rights)*,[74] Baroness Hale said that, '[t]oo ready an interference by the appellate court, particularly if it always seems to be in the direction of one result rather than the other, risks robbing the trial judge of the discretion entrusted to him by the law'.[75] Many participants thought similar concerns applied to relocation.[76]

To explore this argument, we start with the connection between *Payne* and *Poel v Poel*.[77] The historical origins of *Payne* were commented on by several participants,[78] usually with a mixture of concern and disbelief. As one barrister said, *Payne* 'doesn't say anything very different from what *Poel* said 30 years previously, and that was in a completely different world' (EB5). Several participants spoke at length about this development, as this quotation shows:

[72] Again, to ensure anonymity when discussing participants' gender, the identifying tags of judges are omitted in this section.

[73] M Hayes, 'Relocation Cases: Is the Court of Appeal Applying the Correct Principles?' [2006] *Child and Family Law Quarterly* 351, 362. Participants were given a summary of Hayes' argument and asked whether it fitted their experience.

[74] *Re J (A Child) (Return to Foreign Jurisdiction: Convention Rights)* [2005] UKHL 40, [2005] 2 FLR 802.

[75] ibid [12]. This remark was repeated by Lord Wilson, speaking for the Supreme Court, in *Re S (A Child) (Abduction: Rights of Custody)* [2012] UKSC 10, [2012] 2 FLR 442 [35].

[76] See further below, pp 111–12.

[77] *Poel v Poel* [1970] 1 WLR 1469 (EWCA).

[78] See R Taylor, 'Poels Apart: Fixed Principles and Shifting Values in Relocation Law' in S Gilmore, J Herring and R Probert (eds), *Landmark Cases in Family Law* (Oxford, Hart Publishing, 2011).

EJ*y*: *Payne v Payne* reaches back to jurisprudence which was first developed in the Court of Appeal in *Poel v Poel*.[79] I remember that case, and I remember it, about 10 years later, possibly being thought to have been overtaken by a general consideration of welfare, and then, in the late 70s, early 80s, it was explicitly reaffirmed by the Court of Appeal. I have in mind an old case called *Chamberlain v de la Mare*,[80] but there were three or four decisions at that time which brought it back into the forefront.[81] Again, I remember thinking as the 80s passed and as the 90s came, that perhaps that jurisprudence was becoming antiquated, particularly when, in 1991, the Children Act with its welfare criterion and its checklist came in. Nevertheless, in *Payne v Payne* there was an explicit reaffirmation of the jurisprudence which had begun in 1970 and been specifically reaffirmed in the late 70s, early 80s. What troubles me is that in 1970, and in the late 70s, early 80s, contact with the non-residential parent . . . was not regarded as having the importance which it is now regarded as having. . . . Contact . . . was seen as something entirely secondary, and I think that that view was an important factor in the decision in *Poel* . . . and then in its reaffirmation in the late 70s, early 80s . . . because if you don't regard contact with the non-residential parent as particularly important, the arguments in favour of the relocation of the residential parent, wherever she would wish to go and be happy in going, seem almost overwhelming.

Put another way, family relationships after parental separation are conducted (and viewed by the law) differently from 40 years ago.[82] As a barrister explained, 'there were different social norms, where children were generally brought up by their mothers and fathers generally worked . . . [but] now you have got a different type of society' (EB1). The difficulty with *Payne*, therefore, was that 'the approach has [not] really changed in what is now almost 40 years' (EJ*y*), meaning that the law has fallen behind social norms.

The main concern was that this 'old-fashioned' way of thinking about relocation law (EB3) had led to the law prioritising factors in a way which, while perhaps once apt, is now inappropriate. As one solicitor put it, the problem is 'the sort of hierarchy of factors on the list' offered by *Payne* (ES2). This point reflects the criticism made by both English academics and foreign courts. The New Zealand Court of Appeal described the English approach as 'marked by the emphasis on guidelines . . . and by the allocation of particular weight' to particular factors,[83] while Mary Hayes suggests that the effect of *Payne* is 'that a judge . . . does not start his investigation with an open mind'.[84] These arguments were put to participants, and provoked mixed responses.

Participants who supported the English law tended to reject these criticisms, saying, for example, that 'I think the criticism of the New Zealand court is

[79] *Poel v Poel* [1970] 1 WLR 1469 (EWCA).

[80] *Chamberlain v de la Mare* (1983) 4 FLR 434 (EWCA).

[81] See, eg, *Moodey v Field*, 13 Feb 1981 (EWCA), available from the LexisNexis Official Transcripts 1980–1989; *Lonslow v Hennig (Formerly Lonslow)* [1986] 2 FLR 378 (EWCA).

[82] *cf* Thorpe LJ's view that contact with non-residential parents was not given less importance by the courts in previous times: *Payne* [29].

[83] *D v S* [2002] NZFLR 116 (NZCA) [46].

[84] M Hayes, 'Relocation Cases: Is the Court of Appeal Applying the Correct Principles?' [2006] *Child and Family Law Quarterly* 351, 364.

misconceived: I don't think it has quite understood where we are' (EB6). Other participants, though, thought that these views constituted 'a very valid criticism' (ES3): 'it is that concern which is loudest made . . . [and] I agree, generally, with that concern' (EB2). The concern had two manifestations. One group was unhappy about the imposition of *any* hierarchy over the Children Act's stated principles; the other rejected the *particular* hierarchy found in *Payne*, linked back to the law being out of step with current social norms.

Starting with the general concern about the imposition of a hierarchy of factors, two participants put the point particularly clearly:

> **EB5:** I think [*Payne*] takes the code in the welfare checklist and replaces it with a code of its own, for which there is no particular warrant . . . There is nothing at all in section 1 [of the Children Act] that is inadequate to deal with relocation cases.

> **EJ*y*:** I find it curious that we are dispatching every other child case by reference simply to the criteria of the Children Act, but nevertheless in this one compartment of child cases we are instructed to apply a different regime. . . . Thorpe LJ in his judgment [in *Payne*] says in terms, 'first the judge should do this, then the judge should move to this, then thirdly the judge should consider this', and I am unsure why that has crept into this compartment [of cases], when there is total fluidity – governed, of course, by the paramountcy of the welfare of the child – in all other determinations relating to the optimum future of a child.

In other words, these participants were unsure why the Court of Appeal had imposed any particular 'gloss on the welfare principle', as Hayes puts it,[85] rather than leaving judges to determine the best outcome by reference to the Children Act's usual criteria.

It should be noted, however, that there were differences of opinion on this point. While some thought that introducing a hierarchy of considerations meant that 'the welfare principle is being compromised in these cases' (EB3), others thought that this misunderstood what welfare meant. As one judge said, 'if you say, "the test is welfare and should always be welfare", don't you ask the question, "yes, but what aspects of welfare?"' (EJ*x*). In other words, some elements might indeed be more important than others when assessing welfare, and some participants saw no difficulty with the Court of Appeal saying so.[86]

The second concern highlighted the particular hierarchy of welfare imposed by *Payne*, which some participants thought both to over- and under-emphasise important factors. As one barrister put it, 'the emphasis on the effect on the "primary carer" creates the risk that you don't look closely enough at other matters' (EB5). In other words, 'too much importance is placed on the mother and the effect on her if she wasn't to be successful . . . and . . . the loss of contact with the father is too low down' (ES2).

[85] ibid 362.

[86] On the role of guidance from the Court of Appeal, see now *K v K (Relocation: Shared Care Arrangement)* [2011] EWCA Civ 793, [2012] 2 FLR 880; for commentary, see R George, 'Reviewing Relocation?' [2012] *Child and Family Law Quarterly* 110, 115–120.

These participants were not suggesting that the applicant parent's well-being was not important. Rather, they thought that the analysis 'needs to be . . . all on a level to be considered as an all-factor approach' (ES2), without giving any factor presumptive priority. Indeed, participants were clear that they were 'not saying that you shouldn't look very closely at [the effect of refusal on the applicant]' (EB5); they considered that 'in many cases it is . . . a perfectly proper factor to highlight, among others' (EB2). The problem for these participants was that they thought that the weight given to this factor was being treated as a general principle when they thought it a question of fact.

Some participants spoke in detail about the so-called 'distress argument', namely that the distress caused by refusing the applicant leave to relocate will be the most significant factor in the welfare equation.[87] Several participants were unhappy with what they saw as three presumptions hidden within this argument: the presumptive effect on the applicant parent of refusing relocation; the presumptive effect on the child of that effect on the parent; and the presumption that this effect on the child would be more detrimental to the child's welfare than the loss of relationship with the respondent.

Starting with the effect of refusal, many participants thought that the court too readily accepted the 'distress' which would be suffered. There was a concern that 'the [appellate] judges are saying that all women will be equally distressed' (ES5), whereas participants thought that trial judges ought to be able to conclude that 'underneath it all [the applicant] is probably a sensible woman who would get on with life and deal with the . . . unhappiness' (ES1).

There were two problems raised. One was that the distress might not be a result of the refusal of leave, but could have other underlying causes, and relocation would not always improve the situation. As one solicitor put it:

> **ES5:** a lot of depression is caused by issues which don't simply go away. [The court] should be looking at the source of her depression. Is it simply caused by not being in the country that [she] wants to be in, or is it actually unrelated and therefore subject to influences which will be with the parent wherever they live?

The other concern was that participants were unconvinced that refusal of leave would always cause distress (though judicial participants also noted that they 'start off on the basis that there isn't necessarily going to be a devastating effect on the mother if she can't go' (EJ*x*)).[88] Participants noted that in an application 'there is always the emotional part . . . about how upset and devastated you would be if you couldn't go' (ES3), though they thought that there was 'a fine line between exaggerated upsettedness and genuine distress' (EB4). However, it could be hard to make that point in court:

[87] See above, pp 40–42.

[88] In cases decided after the interviews for this research were conducted, it has been noted that the effect, if any, on the applicant of refusing leave to relocate is a question of fact for the trial judge to determine: see, eg, *J v S (Leave to Remove)* [2010] EWHC 2098 (Fam), [2011] 1 FLR 1694 [81]; *Re E (Relocation: Removal from Jurisdiction)* [2012] EWCA Civ 1893, [2013] 2 FLR 290 [11].

> **EB1:** When one of the issues is, 'how is [refusal of leave] going to affect you?', it is very easy to say, 'I am going to be devastated' . . . but it is very easy to say you'll be devastated, and much harder to challenge it. . . . [I]f someone says, 'I'm going to be devastated', apart from saying, 'well, is that really a reasonable response?', how do you challenge it?

In other words, many participants questioned whether applicants would be distressed if they did not relocate, and whether any distress that was present was caused by the refusal of leave, rather than by underlying factors.

Participants then disputed the Court of Appeal's view that 'almost inevitable is the transference of unhappiness from primary carer to child'.[89] One solicitor spoke for several participants when he said this approach gave applicants little credit for their ability as parents:

> **ES3:** [Most applicants] are intelligent people who have put up with good and bad things in their lives the whole way through, and I think the assumption that if there's a primary carer [who] says, 'I will be distraught if I can't go', that that is going to have a knock-on effect on their ability to care for the child, I think patronises the primary carer . . . You are going to be very cross and upset about it, but somehow you have to protect your child from it, and that is what parents do.

Finally, participants queried the view that, where an application is refused, the (presumed) impact on the child of the (presumed) impact on the mother would always be worse for the child than the loss of relationship with the other parent. Again, the problem was that the answer was presumed, rather than being assessed on the facts of each case: '[the primary carer's happiness] is important, but is it more important than the child's family [life] with the other parent in this country? . . . It's judge-led precedent . . . without any data to back it up' (EB1).

This final point, about the lack of research, was the crux of the argument for some. Not only were the answers to these three questions presumed, but

> **EB1:** there is no research to back it up. They are just saying, 'if a parent is devastated it is going to adversely affect the child; that is worse than the child being removed from the current environment and having less contact [with the other parent]'. Where is the research?

Participants compared the approach to domestic violence and criminal law, where expert evidence plays a significant role in guiding judicial thinking.

Some participants put these considerations together – the 'old-fashioned' thinking, the 'hierarchy' of considerations, and the prioritisation of the applicant's well-being within that hierarchy – and concluded that English law amounted to a presumption in favour of relocation. Shortly before research interviews took place, Charles Geekie QC published an article suggesting that *Payne* 'is commonly perceived as walking and talking like a presumption',[90] which offered a useful point for discussion with participants.

[89] *Re G (Removal from Jurisdiction)* [2005] EWCA Civ 170, [2005] 2 FLR 166 [24].

[90] C Geekie, 'Relocation and Shared Residence: One Route or Two?' [2008] *Family Law* 446, 151–52.

Some participants strongly rejected Geekie's argument. One senior barrister, having paused to check that her identity was not going to be revealed, said bluntly: 'I think he's wrong. I think there might have been a time when he was right. . . . [F]ive years ago [ie in about 2004] that may have been right, but I think the discipline in relation to leave to remove is now very much more rigorous' (EB6). Several participants agreed that, while there might once have been a presumption, by 2009 when interviews took place, matters were less clear because the *Payne* criteria were being applied with 'more rigour' (EJ*x*) than they had been previously. As one judge said, 'at one stage, *Payne v Payne* appeared to say, "A plus B plus C always equals relocation", . . . [but] there's been just a bit of a change in the wind' (EJ*y*). Given later judicial developments,[91] it might have been that these participants had picked up early indications of a change of emphasis that later became more pronounced.

If indeed there has been such a shift, though, it was clearly not well established in 2008–09 when interviews took place, since many participants thought that Geekie's view was right. As one barrister put it, 'I definitely would [agree with Geekie] and I'd stick my neck out and say that I think there are few of my contemporary children law counsel who would say otherwise' (EB2). Many participants took the view that *Payne* was 'a presumption in all but name' (EB3), and thought this conclusion clear from the Court of Appeal authorities:

> **EJ*y*:** I think [Geekie's view] is a fair characterisation of the Court of Appeal decisions . . . I would be very surprised if [Thorpe LJ] were to go so far as to say that there was a presumption in favour of relocation, though I think most people would interpret his words as meaning exactly that.

A solicitor similarly said that 'the courts have been very careful to say there is no presumption, but I think to the outside world it is a presumption' (ES2). However, one senior barrister, although agreeing with the sentiment, was unhappy with the word 'presumption':

> **EB5:** I think it would be putting it too high to say that there is a presumption in favour of relocation, but I think that the well-organised, sincere attempt at relocation has the wind in its back, and I think that a well-organised, sincere opposition to relocation has the wind in its face.

It may be interesting to wonder here whether 'having the wind in [your] back' (EB5), 'start[ing] ten points ahead' (EB2), or having 'the cards . . . stacked . . . in favour of . . . the removing [parent]' (ES2) amounts to a presumption or not. A similar situation exists in relation to contact applications: although there is no legal presumption favouring contact,[92] research suggests that, in practice, there is

[91] See, eg, *Re H (Leave to Remove)* [2010] EWCA Civ 915, [2010] 2 FLR 1875; *J v S (Leave to Remove)* [2010] EWHC 2098 (Fam), [2011] 1 FLR 1694; *Re W (Relocation: Removal Outside Jurisdiction)* [2011] EWCA Civ 345, [2011] 2 FLR 409; *K v K (Relocation: Shared Care Arrangement)* [2011] EWCA Civ 793, [2012] 2 FLR 880.

[92] See, eg, *Re L, V, M and H (Contact: Domestic Violence)* [2000] 2 FLR 334 (EWCA).

precisely such a presumption.[93] The current position regarding contact is put well by Nigel Lowe and Gillian Douglas: 'it would be wrong to say *as a matter of law* that there is a presumption that a parent should be permitted contact. Nevertheless, the de facto position is that the courts are predisposed to maintaining contact with both parents'.[94] From practitioners' comments, it may be that a similar conclusion could be reached regarding relocation. Most agreed that 'generally the Court of Appeal has tended to favour these applications' (EJ*y*) and that, as a result, 'generally [the law] is thought to have gone a little bit too far and to be unfair on the opposing parent' (EJ*y*).

Perhaps surprisingly, many participants who were so critical of *Payne* nonetheless stressed that they were 'not about to say that leave to relocate is too easily given – I don't have a strong view about that' (EB5). Participants were mixed in their views about the *outcomes* of relocation cases – some thought leave was too readily given, others did not – but what united them was dissatisfaction with the *process* which *Payne* required.

The final point to consider in relation to these criticisms of the perceived presumption in favour of relocation relates to the role of the Court of Appeal in setting and holding the line taken by the English law.[95] Most participants thought that relocation law constituted 'a presumption in all but name' (EB3), and linked this presumption to the fact that 'the Court of Appeal is being quite prescriptive' (EB3). Participants accepted that the Court of Appeal should give guidance, which was important 'so that [judges are not] reinventing the wheel every time . . . and also so that there should be some conformity of practice' (EB5). However, 'the guidance which is being offered in relocation cases is probably too directive' (EB5).

A number of participants linked this trend to the role of Thorpe LJ, who, they noted, had been involved with virtually all international relocation appeals:[96]

> **EB7:** I know the other judges haven't stepped in to change it, but it really is Lord Justice Thorpe. . . . I think in relocation cases . . . [the other judges] may not absolutely agree with him, but they let him get on with it. . . . The general view [at the Bar] is that when an appeal goes in from a relocation case, Lord Justice Thorpe will be the one who has a look at it. He controls what comes into the Court of Appeal, . . . and he will make sure he is sitting in particular cases.

[93] R Bailey-Harris, J Barron and J Pearce, 'From Utility to Rights? The Presumption of Contact in Practice' [1999] *International Journal of Law, Policy and the Family* 111, 114.

[94] N Lowe and G Douglas, *Bromley's Family Law*, 10th edn (Oxford, Oxford University Press, 2007) 597 (footnotes omitted).

[95] Note the similarity between these points and the argument made by M Hayes, 'Relocation Cases: Is the Court of Appeal Applying the Correct Principles?' [2006] *Child and Family Law Quarterly* 351, 369–71.

[96] Thorpe LJ himself once noted that he 'see[s] almost all those cases': *Re G (Leave to Remove)* [2007] EWCA Civ 1497, [2008] 1 FLR 1587 [18]. It is fair to say that between the interviews for this research and Thorpe LJ's retirement in July 2013, there were a number of reported relocation cases in the Court of Appeal not involving Thorpe LJ, or where another judge gave the leading judgment.

> EJy: The system, satisfactory or otherwise, is that in effect all relocation cases are listed in front of Lord Justice Thorpe, who is Head of International Family Law and is thus regarded as the guru . . . of international relocation.[97]

In other words, participants perceived the Court of Appeal to be taking a particular line on relocation cases (which many practitioners characterised as a presumption favouring of relocation), and they thought this driven primarily by Thorpe LJ.

Practitioners were particularly concerned that, in addition to providing strong guidance on relocation, the Court of Appeal appeared willing to interfere with trial judges' decisions in relocation cases. Outside the relocation context, participants thought that judges had 'such wide discretion that if you really want to appeal a Children Act case you have got to be raving mad' (ES3).[98] However, many participants thought that this general approach was not followed in relocation cases. When asked how much respect the Court of Appeal gave judges' discretion in most children cases, one solicitor said:

> **ES2:** More than in relocation cases, I think is the answer! . . . And if you compare [relocation], not only with other children cases, but if you compare it to ancillary relief cases, . . . [the Court of Appeal says the trial judge's decision] might not have been a decision that [they] would have made, but it was within his discretion. That doesn't seem to apply in relocation cases.

In other words, many participants thought that, in relocation cases, the Court of Appeal was operating outside the general rule that appellate judges 'should not substitute their own discretion for that of the judge by a narrow textual analysis which enables them to claim that he misdirected himself'.[99] It should be noted, though, that it is very difficult to assess the behaviour of the Court of Appeal in this regard, since normally the only cases which become public are those in which permission to appeal is granted. In 2011, for example, the Court of Appeal heard three relocation appeals, but turned down applications for leave to appeal in at least seven other cases.[100] Similarly, in 2012 five cases were given leave to appeal to

[97] Thorpe LJ became Head of International Family Justice in April 2005, but was influential in international relocation cases before that: between Thorpe LJ's appointment to the Court of Appeal in October 1995 and becoming Head of International Family Justice, there were only two reported international relocation cases in which he did not sit: *Re K (Residence Order: Securing Contact)* [1999] 1 FLR 583 (EWCA) and *Re A (Permission to Remove Child from Jurisdiction: Human Rights)* [2000] 2 FLR 225 (EWCA).

[98] Such an approach fits with repeated rulings about the limited appellate function in appeals from discretionary decisions: *G v G (Minors: Custody Appeal)* [1985] FLR 894 (UKHL) 897–99; see also *Piglowska v Piglowski* [1999] 2 FLR 763 (UKHL) 748; *Re J (A Child) (Return to Foreign Jurisdiction: Convention Rights)* [2005] UKHL 40, [2005] 2 FLR 802 [12]; *Re S (A Child) (Abduction: Rights of Custody)* [2012] UKSC 10, [2012] 2 FLR 442 [35]. This approach appears to have survived *Re B (Care Proceedings: Appeal)* [2013] UKSC 33, [2013] 2 FLR 1075, since the judgments make clear that decisions in private law cases continue to be considered 'discretionary' and accept that the *G v G* approach continues to apply to those cases (see [45], [96] and [202])

[99] *Piglowska v Piglowski* [1999] 2 FLR 763 (UKHL) 748.

[100] See R George, 'Relocation Research: Early Ideas from Ten County Court Cases' [2012] *Family Law* 700.

the Court of Appeal, but nine others were refused permission to appeal.[101] Drawing conclusions about the Court of Appeal being 'interventionist' or otherwise may therefore be rather difficult without access to information which is not normally in the public domain.

In summary, participants' evaluations of English relocation law were somewhat varied. One group of practitioners in this study defended *Payne*, arguing that it provided a good discipline for relocation disputes, so long as the questions posed were treated rigorously. However, almost all participants (including those who supported *Payne*) identified aspects which they thought could be improved, and many were unconvinced that *Payne* represented the right approach at all. In taking this view, these participants relied on a combination of three considerations: first, that the law continued to base itself on principles which no longer reflected prevailing norms; that these principles inappropriately prioritised one factor above others; and that the effect, reinforced by a directive and interventionist Court of Appeal, was 'a presumption in all but name' in favour of relocation (EB3).

With these conclusions in mind, we come to ask how practitioners would rewrite relocation law if they were in a position to do so. It will not be surprising that participants were split in their views on how the law should address relocation disputes.

Practitioners' Views on Law Reform

In asking what relocation law should look like, English practitioners in this study divided into two groups, though there was one issue that united many participants, namely that it was time for the Supreme Court to address relocation. Almost all participants were aware of the on-going debate about *Payne*, and people on both sides of the debate acknowledged that their view was 'not everybody's view' (EJ2). Those who criticised *Payne* wanted the Supreme Court to hear a relocation appeal so as to change the approach; but others thought that 'it is not necessarily even that the Court of Appeal has got it wrong, but . . . there is now enough debate around the subject of our relocation law that it is time for it to go to the [Supreme Court]' (EB5). However, although some participants reported that 'there is a general impression at the Bar that the Lords are dying to get this issue' (EB6), there was a degree of scepticism about whether 'this vague aspiration for looking at the test again stands any real chance of turning into something beneficial and concrete' (EJ6).[102] Some participants were unsure what would

[101] See R George, F Judd, D Garrido and A Worwood, *Relocation: A Practical Guide* (Bristol, Jordan Publishing, 2013) [8.37]; R George, 'Relocation Disputes in England and Wales: First Findings from the 2012 Study' (Oxford Legal Studies Research Paper, 2013), online at http://ssrn.com/abstract=2306097, [4.79]-[4.82].

[102] The fact that, five years on from the interviews reported here, there has still been no appeal to the Supreme Court might lend support to this view, particularly since on 4 February 2013 the Supreme Court refused permission to appeal *Re F (Relocation)* [2012] EWCA Civ 1364, [2013] 1 FLR 645.

happen if a relocation appeal were heard: 'would [they] be endorsing *Payne* or what? . . . [A]nd if they did come up with something new, would those opinions be joined-up thinking . . .?' (EB6). Other participants had clearer ideas about how the Supreme Court would, or should, decide the case – though the range of views expressed might in itself reveal the difficulty inherent in finding a legal approach which satisfies everyone.

Unsurprisingly, supporters of *Payne* thought that the core of the English approach to relocation law was correct; they might make minor amendments but were not seeking wholesale reform.[103] One judge, who generally supported *Payne*, said:

> EJ*x*: The problem with relocation cases is that, in most relocation cases, each parent has an equally valid position, but they are very stark decisions, and I think you have to have a starting point, and I think the starting point of *Payne* is a good discipline . . . I do not think it would make things better all round to have a different test, because I think a different test would just create more heartache in a different direction.

The other main group of participants wanted to remove *Payne*'s 'discipline' and to leave all factors to be balanced at trial, thus allowing 'competent judges to make decisions about relocation with rather more light-handed guidance' (EB5). One solicitor said simply that she wanted to see 'a checklist without there being any order in the checklist' (ES2); a barrister similarly said he 'would demote the *Payne* factor of the likely emotional effect on the residential parent' (EB2) to make the enquiry more balanced.

Most practitioners who sought a change in approach thought that the Children Act provided adequate tools for disposing of relocation disputes: 'you have got the welfare checklist under the Children Act . . . and I think [using] that would be better' (ES2). One barrister, who agreed that 'there is nothing at all in section 1 [of the Children Act] that is inadequate to deal with relocation cases' (EB5), thought that the Supreme Court could easily achieve this goal:

> EB5: I wouldn't be surprised if the [Supreme Court] . . . were to say . . . 'let's go back to what the statute says'. . . . The change would be, rather like a picture restorer, . . . to take off some of the varnish. . . . So I wouldn't be surprised if there wasn't, not the addition but rather the stripping away of some of the considerations that have been put forward.

This view fitted with what one judge described as his 'ideal jurisprudential world':

> EJ*y*: Of course, the welfare of the child should be paramount, should direct the outcome, and in the assessment of welfare there has to be the most sensitive consideration of the rival detriments to granting and refusing [leave to relocate] – the effect on the applicant of refusal and the effect of grant on the [child's] relationship with the respondent.
>
> Q: So, does that amount to a section 1 plus 1(3) welfare decision, but with those two factors highlighted as needing to be assessed by the judge?
>
> EJ*y*: Assessed and balanced. Yes, quite.

[103] Some actively supported *Payne*; others went only so far as to say that 'I can't think of anything at the moment that I would change particularly' (EJ*x*).

A similar outcome was sought by EB3 but, worried that the Supreme Court might 'fudge the issue', he thought that legislative amendment might be necessary, with a detailed checklist of factors for relocation cases added to section 13 of the Children Act. The aim for these practitioners was to examine all factors as they appeared from the evidence and, taking into account both long-term and short-term consequences, to decide which option was best for the child without pre-determining any issues.

Discussion

Participants' understandings of relocation law in practice fit with the findings of chapter two, suggesting that the practice in the trial courts conforms with the approach set by the Court of Appeal. However, while the law was well understood, there were varied views when evaluating that law. One group of participants was, in general, supportive of *Payne*, seeing it as a good approach to a difficult area. This group identified particular aspects of *Payne* which they would change, but thought generally that the Court of Appeal had identified the correct approach. Other participants disagreed, and were uncomfortable with the reasoning which underpinned *Payne*. This group thought that *Payne* unjustifiably promoted the applicant's well-being over other factors, while simultaneously under-valuing the child's relationship with the respondent. There were, in particular, questions raised about the connection between the current law and the welfare principle. Some thought that *Payne* marked an application of the welfare principle, identifying particular aspects of welfare which were relevant to relocation; others thought this approach was 'compromising' the welfare principle (EB3).

It followed from this divergence of views that some participants saw little that needed changing, while others sought to reconsider the entire approach to relocation. The change which these participants hoped to achieve was a return to 'the welfare principle . . . with a small amount of underlining and emphasis – I don't particularly see the need to impose a code on top of it' (EB5). These participants favoured an approach which gave trial judges more room to approach each case on its particular facts. (Those who supported *Payne* thought that removing its guidance risked missing important long-term considerations.)

Those English and Welsh practitioners who sought legal change favoured an approach which bears considerable resemblance to the New Zealand law. The criticisms of *Payne* made by many reflect those of the New Zealand courts, in particular that *Payne* involves 'presumptive or *a priori* weighing' of factors.[104] As one New Zealand case put it:

[104] *D v S* [2002] NZFLR 116 (NZCA) [47].

> *Payne*... effectively constricts the welfare test by assuming too readily that the enhanced happiness of the custodial parent who is allowed to relocate will necessarily enhance the welfare of the child to a greater degree than the child's continuing regular contact with the other parent. In some cases, that may be true, but as a generality its validity and logic are surely open to question.[105]

Given that many English practitioners favoured an approach broadly similar to the New Zealand law, it is worth looking at how New Zealand practitioners view that law in practice. We saw in chapter three that, when applied to hypothetical cases, the New Zealand approach appeared markedly different from the English law, and seemed less favourable to relocation. In order to assess whether the grass truly is greener in New Zealand, it is necessary to ask whether New Zealand practitioners are more satisfied with the application of that law than are English practitioners with the application of *Payne.* The New Zealand experience may also tell us something about potential pitfalls which accompany the kind of reforms which some English practitioners sought.

[105] *Gray v McGill* [2001] NZFLR 782 (NZFC) [6].

5

Evaluating Relocation Law in New Zealand

New Zealand's courts rejected the approach to relocation disputes adopted by the English courts and epitomised by *Payne v Payne*.[1] That approach was said in New Zealand to be 'marked by the emphasis on guidelines . . . and by the allocation of particular weight to the reasonable proposals and emotional and psychological wellbeing of the primary carer', whereas the New Zealand Court of Appeal considered that the better approach was to apply a 'wider all-factor child-centred approach'.[2] Although now guided by the statutory 'principles relevant to child's welfare and best interests',[3] that remains the core of the New Zealand law.[4]

In chapter three, we suggested (based on practitioners' responses to three hypothetical cases) that the application of the New Zealand approach might lead to relocation applications being treated less favourably than they would be under the English law. We then saw, in chapter four, that many English practitioners were uncomfortable with the current approach in England. Although some English practitioners strongly defended *Payne*, a significant group favoured changing the law to 'take off some of the varnish' and leave judges 'to make decisions about relocation with rather more light-handed guidance' (as one English barrister put it: EB5). This approach might be similar to that adopted in New Zealand, which raises the question of whether New Zealand practitioners are more content with their law than are many English practitioners. We should also ask whether approaching relocation disputes 'the New Zealand way' might involve any pitfalls of which practitioners in England should be aware.

In this chapter, therefore, we explore the views of the 22 New Zealand practitioners who participated in this research.[5] We examine their experiences of how relocation law is applied 'on the ground' in New Zealand (that is, in day-to-day cases, rather than those of special difficulty or interest which reach the law reports),[6] and ask how practitioners evaluate or critique the law. It will be seen that the story which New Zealanders tell is in many ways very different from the

[1] *Payne v Payne* [2001] EWCA Civ 166, [2001] 1 FLR 1052 [hereafter, *Payne*].

[2] *D v S* [2002] NZFLR 116 (NZCA) [hereafter, *D v S*] [46]–[47].

[3] Care of Children Act 2004 [hereafter, COCA], s 5.

[4] *Kacem v Bashir* [2010] NZSC 112, [2010] NZFLR 884; R George, 'Principles Relevant to Child's Welfare and Best Interests' [2011] *New Zealand Family Law Journal* 26.

[5] For a note about participants, see above, pp 58–60; on methodology, see Methodological Appendix.

[6] Note, however, that a higher proportion of first instance decisions from the Family Court are reported in the New Zealand Family Law Reports than reach England's specialist reports.

English version in chapter four. New Zealanders had a clear understanding of the law and were generally satisfied with the approach set out by the higher courts. However, while practitioners agreed that the New Zealand Court of Appeal had set out the appropriate approach to relocation disputes, there was a concern amongst many that the law in practice had deviated from that approach in the mid-2000s. There was a clear group of practitioners who, in early 2009 when these interviews took place, thought that the practical application of the law had turned too far against relocation, though it is worth bearing in mind that subsequent cases may have had the effect of shifting this balance a little.[7]

Practitioners' Experiences of Relocation Law in Practice

As an initial point, it may be noted that, in contrast to the English position whereby practitioners reported rarely being involved with a contested internal relocation case, New Zealand participants estimated that internal moves within the country accounted for between half and two thirds of their relocation cases. Consequently, it should be kept in mind that many of the experiences being reported here were focused on moves within New Zealand. The significance of that point may be lessened given that, consistently with what we saw in chapter two, participants were clear that there was only one legal approach to relocation in New Zealand – that is, the approach under *D v S* – unlike the three distinct approaches seen in England. Consequently, although there may be factual differences between an internal relocation case and an international one, the New Zealand legal framework is unaffected by those differences.

As seen in chapter two, New Zealand law takes an 'all-factor child-centred approach',[8] meaning that all relocation disputes are addressed within that same analytical structure, and different background facts (care arrangements, proposed destination, etc) are taken simply to be relevant factors. The *D v S* approach has to be read alongside the statutory framework later imposed by the Care of Children Act 2004 (COCA). However, although judges need to consider each of the factors listed in section 5 of COCA,[9] there is no reason to think that the Act's provisions themselves make relocation applications inherently more difficult:[10] the approach to relocation remains that set out in *D v S*.[11]

New Zealand participants outlined *D v S* in their summaries of the law. As one judge put it, 'we look at all the facts as they are and weigh everything in the balance and come to a decision. . . . [W]e have no *a priori* assumptions, and each case

[7] See especially *Kacem v Bashir* [2010] NZSC 112, [2010] NZFLR 884 and *Millett v Clyde* [2012] NZFLR 351 (NZHC).

[8] *D v S* [47]

[9] *Kacem v Bashir* [2010] NZSC 112, [2010] NZFLR 884 [19]

[10] ibid [18], [23], [28] and [29].

[11] ibid [36].

is weighed on its own merits' (NJ3). Many participants stressed that the court would engage in 'a multi-factorial analysis' (NB6),[12] and that 'the court is going to look at this from the point of view of the child' (NB5).

Participants frequently listed relevant questions for a court faced with a relocation case:

> **NJ6:** What are the child's needs? How do we meet those needs? What would happen if there was a relocation? How would it impact on this child? . . . [P]robably you would look at the nature of the relationship between the child and each of the parents. The parent who would have his or her contact diminished by the relocation, how strong is his or her relationship? How will that relationship be sustained if the relocation goes ahead? Do the parents co-operate? Is it likely that, with relocation, the father (or the mother) is not going to be able to afford to have contact? How will that affect the child? Is the relocating parent really doing it for the child's benefit, or for his or her own benefit . . .? That's how I would think about it – always from the child's perspective.

In terms of the effect of the Care of Children Act, practitioners frequently mentioned the 'section 5 imperatives' (NJ5) – the list of six 'principles relevant to child's welfare and best interests' – but there was some divergence of views on whether they marked a practical difference in approach from the previous law. One judge thought there was some change: 'Pre-COCA, I didn't *have* to take anything into account, [but] now I do: if they are relevant, I *have* to take into account those matters in section 5, so there must be a difference' (NJ5). However, another judge spoke for most participants, explaining that 'although *D v S* was before the Care of Children Act, I think the legislation has codified, in effect, what *D v S* said, and has put it very clearly in terms of the principles that we have to apply, the section 5 principles in the Act' (NJ1). In other words, the section 5 principles were a statutory expression of principles which had already underpinned *D v S*,[13] which is broadly in line with the subsequent decision in *Kacem v Bashir*.[14]

A more substantive modification to all disputes involving children was seen in section 6 of COCA, requiring that the child 'must be given reasonable opportunities to express views on matters affecting the child' and that any views expressed 'must be taken into account'.[15] Participants thought that this section placed 'a stronger emphasis on the views of children' (NB2) than the previous legislation had.[16]

Overall, therefore, participants thought that *D v S* continued to be their guiding authority, albeit supplemented by COCA. However, although participants were clear that there was only one legal approach, they also thought that it was possible,

[12] For similar phrases in reported cases, see, eg, *NW v MW [Parenting Order]* [2006] NZFLR 485 (NZFC) [10]; *ACCS v AVMB [Parenting Orders]* [2006] NZFLR 986 (NZHC) [55]; *LH v PH [Relocation]* [2007] NZFLR 737 (NZHC) [8]; *S v L [Relocation]* [2008] NZFLR 237 (NZHC) [26].

[13] See also D Inglis, 'The Care of Children Act and Separated Parents' [2005] *New Zealand Law Journal* 233, 234, saying that COCA 'reinforces' the *D v S* approach to child law.

[14] *Kacem v Bashir* [2010] NZSC 112, [2010] NZFLR 884.

[15] COCA, s 6.

[16] Guardianship Act 1968 (New Zealand), s 23.

looking at the practice of the courts, to categorise relocation cases. Two senior barristers, interviewed together, said they thought that the court's approach depended on the applicant's reason for relocating, though they did not think that this demarcation was explicit:

> **NB4:** Broadly speaking, our courts have adopted a three-tier approach, looking at the purpose of the relocation. If you suddenly decide that you'd like to go and live [somewhere else] because you have always heard that [it] is a lovely place and you think you can get a good job, but you have no family support or anything else, it just seems like a really good idea, the answer is no.
>
> **NB5:** Or if you're trying to get away from the bastard, the answer will be no.
>
> **NB4:** At the other end is the person who wants to return to the bosom of the family, who . . . has tremendous family support, family ties and all the rest of it – that has got a much greater chance of success. And then you have got the one in the middle, of the person who has separated, has re-partnered, and the new partner is offered a work opportunity, which is completely genuine [or something like that]. Those are the really difficult cases. . . . Those are the ones that we can't generalise about.

A judge agreed that the reason for relocating might be significant: 'if you categorise them into return cases and other reasons, return cases have much higher chance of success than other cases, [such as] job reasons or lifestyle. . . . [Lifestyle cases] are much harder' (NJ3).[17] This judge also thought that the personalities of the parties could be crucial, and referred to one 'test' in particular:

> **NJ3:** It often comes down to what I call 'the bastard factor', which is an unwritten rule . . . – sometimes called 'the prick factor' – [that] if you get one party who is a prick, so you come to the conclusion that the child isn't going to get that much out of a relationship with this person – nearly always the man – . . . then you would be more inclined to allow the relocation.[18]

It is also notable that, within the 'all-factor child-centred approach',[19] participants consistently identified one factor as being particularly significant, namely the child's relationship with the non-relocating parent. This point is addressed in detail below,[20] but in summary many participants stressed that 'the courts are anxious to ensure that a child has a constructive relationship with both parents, and would not lightly agree to an arrangement that didn't promote that' (NB7).

Two points in relation to the practice of the law can be noted here. The first relates to so-called 'unilateral moves' (where a parent moves with the child without first obtaining permission from the other parent or the court), while the second questions whether the non-moving parent ought to relocate as well to be near the child. Both relate to the significance of the child's relationship with the non-relocating parent because they are about keeping the child in the same

[17] English practitioners similarly thought that lifestyle cases were the most difficult to succeed in bringing: see above, pp 101–102.

[18] *cf* above, p 67, n 30: in Tom's case, NJ3 thought that 'unless . . . this father was a bit of a prick, I wouldn't think [the mother had] much chance of success'.

[19] *D v S* [47].

[20] See below, p 128.

location as both parents. As we will see, unilateral moves are strongly discouraged and parents frequently ordered to return with the child; conversely, in cases where relocation is being considered, the court often enquires as to whether the other parent might move as well.

Starting with unilateral moves, many participants suggested that, in advising a client, '[t]he first message is not just to [move], because . . . parents have been required to come back' (NS4). A senior barrister described moving without first obtaining permission as 'a bad mistake – we never advise clients to do that' (NB5). There were two reasons why unilateral moves were so inadvisable. The first was simply that such a move 'would put you on the back foot' when the court heard your substantive application (NS5). However, while many participants made similar points, it is worth noting the rather different tone of Kós J's judgment in *Millett v Clyde* in 2011.[21] Contrary to practitioners' experiences in 2009, his Honour thought that a unilateral move should be seen simply as 'one of the circumstances we must deal with under ss 4 to 5 [of COCA 2004]. It is a fact, as it is a fact that the [respondent] remains in [the original location]'.[22] This case may therefore have caused some practitioners to re-evaluate their views on unilateral moves, though the effect of the judgment in the Family Court is yet to be seen.

The second, more serious reason was the very real chance that the court would order the child returned. Many participants reported direct experience of having children ordered back, either by the parent having to return, or by a change in residence: 'some judges think so ill of that attitude that they will change [the child's primary] care' (NB6). Another barrister's experience was typical:

> **NB4:** without reference to the father, [the mother] relocated [about 90 minutes' drive away]. The father immediately applied to have the children brought back, . . . and at first call [the judge] said, 'I give you 24 hours, mother, to bring those children back. If you don't, custody changes to the father instantaneously . . . I will not have children removed without the consent of this court.'

There were mixed views about this approach, as we will see in the following section.[23] It might be noted at this point, though, that there are significant gender issues involved in a legal approach which forces a parent to return to a particular location or lose the care of their child.[24] Two aspects are particularly noteworthy. One is that women sometimes migrate internally, often over relatively short distances, to escape domestic violence.[25] Summarily ordering their return may risk

[21] *Millett v Clyde* [2012] NZFLR 351 (NZHC).

[22] ibid [50].

[23] See below, pp 130–31.

[24] See, eg, J Behrens, 'A Feminist Perspective on *B and B* (The Family Court and Mobility)' (1997) 2 *Sister in Law* 65; S Boyd, 'Autonomy for Mothers? Relational Theory and Parenting Apart' (2010) 18 *Feminist Legal Studies* 137; R George, 'Regulating Responsibilities in Relocation Disputes' in J Bridgeman, H Keating and C Lind (eds), *Regulating Family Responsibilities* (Aldershot, Ashgate, 2011).

[25] See, eg, J Bowermaster, 'Relocation Custody Disputes Involving Domestic Violence' (1998) 46 *University of Kansas Law Review* 433.

exposing them (and their children) to significant physical or psychological harm.[26] The other is that moves are often motivated by job opportunities, new partners, or to be nearer family and support networks.[27] All these reasons have significant connection to women's capacity to escape or avoid poverty, either by providing money or by providing childcare assistance which in turn enables the mother to undertake additional paid employment.[28]

The other aspect of the New Zealand practice to note at this point is the possibility that the parent opposing the relocation ought to consider moving to the new location as well.[29] In one reported case, a Family Court judge said that '[t]he party endeavouring to stop relocation . . . has as much an obligation to show why he or she cannot shift to the new place as to why the children should not be allowed to shift'.[30] Several participants adopted a similar view, usually linking it to gender equality and fairness – that is, since non-residential parents (usually fathers) are free to relocate without the court's permission, there was a perceived unfairness in imposing restrictions on the movement of resident parents (usually mothers) without at least asking whether both parents might be able to move instead:

> **NJ2:** I am often aware of a double standard that is applied, and I think it is a gender issue really . . . As between the parents, there is not a lot of justice in it . . . The aim is to keep both parents within a reasonable radius of the child, so . . . why don't both parents move? . . . I do sometimes ask that.
>
> **NJ4:** I am always open to hearing why somebody wants to move, and a lot of that is based on the fact that the non-custodial parent – we don't call them that – can do what they like. They can up and move and leave and nobody makes them accountable . . . I really do make sure that there is a lot of cross-examination on whether the father can actually get up and move. . . . And . . . if these fathers really want to have a relationship with their children, why wouldn't they follow them around the world?

This final remark was echoed by a senior barrister when he said that long-distance relocation usually means the end of a significant relationship between the non-moving parent and the child 'unless [that parent is] prepared to relocate – and if their focus was on the child, they should be' (NB7):

[26] *cf BDD v IBG [Relocation]* [2007] NZFLR 1 (NZFC) [53], where serious violence against the mother carried little weight: 'Notwithstanding what I am sure was an abusive relationship with [the father], the fact is that stability existed . . . and a long running care arrangement was in place'.

[27] See, eg, R Kaspiew, J Behrens and B Smyth, 'Relocation Disputes in Separated Families Prior to the 2006 Reforms: An Empirical Study' (2011) 86 *Family Matters* 72, 74. From a study of 174 court judgments in Australia, the authors say this: 'Two types of reason [for seeking to relocate] were frequently emphasised: a desire to be closer to family support (33%) and to be with a new partner (30%). The next most frequently raised reason was to pursue work opportunities in the new location (16%).'

[28] See, eg, M Hetherington and J Kelly, *For Better or For Worse: Divorce Reconsidered* (New York, Norton, 2002) esp 88 and 165; M Daly and K Rake, *Gender and the Welfare State: Care, Work and Welfare in Europe* (London, Polity Press, 2003).

[29] See M Weiner, 'Inertia and Inequality: Reconceptualizing Disputes Over Parental Relocation' (2007) 40 *University of California Davis Law Review* 1747.

[30] *NW v MW [Parenting Order]* [2006] NZFLR 485 (NZFC) [10]; see also *V v F* (HC Wellington, CIV-2006-485-1573, 1 Dec 2006) [131]; *KAR v PWM [Parenting Order and Relocation]* [2009] NZFLR 915 (NZFC) [37].

> **NB7:** All these relocation issues could be solved by the relocating parent being allowed to leave and the so-called left behind parent saying, 'I'm not going to be left behind, I'm coming too!' So there is another solution. . . . It is all about choices, and I do think that is something that needs to be looked at, not from a legal perspective but by standing back and [asking]: when all this is over, when all the decisions have been taken and the appeals have been lodged and lost, was there another solution? Yes, there was: let her go – and follow her.

Again, the gender implications here are significant, and participants thought that the law might go some way towards rectifying that imbalance by enquiring whether the non-resident parent might relocate as well, if his relationship with the child justified considering restrictions on the mother's relocation.

To summarise this section, the story told by New Zealanders shows a strong correlation between *D v S* and the daily practice of relocation law. The New Zealand law looks at all the factors relevant to the child's life when assessing relocation applications, guided in particular by the six statutory principles.[31] Practitioners' experiences showed that, within this approach, different reasons for relocating were viewed differently by the courts in some respects, and that a significant aim for the law was to preserve relationships between the child and both parents.

With these findings in mind, we look at practitioners' evaluations of relocation law. These evaluations fall into three broad areas: a general assessment of the law as set out by the Court of Appeal; a critique of the law as applied in the trial courts; and a discussion of case outcomes. We will see that practitioners were strongly supportive of the legal approach to relocation, but were concerned that that approach was not always applied appropriately. In particular, some participants thought that the courts were placing too much weight on the child's relationship with the respondent (non-moving) parent, and too little weight on the well-being of the applicant (moving) parent. Consequently, some participants were worried that the law was, in effect, making it overly difficult to relocate.

Practitioners' Evaluations of Relocation Law in Practice

Participants were asked about the advantages and disadvantages of the New Zealand approach to relocation; about the ways in which it was helpful to them and about the problems it created in practice; and about whether there were aspects of the law which they thought could be improved. As with English practitioners, New Zealanders were mixed in their response. Some directed their responses to their day-to-day experiences, while others offered more jurisprudential, overarching analyses. We start by looking at practitioners' views on the principles laid out in *D v S*.

[31] COCA, s 5.

Evaluating New Zealand Law in Principle

Participants uniformly praised the approach to relocation outlined in *D v S*, though many thought that it made each case difficult:

> **NJ5:** The principles [in *D v S*] don't help you in your determination at all – far from it! They can tell you where you have gone wrong, but they can't help you to get it right. All I know is, I must take a relevant matter into account and give it such weight as is appropriate on the evidence – but it is still up to me to know what is relevant and make those findings of fact. . . . [R]elocations remain some of the hardest [cases] because they are the most finely balanced, often. Truly hard.

Despite this difficulty,[32] there was very little criticism of the principles themselves.[33] The judge quoted above, asked whether anything should be changed about relocation law, replied: 'Absolutely not! I wouldn't change the approach in *D v S* at all' (NJ5). The Court of Appeal's approach was described as 'very sensible, very straightforward' (NS3), and was praised in strong terms:

> **NB6:** I think *D v S* has got it very right. . . . Many of us in the profession were just applauding *D v S* [when it was decided]. . . . I think it is a really very sensible, child-focused approach [and] that is what it should be, as with other parenting matters. It would be ridiculous to do anything other than that.

> **NJ5:** I think we are very lucky in New Zealand to have an unfettered approach to what is in the child's welfare – it is completely unfettered – because each case is so heavily fact-specific, and so subtly fact-specific. . . . I don't think that we should change *D v S*, because it actually forces you to think very hard and articulate whatever it is you think.

While some participants identified particular aspects which they thought needed modification, all participants agreed that the core approach was right. It was with some relief, therefore, that most thought that the Care of Children Act 2004 had not affected the *legal principles* applicable to relocation. Interviews for this research took place in early 2009, before the Supreme Court's ruling in *Kacem v Bashir* which clarified that COCA did not herald any change of approach from that set out in *D v S*.[34] While not all practitioners interviewed for this research would have predicted that result,[35] most argued that COCA should not affect the approach set by *D v S*:

[32] Others thought that, although cases might be difficult on their facts, the legal principles were straightforward: 'there is no reason why [relocation] should not be dealt with in the same way as any other parenting case' (NB7).

[33] For criticisms of its application in practice, see below, pp 124–28.

[34] *Kacem v Bashir* [2010] NZSC 112, [2010] NZFLR 884; see above, pp 54–55.

[35] See, eg, NS3: 'I thought [COCA] would [make a difference to relocation law], and . . . we all believed relocation cases were going to get a lot harder to win because of the Care of Children Act and that compulsion on parents to make parenting arrangements that were going to promote relationships.'

NJ1: the law reflects what the Court of Appeal had articulated in *D v S*. . . . I said in one of my first cases decided under the Act . . . that I didn't consider that the Act had changed the substantive law. . . . I don't think the Court of Appeal said anything different in *D v S*. . . . I don't think it is a change of approach.

NJ3: In one of my decisions, one of the first issues I had to decide was whether the introduction of sections 4 and 5 [of COCA] actually made a change, and I held that they didn't and that the law as laid out in *D v S* continued.

Referring to a 2006 High Court judgment in which Priestley J said that relocation law was unaffected by the introduction of COCA,[36] a senior barrister said that 'Justice Priestley of course is right: nothing really changed in terms of the applicable principles [when COCA entered force]' (NB7). However, while participants were strongly supportive of *D v S* and thought those legal principles unaffected by COCA, they were less certain when it came to the practical application of the law.

Evaluating New Zealand Law in Practice

Although participants thought that the 2004 legislation did not change the legal approach to relocation, many nonetheless thought that COCA had marked 'a toughening up of Family Court judges' attitudes and a stronger resistance [to relocation]' (NB7). As one solicitor explained, '[i]n the last five years [that is, 2004–2009], I think that the advice that practitioners have given has changed from being more ready to support a relocation application . . . [to] advising [applicants] that their prospects of success are limited' (NS2).

While participants frequently noted that this change in attitude coincided with the introduction of COCA, many were sceptical as to whether COCA itself was the cause. For some, COCA was simply 'a platform for our Principal Family Court Judge to come out and say, "I think there is going to be a third way",[37] but I think [the change] was happening before that' (NS2).[38] This view, of a pre-existing trend of which COCA was merely a 're-emphasis' (NJ1), was found in several accounts:

[36] *Brown v Argyll* [2006] NZFLR 705 (NZHC). While the matter was still contested in 2009 when interviews took place, the Supreme Court later reached the same conclusion as Priestley J about the effect of COCA on relocation law: see *Kacem v Bashir* [2010] NZSC 112, [2010] NZFLR 884.

[37] According to Judge Boshier's paper: 'There is disagreement between those jurisdictions where the welfare of the child is the key consideration in relocation cases. There are two broad approaches. The first is that the [child] is so dependent on the welfare of the primary caregiver, that to restrict the movement of the caregiver, and force them into a life they may not be happy in, will have a detrimental impact on the child. . . . The second general approach is the view that the welfare of each child is different and must be assessed on its merits. . . . The Care of Children Act may herald the onset of a third approach, where enabling the child to have a relationship with both parents is to be accorded greater weight over any other consideration. This would militate against relocation in many cases': P Boshier, 'Relocation Cases: An International View from the Bench' [2005] *New Zealand Family Law Journal* 77, 78. This view was specifically disapproved by the Supreme Court in *Kacem v Bashir* [2010] NZSC 112, [2010] NZFLR 884 [28].

[38] Precisely when this trend began is hard to say. Participants thought the change had occurred 'in the 2000s' (NS5), citing cases like *W v C* [2000] NZFLR 1057 (NZFC) (NS2) and *D v S* (NJ5).

NB6: The Family Court seems to be quite persuaded by the principles in [COCA], which are about the continuity of care arrangements. I wonder, though, whether it is less a legislative shift . . . [and more that] there has been a shift in the approach of the Family Court generally in terms of fathers having more contact with their children, and I think it is an amorphous and difficult-to-quantify shift in perception, far more ephemeral than actual change in the legislative focus. . . . [T]hat change has a flow-on effect on relocation, but I think that is far more subtle and not legislative, and that was already there before the new Act.

NJ5: My pip is that it is harder now to relocate after COCA than before, but that might not be about COCA, that might just be about how we grew and developed and thought about family law problems and put more store in joint guardianship, moving away from the influence of *Payne v Payne*. . . . [T]hings change in imperceptible ways. That is the change, and I could not tell you if it came as a result of COCA.
Q: So that shift may have been—
NJ5: Coming anyway, as a result of changing nuances, psychologists changing their thinking.
Q: And you can see that in *D v S*.
NJ5: Oh, very much the genesis of it, yes.

There were two practical expressions of this 'hardening of attitude' (NB4) to relocation which some participants identified, though they can be seen as two sides of the same coin. One aspect was the increased weight put on maintaining the child's relationship with both parents. Many participants thought that the courts' practice was to 'put a stronger emphasis on the shared parenting role . . . and I think there is much greater emphasis on fathers to start off with that equal sharing role' (NS6). Generally, participants thought that fathers were 'more front-and-centre for judges' (NS1) than they had been previously. In other words, 'the courts are anxious that a child has a constructive relationship with both parents, and would not lightly agree to an arrangement that didn't promote that' (NB7), because 'the law believe[s] that the on-going involvement of both parents in the child's life is . . . a good to be pursued' (NS5).

The other aspect was a corresponding reduction in the significance accorded to the well-being of applicant parents.[39] The relevance of the psychological and emotional well-being of applicants was discussed in *D v S* when the New Zealand court analysed (and rejected) the English case of *Payne*. The Court of Appeal said that *Payne* involved 'the allocation of particular weight to the reasonable proposals and emotional and psychological wellbeing of the primary carer. . . . [P]resumptive or *a priori* weighing is inconsistent with . . . New Zealand law'.[40]

This position, as seen, was strongly supported by participants. However, 'there is the formal statement of the law, and then there is the reality of it, and they are not on all fours with each other' (NS2). The development of this disjuncture was explained by one lawyer:

[39] See above, pp 56–57.
[40] *D v S* [46]–[47].

> **NS1:** [The position now marks] an interesting transition from a situation where, 20 years ago, when mum wanted to relocate there would be a sense that mum needed to be where she needed to be . . . to a stage where you said, 'best interests of the child, but there is no presumption of mum going' – which is really what *D v S* is saying – . . . through to a stage where you are then saying, 'not only isn't there a presumption that mum can relocate, but before she can relocate we want to see some real evidence of damage'.

Many participants discussed this trend with reference to *B v B [Relocation]*,[41] which was the most recent High Court relocation case when research interviews took place. In that case, Duffy J said:

> Relocation will only be in the child's best interests if his mother is so harmed by having to remain in New Zealand that her emotional and psychological health will deteriorate to a point where it will impact detrimentally on the child.[42]

Participants thought that this view 'is really over-stating it' (NS4) and, as a statement of what the law should be, 'puts it too high' (NJ2). However, they were less certain as to whether Duffy J's comment reflected the current practice in the Family Court. Some participants were simply unsure – 'The short answer is I don't know if we have got to that point' (NJ1) – but many saw *B v B* as fitting their experience in the trial courts:

> **NB1:** That is what I picked up even before [*B v B*]. . . . [T]hat is my experience, and perhaps I hadn't elevated it to the extent of clinical depression or anything like that, but . . . [applicants] need to be seeing a psychologist.

> **NJ4:** [An applicant] has got to actually probably be pretty depressed, and she has got to have doctors' letters and there has got to be a psychological report to the court . . . You would probably have a list of reasons [for granting a relocation], and that could be one of them, but I don't think in itself that would be enough nowadays.

This view was also reflected in relation to the strength of the evidence required if a parent was going to seek to relocate based on her own psychological or emotional state:

> **NS5:** Not just [evidence from] your doctor, it would have to be from a psychologist or from a counsellor – but not a wussy counsellor! It would have to be someone of standing.

> **NB6:** If you are going to try and make a relocation application on the basis of, 'can't cope, totally depressed, trapped', [then you need] psychological evidence. I wouldn't bother with a counsellor. I would get [a client] to be assessed by somebody who was well known and respected within the Family Court system, who is a psychologist, and it is always a careful balance because you don't want [the psychologist] going so hard that [your client] looks like a complete loon, but you do want somebody who is expert and is able to say . . . 'the effect of being able to relocate . . . is going to enhance [them] and therefore the children are going to benefit'. It's that causative link that is hard to get.

[41] *B v B [Relocation]* [2008] NZFLR 1083 (NZHC).
[42] ibid [62].

For these participants, then, Duffy J's comments simply reflected their own experiences of cases where the applicant was making an application in part based on her own psychological well-being. By contrast, other participants thought that *B v B* was 'not representative of very much at all . . . [Family Court judges] are not saying [that not] until you are nearly institutionalised will they listen to the evidence properly' (NB5). Two senior barristers gave the case particularly short shrift, one saying 'I don't think legal scholars should pay much heed, to be blunt' (NB7), the other saying 'I would just tear it up if I were you' (NB4). Family Court judges are not, of course, at liberty to 'tear up' High Court decisions, but participants had their own solutions:

> **NJ6:** I would think that as a general proposition [Duffy J's approach] may be too stark for me. Of course I am bound by the High Court, but again it is a question of how I assess the degrees of risk.

In assessing these developments in the practice of relocation law, practitioners tended to take one of two positions. For one group of participants, the concern was that the later practice of the courts had introduced a hierarchy of factors, whereas *D v S* (which they strongly supported) stated that any *a priori* weighing of factors was inappropriate. Although these participants commented on the specific elements of the hierarchy (the importance of mothers' psychological wellbeing and of father-child relationships), the generalised way in which they discussed these points suggests that they would have had a similar reaction regardless of the particular factors which were in the hierarchy. The point was particularly well expressed by one judge when discussing *B v B [Relocation]*:[43]

> **Q:** In *B v B*, Justice Duffy said that 'Relocation will only be in the child's best interests if his mother is so harmed by having to remain in New Zealand that her emotional and psychological health will deteriorate to a point where it will impact detrimentally on the child'.
> **NJ5:** She rather elevates that [point] to a presumptive principle. It is the use of the word 'so', I think, if you read it carefully. I can't read her ratio any other way . . . I read that as maybe unfortunate semantics, but the effect is . . . rather presumptive.
> **Q:** Is it the same flaw that the Court of Appeal [in *D v S*] criticised *Payne* for, but [highlighting a factor which pulls] the other way?
> **NJ5:** Yes! Yes, yes, yes, yes!

A solicitor similarly thought that recent developments were not 'within the spirit of the Court of Appeal cases' (NS1).

For the other group of practitioners, although there was frequent reference to the divergence from *D v S*, the greater concern seemed to be with the *particular* hierarchy that had been introduced into New Zealand law. In other words, they seemed more concerned about the detail of the hierarchy than about the existence of a hierarchy. One solicitor was a particularly good exponent of this approach:

[43] ibid.

> **NS2:** I think the emphasis on the relationship with the non-relocating parent has been elevated to a position of [there] almost [being] a presumption that that equates with the welfare and best interests of the child, so that it is almost impossible to satisfy the court, based on all the other factors that might be present, that it will be in the welfare and best interests of the child to [relocate]. . . . [T]hat is the point we have come to: the mental health and happiness of the mother is so downplayed and so ignored that it is like the contrary *Payne* position. . . . In New Zealand, we have got *Payne* being rejected, [and *D v S* said]: 'the mental health and happiness of the mother should not be elevated; all factors are the same; no *a priori* weighting; don't start from any particular position'. Right, okay. And then we have got what is happening, which is that the mental health and happiness of the mother is absolutely sent out the back door, and shared care relationships, as *being* the welfare and best interests [of the child], are elevated right up there . . . So we have reintroduced *Payne*, but in a different way and with different factors.

In other words, the worry that these participants had was that *D v S* was being used to justify ignoring the applicant's well-being, when all it said was that this factor should not be given presumptive importance.

One participant, contrasting their own approach of having no presumptions, said that 'you have some judges who just have this view that non-caring parents' rights of guardianship should not be devalued, [that] their children's ability to have regular contact is almost paramount' (NJ5).[44] Another judge, when discussing *B v B*, said: 'if we have got to that point, it would worry me . . . and if we have . . . then I think we have gone too far' (NJ1).

However, although there were two sources of concern about the apparent trends in the Family Court, there was considerable overlap between the groups, since they shared the same concern about prioritisation of factors being inconsistent with the Court of Appeal's approach. We have seen, therefore, that although New Zealand practitioners were strongly supportive of the legal approach of *D v S*, there was concern that the practice of the law was not 'within the spirit of the Court of Appeal cases' (NS1). Practitioners thought that COCA had been used by the courts to shift the focus in relocation disputes. The main effect of this change of emphasis, in practical terms, was an increased focus on children's relationships with respondent parents, and less weight being given to the emotional and psychological well-being of applicant parents. This de facto position, apparently divergent from the clear instruction of the Court of Appeal in *D v S*, may be particularly significant with regard to the reforms proposed by some English practitioners.

Case Outcomes under New Zealand Law

It was in response to these concerns that some participants worried that 'we have got ourselves into a position where we are seeking, through the court, to stop relocation from happening at all, and that is simply a lack of recognition of the reality

[44] On judicial variation, see below, pp 131–32.

of modern life – so we have got to do something about that' (NS2).[45] As another solicitor put it:

> **NS6:** I think we have gone too far in saying that the relationship between the child and the non-custodial parent has to be maintained at the level it was at . . . [I]t has gone to that extreme where you are saying to people, 'you can't [relocate], there is no point, I am not even going to run that case', because you can see what the outcome will be.

This sense of the difficulty of obtaining leave to relocate, even over fairly short distances,[46] was reflected in many interviews. Lawyers 'generally impress upon people . . . the difficulty of it' (NS5), and 'make sure, if it is the person who wants to relocate, that they are aware that it is an uphill struggle' (NS4); indeed, some 'would actually be advising [applicants] that their prospects of success are limited . . . that in New Zealand relocation is militated against' (NS2). As a senior barrister explained:

> **NB7:** you have to make a good case to relocate . . . There is a task ahead of you, . . . it [is] by no means a straightforward process. . . . One of the great sadnesses of these cases is often the fact that they have come to trial, because . . . if . . . you look at them from the outside, you think, 'this should never have come to trial: someone should have told somebody where the inevitability of this was going to be'.

For most participants, that inevitability was usually that relocation would be refused. Moreover, because relocation was perceived as so difficult to achieve, when leave was granted, practitioners were concerned about the prospect of the decision surviving an appeal:[47]

> **NB5:** A case I had last year, . . . the court did allow [the mother] to go back [to her home country]. . . . When the decision came out, I said, 'get on the plane straight away', even though she had wanted to do the thing of letting [the father] say good bye to [the child], but he was going to appeal. He appealed when she was in the sky. I hate stooping to that sort of thing, but that is the reality about these sorts of decisions.

The reason that obtaining permission to relocate was perceived to be so difficult stemmed from the way factors were prioritised; promoting the child's relationship with the non-relocating parent tended to be seen as more important

[45] This view was not universally held, though, as this exchange with another lawyer shows:

> **NS4:** Can I say that the courts normally get [relocation cases] right? No, I can't honestly say that.
> **Q:** Do you think they normally get them wrong in one direction rather than the other, refusing [relocation] when they should allow or allowing when they should refuse?
> **NS4:** I think it is probably mostly the latter, that they have allowed [relocation] when they should have refused.

[46] Many participants had experience of short-distance relocation cases. NB4 was currently involved with a case where the mother wanted to move 'about 35 minutes drive north', while another barrister spoke of a case where leave was refused to move from Devonport (a coastal suburb of Auckland) to Waiheke Island, which is part of greater Auckland and 'which you can actually see from the end of Devonport wharf' (NB7).

[47] Note that Family Court decisions may be overturned simply because the High Court Judge takes a different view of the merits: see above, pp 27–28.

than improving or safeguarding the relocating parent's well-being. Another example of this prioritisation of factors was seen from one lawyer who was concerned about the court treating the child's relationship with the non-relocating parent as 'almost paramount':

> **NS2:** Not only are [judges] putting greater weight on [contact], but I sense that they are also starting from the position that the ideal is that there is a shared day-to-day care [arrangement] in place. . . . [You can go into court applying for relocation] and end up with a shared day-to-day care arrangement [in a case where] that wasn't even in place before!

We saw in chapter three that New Zealand participants tended to think that the courts would favour shared care arrangements. The strongest example was Tom's case: New Zealanders thought relocation would probably be refused but, moreover, several said that a more likely outcome was that Tom would move into an increasingly shared care arrangement.[48] As one judge said in relation to Tom's case (but with more general applicability):

> **NJ5:** If [a child's] overall interest is to increase [contact], clearly it is not to relocate. Very few practitioners argue it that way, and they should [because] it is a very powerful way to argue it: 'Judge, not only am I opposed to relocation, I want shared care'. All of a sudden, you have got a very different analysis.

Participants had different views on this practice, but several found it concerning that the court would use the opportunity of a relocation application to start shared care. For some, it was another reason to think that 'the litigation risk is so high' and that 'only the very best relocation situations should ever be put to the test' (NS2).

Similar points about the difficulty of relocation were seen in relation to the courts' attitude to unilateral moves – that is, cases where the parent moves before obtaining permission, where the application before the court is from the other parent seeking to have the child returned.[49] Participants' experience was that the courts were strongly critical of such moves, and would often require the child be returned immediately so that the issue of relocation could be addressed in the former location. There were mixed views on this approach.

Some participants thought that the damage caused by unilateral moves necessitated a strong response:

> **NB6:** I think the judges are right to be robust about that. . . . I don't think the court should be encouraging people to take matters into their own hands. It is really detrimental to the children, and is an attempt to say 'it's none of the court's business', and it is the court's business because the court has got jurisdiction over what is in the child's

[48] See above, p 64. *cf* the recent English High Court case of *Re L (Relocation: Shared Residence)* [2012] EWHC 3069 (Fam), [2013] 1 FLR 777: the mother's application to relocate to the USA with the 3 year old child was refused, with the Deputy Judge saying that the boy's relationship with the father 'should be on an upward trajectory' best promoted by a shared residence order (which had not been in place previously).

[49] See above, pp 119–20.

> best interests. An attempt to oust the court by doing your own thing is appalling, and not the way civilised societies conduct these sort of proceedings.

Similarly, one judge favoured a presumption of immediate return unless there were exceptional circumstances 'because it is so debilitating [and difficult] to get ground back once there has been an effective removal – you can't apply a *D v S* analysis with any degree of equality' (NJ5).

However, other participants thought that ordering an immediate return 'is not always in the child's interests, depending on the facts, [especially] if the kid has been enrolled at a school, or whatever' (NB5). They thought that the disruption caused by having to return was a significant factor, especially if the court might then permit the relocation after the child had been returned. There was also an awareness that there might be good reasons for moving without waiting for permission: as one psychologist said of a case he was doing, 'I know that mum was a naughty girl for relocating without the court's permission. . . . On the other hand, I don't blame her for getting outside of the influence of this controlling and physically violent man' (NC1).[50]

In addition to these aspects which participants thought demonstrated a general resistance to relocation in the practice of the law, many thought that different judges took different approaches to relocation, which made cases difficult to manage. As one judge put it, relocation 'is an area in which different judges use different yardsticks, which is why it is such a vexed area for litigants' (NJ2). Several participants noted that judges took different views on what distance counted as relocation,[51] as well as whether they looked more or less favourably on relocation.

An unusual example, where judicial variation worked in favour of the relocating parent, was reported by one barrister who described

> **NB7:** a case that might not have been perceived as particularly hopeful [which] was surprisingly won by the mother . . . Now, the only real explanation for that was the individual input of the judge, because that was a case that, with a different judge, might well have been crushingly lost.

More typical were comments that there were 'some judges who just do not think that children should relocate, so they will find a way to make sure they can't' (NS4). As another solicitor explained:

> **NS2:** We do get deviation according to which judge is doing it, because they do have their own pre-conceived positions. With some, you wouldn't bother going to court – you would just tell your client, 'go away and get a medical certificate, you'd be wasting your time here'. With another judge, you'd think, 'you'll get a fair hearing here, let's just have a go'.

[50] On the gendered implications of the New Zealand law, see above, pp 120-21.

[51] Several participants observed that 'one judge may perceive one side of [town] to the other as relocation, while another may not' (NB7). One participant spoke for many in saying that treating such moves as relocations 'may be understandable, but it is also petty' (NJ2).

These findings suggest that, although the principles enunciated in *D v S* were strongly supported by practitioners, the practice of the law was often quite different from those principles. Many participants thought that the de facto prioritisation of factors meant that, in practice, 'relocation is militated against rather than militated for' (NS2). We saw in chapter four that *Payne* was perceived by many English practitioners to be a presumption in favour of relocation. It might be that the same perceived presumption exists in practice in New Zealand, albeit in that case a perceived presumption against relocation, rather than in favour of it. It might also be suggested that proposals from English practitioners to have 'rather more light-handed guidance' (EB5) in relocation cases risk significant variation between judges because of 'their own pre-conceived positions' (NS2);[52] this aspect may be another factor for those who would reform the English law to consider.

Having thus seen New Zealand practitioners' views on the legal principles and the practice of relocation law, in the next section we look at their assessments of whether there should be any reforms. It will not be surprising to find that there was considerably less call for any reconsideration of the law in New Zealand than we saw in relation to English law.

Practitioners' Views on Law Reform

In keeping with their general praise of *D v S*, most participants did not seek changes to the legal principles governing relocation. Participants said, for example, that 'the New Zealand approach is a very good approach: it is very balanced and it is entirely child-focused, which is what it should be' (NB6), and that 'I wouldn't change any of the approach in *D v S* at all' (NJ5). As one barrister explained:

> **NB7:** There is a whole lot we could do better in the Family Court as a general proposition, but if the question is, 'can we do something to make relocation cases better?', [the answer is] 'no, nothing that we can't do to improve the Family Court generally'.

It is worth noting the contrast between this opposition to change amongst New Zealand practitioners, and the views of most English practitioners. In England, even those who were generally supportive of *Payne* identified aspects that they would amend, and a significant group of practitioners sought a full reconsideration of the legal approach. In New Zealand, on the other hand, the consensus was that the court had found the correct approach, and there was nothing to change in terms of the legal principles.

There was some concern about how to ensure that the practice in the Family Court fully reflected the *D v S* approach, though. Some practitioners thought that

[52] A similar situation exists in Canada: R Thompson, 'Ten Years After Gordon: No Law, Nowhere' (2007) 35 *Reports of Family Law* (6th) 307.

the High Court was 'trying to correct things a bit' (NB5), though whether this attempt was succeeding or not was unclear. Another practitioner, convinced that the problem was not solved, nonetheless thought that rigorous appeals of flawed Family Court decisions might be a good solution, because 'that would enable the High Court to correct this trend in the Family Court . . . which . . . is making it so hard to successfully get a relocation' (NS2). Subsequent discussions with some participants in this research suggest that the Supreme Court's decision in *Kacem v Bashir*[53] may have had some effect on 'loosening up' relocation applications (NS2), perhaps tempering some of the perceived anti-relocation impression that many participants had in 2009.

Two other practical points were suggested, both designed to help the trial courts to implement *D v S* more effectively. One suggestion was 'to try to get a list of factors to be taken into account' by trial judges when deciding a relocation case (NJ3 and similarly NJ6). While these participants were aware that the High Court had criticised the use of checklists[54] because they could distract from the individualised assessment of the particular child's welfare,[55] some thought that 'it may be helpful' nonetheless (NJ6). Proponents of checklists thought they might lend the law greater certainty, because 'on each factor you would have judges making decisions more commonly, so that practitioners could read those decisions and get a better feel for judicial thinking, which may help in predicting the outcome of the case for their particular client' (NJ3).

However, even those who made this suggestion were cautious, noting that 'by putting in particular provisions, you [risk] overlooking other issues' (NJ6). Other participants specifically rejected using a list of factors, warning that 'a checklist can be a trap – you can find yourself going to the checklist . . . and doing that with respect to every case becomes a burden and unnecessary and can even bring in irrelevancies to that case' (NJ1). As another judge put it, 'I am not a fan of templates because in an individual case there are fewer factors that are really *moving* factors, and the rest kind of fall into line. I see it as being an art rather than a science' (NJ2).

The other practical suggestion was not entirely unconnected, and proposed legislative amendment to attempt to 'normalise relocation' and make clear that relocation should sometimes be allowed (NS2). This participant saw the current trend in the law as 'seeking . . . to stop relocation from happening at all, and that is simply a lack of recognition of the reality of modern life' (NS2). The aim, therefore, was to clarify that allowing relocation should not be an exceptional outcome. To achieve this aim, she suggested amending two sections of COCA:

> **NS2:** [First, there should be a] reintroduction into the Care of Children Act of a section from the Bill that was thrown out, so that in addition to being a guardianship decision, [relocation] becomes an incident of day-to-day care – it is both – so that it doesn't give

[53] *Kacem v Bashir* [2010] NZSC 112, [2010] NZFLR 884.
[54] *Brown v Argyll* [2006] NZFLR 705 (NZHC) [38]; *S v L [Relocation]* [2008] NZFLR 237 (NZHC) [28]–[30]; but see now *Kacem v Bashir* [2010] NZSC 112, [2010] NZFLR 884 [19], saying, contra *Brown v Argyll*, that judges should go through the COCA s 5 principles as a form of checklist.
[55] COCA, s 4(2).

> carte blanche to the care-giving parent to be able to shift without consulting the [other] guardian, but it does presume that shifting is an incident of day-to-day care in a way that isn't at the moment, so that will normalise things. . . . [Second,] the section 5(b) principle [should] be amended [so that], where it has got in brackets, 'and in particular the child should have a continuing relationship with his or her parents', I don't think it would be difficult to insert after that, 'and especially after the relocation of one or both of them', because that is the very time when you have to look at how you are going to keep this relationship alive. You are not looking at how you are going to stop the relocation any more, you are looking at, given that the relocation is going to happen, how do you keep the relationship alive with the other parent?

The idea was to make clear that 'relocation will and can happen as part of everyday life' (NS2), though it may be that the Supreme Court has subsequently made much the same point.[56] Moreover, promoting and maintaining strong relationships between the child and both parents did not necessitate them being confined to the same geographic location, especially where the proposed move was over a relatively short distance.

In short, although there were suggestions for minor changes, they were intended to compensate for shifts in the practice of the courts, which were seen as deviating from the law as prescribed by *D v S*. The legal approach laid down was strongly supported by New Zealand practitioners, and the 'changes' suggested were designed to ensure that everyday cases followed that legal approach.

Discussion

The three chapters based on empirical interviews with practitioners in England and Wales and New Zealand have shown a significant divergence in the approaches of the two jurisdictions in practice. In chapter three, the analysis of three hypothetical relocation disputes showed differences in both the reasoning and the outcomes reached by the two national groups. In all three vignettes, the English thought relocation more likely to be allowed than the New Zealanders, even though in two cases the predicted outcome was the same in both systems. Crucially, though, it was Tom's case where the difference in outcome was seen: on the facts which are most prevalent in English cases, New Zealanders thought relocation likely to be refused, while English practitioners considered it a strong case for relocation.

The chapters which followed explored the two legal approaches in more detail. English practitioners were seen, in chapter four, to have a clear understanding of the law, but to be mixed in their assessments of it. While some were strongly defensive of the *Payne* approach, others thought that its effect was to 'compromise' the welfare principle (EB3), forcing courts to focus on one factor which

[56] *Kacem v Bashir* [2010] NZSC 112, [2010] NZFLR 884 [28].

might not always be the most important aspect of the child's best interests. Those who offered this criticism favoured an approach which involved less guidance and left judges to assess the child's welfare with fewer strictures.

This chapter has explored New Zealand practitioners' experiences of relocation law which largely represents the approach favoured by many English practitioners. Participants' understandings of the law fit with the conclusions of chapter two: *D v S* continues to be the leading authority on relocation, with COCA augmenting rather than amending that approach.[57] However, it was also suggested in chapter two that the practice of New Zealand law might have turned against relocation. This chapter has shown that practitioners shared these conclusions. Most practitioners thought that, in general, the courts now favour shared day-to-day care arrangements and place greater weight on a child's relationship with a non-resident parent. At the same time, the importance of a carer's emotional and psychological well-being was being seen as a secondary factor when assessing children's welfare in the relocation context. As a result, there was a general view that 'in New Zealand relocation is militated against rather than militated for' (NS2).

In terms of the core legal approach, New Zealand practitioners did not seek changes to the law; indeed, they strongly supported *D v S* and thought that 'it would be absurd to do anything other than that' (NB6). There was, however, some suggestion that there needed to be a change in the application of the law because, in practice, it was becoming too difficult to achieve relocation. We saw in chapter three that New Zealanders were consistently less likely to predict that relocation would be allowed than were English practitioners when assessing hypothetical cases. Many New Zealanders were unhappy with the outcomes which they predicted in chapter three, and that discomfort was mirrored in their general view seen in this chapter that obtaining leave to relocate was 'an uphill struggle' (NS4).

We began our analysis of New Zealand practitioners' experiences by noting that *D v S* bears considerable resemblance to the 'ideal jurisprudential world' (EJ1) of some English practitioners, as seen in chapter four. We asked whether New Zealand practitioners were more satisfied with their relocation law than were English practitioners, and whether adopting an approach similar to that taken in New Zealand would satisfy the concerns of those English practitioners who criticised *Payne*. The findings of this chapter suggest that the answers to these questions might be somewhat mixed. On the one hand, the approach set out by *D v S* was strongly supported by practitioners, who thought (as did many English practitioners) that assessing each relocation case on its facts, with no preconceived ideas about the importance of any one factor, was the most appropriate way to resolve these difficult problems.

However, the practice of New Zealand law suggests that there are potential pitfalls to leaving trial judges without guidance. In particular, the practical reality of New Zealand law seems to be that a parent's emotional and psychological

[57] For subsequent affirmation of that conclusion, see *Kacem v Bashir* [2010] NZSC 112, [2010] NZFLR 884.

well-being is routinely given less significance than many practitioners think it deserves. In other words, English practitioners may be right to say that one of the benefits of *Payne* is that it focuses attention on 'what the true impact on mother is going to be if she is not permitted to go' (EJ2), and thereby 'emphasise[s] that one should take the medium to long-term view of the situation. . . . *Payne* does have the effect of stopping short-termism' (EB5).[58] While New Zealand practitioners did not express themselves in these terms, it might be that at least some would have agreed that the practice of down-playing a primary carer's well-being risks ignoring the long-term effect on that parent and, consequently, on the child.

It might be that one lesson which those assessing the English law could learn from the New Zealand experience is that there are perils involved in removing any 'gloss on the welfare principle'.[59] When practitioners are as 'conditioned by the current law' as the English are by *Payne* (EJ1), not only would it 'take time to move out of that mode' (EJ1), but the move itself would need to be done carefully. In moving from a position where factor *x* is given particular emphasis to a rule which says 'all factors are equal', factor *x* is being given less weight than before; the difficulty then is in knowing how much weight to give that factor.

The risk which the New Zealand experience highlights is that factor *x* ends up being given too little weight instead of too much. As one New Zealand practitioner explained, 'we have actually gone too far – the English are at one end of it and we have got the other' (NS6). In an effort to shift away from *Payne*, it may have been forgotten that '*D v S* intends only to avoid giving presumptive weight to any one factor; it does not follow that the applicant parent's emotional and psychological wellbeing might not, on the facts, be the decisive factor'.[60] Part of the explanation for this over-compensation may stem from the introduction of COCA in 2004, but as we saw the shift was taking place before that Act came into force.[61] Consequently, it seems plausible that the risks involved in reforming the guidance in relocation cases which the New Zealand experience highlights are of broad relevance, regardless of the detail of the legislative background.

[58] See above, p 98.

[59] M Hayes, 'Relocation Cases: Is the Court of Appeal Applying the Correct Principles?' [2006] *Child and Family Law Quarterly* 351, 362.

[60] R George, 'The Shifting Law: Relocation Disputes in New Zealand and England' [2009] *Otago Law Review* 107, 125.

[61] See above, pp 124–25.

6

Reforming Relocation Law?

One of the common threads of the relocation debates in many countries is a question – sometimes open and vociferous, sometimes rather less forceful – about whether the law might need to be reviewed. This thread can be found seemingly regardless of the particular country's approach to relocation disputes in theory and in practice.

In England, critics of *Payne v Payne*[1] have successfully established a now well-known narrative that the law is effectively operating as a presumption in favour of relocation applications.[2] Many proponents of this critique present their view as representing the dominant experience of litigants and professionals, though the extent to which that representation is true is difficult to ascertain. Certainly the experiences of practitioners interviewed as part of this research suggest more variety of views and assessments than the initial chorus might imply.

Despite the rather different legal context of relocation disputes in New Zealand, the debates there have surprising similarities to those in England. The core question being discussed in both countries (and, indeed, in most countries around the world) is the same: how should the law resolve a dispute where the two sides have such compelling cases? Is it possible to find a legal approach that allows both sides of these difficult cases to be fully explored without imposing a solution which might not be the best available in any given case? This chapter assesses some of the lessons that might be learned from the experiences of those two jurisdictions, and discusses some alternative approaches to relocation disputes.

Learning Lessons about Relocation Law

A number of important points have arisen from the exploration of relocation law in this study, and the experiences of practitioners in both jurisdictions may offer important lessons for those who favour law reform. Some of those lessons can

[1] *Payne v Payne* [2001] EWCA Civ 166, [2001] 1 FLR 1052 (hereafter, *Payne*).

[2] See, eg, C Geekie, 'Relocation and Shared Residence: One Route or Two?' [2008] *Family Law* 446; M Robinson, 'Relocation and Leave to Remove' (2009), online at www.thecustodyminefield.com, 12; D Hodson, 'Every Family Matters: An In-Depth Review of Family Law in Britain' (London, Centre for Social Justice, 2009) 165.

perhaps be shortly stated. From the English interviews, for example, it is possible to see that there is a clear group of practitioners, some of them very senior, who think that the law is approaching relocation cases in more or less the right way at the moment. This group of supporters would not perhaps be readily apparent from the public debate about relocation law, which is dominated by those who seek reform. It is impossible to tell from this study what proportion of experienced practitioners would be in support of the current law in England, but the more important point may be to realise that there is a body of generally silent supporters.

Another lesson to learn from the current English guidance is the importance of testing relocation proposals for the applicant's bona fides, as well as making clear that a significant amount of planning will be required before a relocation application is brought. This is a valuable point to retain, especially in the light of the judicial recognition that there may be a difference in the degree of planning required in, say, a case where a parent is moving back to a location where she has previously lived for many years, compared with a case where a parent is moving somewhere new for the first time.[3] Other lessons from this study require rather fuller discussion.

The Value of a Single Approach

Compared with almost all other countries, England is unusual in having a number of different legal approaches to relocation disputes – one approach for internal relocation within the UK, another for international moves by a primary carer, and a third for international moves in truly shared care cases. The reasons underlying this division, while rarely made explicit,[4] seem to relate to a desire to be aware of context: each of the three approaches relies on certain factual characteristics being present, and when they are missing that approach struggles to accommodate the case. In theory at least, this multi-angled approach ought to allow the law to be nuanced and attuned to the particular elements present in each type of case, which would be a potential advantage of the English law. So, for example, the focus in *Payne* on assessing the effect of refusing relocation on the applicant primary carer is only relevant where there is indeed a primary carer;[5] where there is shared care, this factor is of less central relevance, hence the different approach in *K v K (Relocation: Shared Care Arrangement)*.[6]

[3] See, eg, *Re F and H (Children: Relocation)* [2007] EWCA Civ 692, [2008] 2 FLR 1667 [9]; *S v T (Permission to Relocate to Russia)* [2012] EWHC 4023 (Fam), [2013] 2 FLR 457 [6(1)].

[4] See below, p 140.

[5] The fact that the person identified as the primary carer must also be the applicant parent in order for the logic of *Payne* to apply appears to get lost in some cases: see *Re F (Relocation)* [2012] EWCA Civ 1364, [2013] 1 FLR 645, where the trial judge identified the father as the primary carer and then went on to apply the *Payne* guidance to the mother's application to relocate. The Court of Appeal dismissed the father's appeal.

[6] *K v K (Relocation: Shared Care Arrangement)* [2011] EWCA Civ 793, [2012] 2 FLR 880 (hereafter, *K v K*).

However, this theoretical benefit is countered by some practical difficulties associated with the three-fold approach to relocation disputes. For the divide between shared care and sole care in international cases, one danger was highlighted by Black LJ in *K v K*:[7] having different approaches risks initial pre-trial disputes between the parties about the nature of their care arrangements, since being in one legal category or the other will (be perceived to) affect each party's chances of success.[8] A similar point was made by Wall LJ in an internal relocation case when his Lordship explained that he considered it to be 'wrong in principle' to have differing approaches based on whether residence was shared or not.[9]

In practice, it is hard to see how initial disputes about the existing care arrangements and their importance to the child could be avoided if the law has different legal approaches to relocation based on the assessment of that question. Some practitioners in this study also pointed out that such an approach to relocation incentivises a 'tactical approach' to residence arrangements long before relocation becomes a live issue:

> **EJ2:** in anticipation of there being a relocation application further along the line, one of the parents, usually the father, will do his utmost to achieve a shared care arrangement, not just for its own sake but also in order to make the prospect of leave to remove more difficult. So you get an awful lot of manoeuvring, establishing of position at the outset of proceedings.

The other difficulty highlighted by some participants was that there were many cases where it was unclear whether a case should properly be categorised as sole or shared care, based on the child's day-to-day living arrangements. As one senior barrister explained, there were many care arrangements where 'it would be very hard from the child's point of view to say whom they regarded as being their primary carer' (EB5). A similar point was made by Munby LJ in *Re F (Relocation)* when deploring the development of a complex taxonomy of relocation case-types:

> The last thing that this very difficult area of family law requires is a satellite jurisprudence generating an ever-more detailed classification of supposedly different types of relocation case. Any move in that direction is, in my judgment, to be firmly resisted. . . . Asking whether a case is a '*Payne* type case', or a '*K v K* type case' or a '*Re Y* type case', when in truth it may be none of them, is simply a recipe for unnecessary and inappropriate forensic dispute or worse. It is to be avoided.[10]

At the same time, while there is value in having a single set of guidelines for all relocation disputes, one must question the wisdom of the apparent attempt by some judges to interpret *Payne* in such a way that it will form the basis of that single approach.[11] Not only might this approach conflict with binding authority

[7] ibid [145].

[8] This point was specifically endorsed by Munby LJ in *Re F (Relocation)* [2012] EWCA Civ 1364, [2013] 1 FLR 645 [58].

[9] *Re L (Internal Relocation: Shared Residence Order)* [2009] EWCA Civ 20, [2009] 1 FLR 1157 [36].

[10] *Re F (Relocation)* [2012] EWCA Civ 1364, [2013] 1 FLR 645 [60].

[11] See Black LJ in *K v K* and Munby LJ in *Re F (Relocation)* [2012] EWCA Civ 1364, [2013] 1 FLR 645.

which, at the least, needs to be addressed,[12] but more importantly it is doubtful whether *Payne*, even on a broad reading, ought to be applied to all relocation cases. The author of the principal guidance in that case, Thorpe LJ, has made plain that he considers *Payne* to be confined to cases where the applicant is clearly the child's primary carer.[13] If there is now a move towards a single approach, the *Payne* guidance cannot be its basis.[14]

The existence of a division between internal and international relocation applications raises rather different issues. There is no practical complication to categorising cases: the destination either is or is not within the UK.[15] However, there may nonetheless be two problems arising from the distinction.

The first issue is that, when thinking about the effect of the relocation on the child involved, the distinction can appear somewhat arbitrary. The original rule that wards could not be removed from the jurisdiction stemmed from a judicial concern to retain oversight of the child;[16] the rule later morphed to say that moves within the jurisdiction (and then within the UK, as the Family Law Act 1986 and the Children Act 1989 entered force) would be more readily allowed than moves overseas.[17] However, although that original justification seems to have fallen away, the rule itself remains, now explained by the greater impact on the child of an international rather than a domestic move.[18] At a practical level, though, some people consider the effects of this rule somewhat unprincipled. As several practitioners in England noted in this study, the law makes it easier to move from

[12] See *Re C and M (Children)*, 30 July 1999 (EWCA), discussed above, p 43.

[13] The words 'primary carer' appear no fewer than 14 times in Thorpe LJ's judgment in *Payne*, including twice in the 'discipline' of paras [40] and [41]. His Lordship has elsewhere clarified the restriction of that guidance to primary carer applications: see, eg, *Re C and M (Children)*, 30 July 1999 (EWCA); *Re J (Children) (Residence Order: Removal from Jurisdiction)* [2006] EWCA Civ 1897, [2007] 1 FLR 2033 [27]; *Re H (A Child)* [2010] EWCA Civ 789 [13] and [15]; *K v K* [41].

[14] See further R George, 'International Relocation, Care Arrangements, and Case Taxonomy' [2012] *Family Law* 1478.

[15] On possible complications with Scotland and Northern Ireland, see above, p 29.

[16] See, eg, *De Manneville v De Manneville* (1804) 10 Ves 52, 32 ER 762; *Campbell v Mackay* (1837) 2 My&Cr 31, 40 ER 552; see generally J Seymour, 'Parens Patriae and Wardship Powers: Their Nature and Origin' [1994] *Oxford Journal of Legal Studies* 159.

[17] See, eg, *Practice Direction (Custody Order)* [1953] 1 WLR 707, providing that children who were the subject of custody orders must not be removed from the jurisdiction without court leave; Children Act 1989, s 13(1)(b) later broadened this provision to include the three jurisdictions of the United Kingdom, and in *Re E (Residence: Imposition of Conditions)* [1997] 2 FLR 638 (EWCA) the Court of Appeal interpreted this provision to imply that no leave was required to move within the UK.

[18] See *Re H (Children) (Residence Order: Condition)* [2001] EWCA Civ 1338, [2001] 2 FLR 1277 [20] (Thorpe LJ): 'What then is the rationalisation for freer movement of the primary carer within the United Kingdom? It seems to me to be obvious. Within the same sovereignty there will be the same system of laws, with the same rights of the citizen, rights for instance to education, health care and statutory benefits. Equally, it can be said that within Europe, whilst perhaps the burden on the applicant may be greater, it is equally mitigated by the fact that within the Community there is the same fundamental approach to social issues and a real endeavour to achieve harmonisation, obviously in social policy but also in family justice. If, moving to the third alternative, the application is for relocation outside the European region, the necessary adjustment may be rationalised on the basis that the social and other circumstances involved in relocation may require much greater adjustment for the children; alternatively, that the obstacles to contact may be enhanced.' But *cf Payne* [36]–[37], quoted below, n 22.

London to Penzance or Bangor than to Paris or Brussels, even though in some ways the international destinations may be easier to move back and forth between than the national ones. It is fair to say though that this view presumes that post-relocation contact will proceed smoothly, since the legal and practical options available to a parent whose contact is being obstructed are different in cases where the child remains in the same jurisdiction compared to cross-border cases.[19] In that regard, it is important to remain aware that post-relocation contact does not always proceed smoothly.[20] (That said, some evidence raises questions about whether the relocation is always the cause of the loss of contact: in the words of once New Zealand study, '[s]ome children reported difficult, strained or distant relationships with their contact parent. In most cases this did not appear to be due to the relocation or the geographical distance but was a feature of their relationship prior to the relocation'.[21])

The second potential problem, seemingly not yet argued before the courts, is a legal one stemming from the provisions of EU law.[22] As Ruth Lamont explains:

[19] Within the EU, contact orders are automatically enforceable under the Brussels II Revised Regulation, Council Regulation (EC) No 2201/2003 of 27 November 2003, though it is debatable how well the system works in practice. Outside the EU, there are possible remedies under the Hague Convention on the Civil Aspects of International Child Abduction 1980 and the Hague Convention on Jurisdiction, Applicable Law, Recognition, Enforcement and Co-operation in Respect of Parental Responsibility and Measures for the Protection of Children 1996, if the country in question is a signatory of those Conventions.

[20] Reports of parents losing all contact after relocation are not uncommon, though the extent to which such cases are generally representative is unclear: see, eg, M Freeman, *Relocation: The Reunite Research* (London, Reunite, 2009) 26.

[21] N Taylor, M Gollop and M Henaghan, *Relocation Following Parental Separation: The Welfare and Best Interests of Children* (University of Otago, Dunedin, 2010) 126.

[22] It is surprising that no one has yet made this argument, since Thorpe LJ explained it in some detail in *Payne* [36]–[37]:

> But despite the fact that this appeal has raised only the asserted Art 8 rights of the secondary caring parent, we should not lose sight of the Art 8 rights of the primary carer, although not specifically asserted in argument. However an appeal may well arise in which a disappointed applicant will contend that s 13(1)(b) of the Children Act 1989 imposes a disproportionate restriction on a parent's right to determine her place of habitual residence. This right was recognised by the decision of this court in *Re E (Residence: Imposition of Conditions)* [1997] 2 FLR 638 within the confines of the jurisdiction of the court and indeed beyond within the UK. But why should the same right not extend to anywhere within the European Union (having regard to Art 48 of the Treaty of Rome) or, beyond that, within wider Europe? From that point to a right to world-wide mobility seems but a short step. The European Convention for the Protection of Human Rights and Fundamental Freedoms 1950 does specifically recognise this right of mobility in Art 2 of Protocol 4 which provides:
>
> 1. Everyone lawfully within the territory of a state shall, within that territory, have the right to liberty of movement and freedom to choose his residence.
> 2. Everybody shall be free to leave any country, including his own.
> 3. No restrictions shall be placed on the exercise of these rights other than such as are in accordance with law and are necessary in a democratic society in the interests of national security or public safety, for the maintenance of public order, for the prevention of crime, for the protection of health and morals, or for the protection of the rights and freedom of others.
>
> Although Protocol 4 has yet to be ratified by the UK, it undoubtedly lends force to the argument that a failure or refusal to recognise a right of mobility beyond the somewhat fortuitous jurisdictional boundary represents a stance of disproportionate parochialism.

> Free movement of persons is central to the European conception of citizenship and the principle is strongly protected and promoted by the EU and the European Court of Justice. Restrictions on free movement affect the realisation of this right so, to be maintained, any restriction must be objectively justified and proportionate. A legal measure that restricts the free movement of persons can be subjected to a proportionality assessment.[23]

As Lamont goes on to explain, the potential of relocation law to limit free movement within the Union brings domestic family law within the scope of EU law, which is particularly important given that the two approaches to relocation in English law may constitute indirect discrimination on the ground of nationality which would then have to be objectively justified.[24] The European Court has yet to address this issue directly, but Lamont's discussion of general principles leads her to suggest that, as long as the welfare analysis is individualised and not mechanistic, a decision to refuse relocation may well be proportionate as long as there are 'objective, identifiable reasons for the refusal of an application that respond to circumstances'.[25]

Lamont is understandably cautious in her conclusion on this point. She notes, for example, the primacy of the child's welfare and the explicit EU recognition of a child's right to a relationship with both parents,[26] observing that these factors may 'legitimise the restriction on movement posed by relocation law'.[27] On the other hand, though, with Family Court orders relating to the upbringing of children now automatically enforceable across the EU,[28] it may be increasingly hard to provide an objective justification for rules which make relocation within the UK easier than relocation within the EU, even if each case applying those rules is said to be promoting the best interests of the child. At any rate, EU law raises a potential complication which is more difficult to resolve because of the legal difference between intra-UK moves and intra-EU moves.

Given both the practical and the legal complications which arise from having several approaches to relocation disputes, there seems to be merit in the unity of legal approach found in New Zealand (and, indeed, in most jurisdictions outside the United Kingdom). If the law itself places no preconceived weight on the relevance of care arrangements or destination, then trial judges will be able to assess

[23] R Lamont, 'Free Movement of Persons, Child Abduction and Relocation Within the European Union' [2012] *Journal of Social Welfare and Family Law* 231, 231.

[24] ibid 241. The argument would be that since UK nationals are more likely to be involved with an internal move within the UK, and non-UK EU nationals are more likely to be involved with an international move within the EU (returning to their home country, most likely), the more restrictive rules on international relocation are, de facto, more likely to affect a non-UK EU national, and obviously do so in an adverse way from the point of view of the parent seeking to relocate.

[25] ibid 241.

[26] Charter of Fundamental Rights of the European Union (OJ No C303, 14 Dec 2007), Art 24(2).

[27] R Lamont, 'Free Movement of Persons, Child Abduction and Relocation Within the European Union' [2012] *Journal of Social Welfare and Family Law* 231, 241.

[28] See the Brussels II Revised Regulation, Council Regulation (EC) No 2201/2003 of 27 November 2003 concerning jurisdiction and the recognition and enforcement of judgments in matrimonial matters and the matters of parental responsibility.

the importance of those factors alongside all others on a case-by-case basis. Childcare arrangements, for example, raise three core questions. First, is it realistic for the non-moving parent to have main care of the child? Second, what will be the likely effect on the child of the diminution in the relationship with the non-moving parent if a relocation goes ahead? And third, what will be the likely effect on the child of a refusal of relocation, whether in terms of a transfer of main residence and the diminution in the relationship with the moving parent, or in terms of the impact on the would-be moving parent if she decides not to move?

Similarly, when it comes to the proposed destination, the main issue is the same regardless of whether the move is international or not, relating to the practical and legal ability of the child to maintain a positive relationship with the non-moving parent if the relocation goes ahead. (A secondary question may be about how easy it would be for the would-be relocating parent to mitigate any negative impact from a refusal of relocation by travelling regularly to the proposed destination himself.) Consequently, if an approach to relocation law which applies equally regardless of these factual variations can be formulated, there may be advantages to adopting that approach.

The Value of Guidance

One of the criticisms made of the existing law in New Zealand by participants in this study is that its broad all-factor approach gives inadequate guidance to decision-makers and, by extension, legal advisers and parents.[29] Many participants expressed a desire for greater clarity about the process by which relocation cases are decided, and about the factors which judges take into consideration.

One effect that can flow from a lack of guidance is that individual judges have increased scope to create their own approaches to relocation. New Zealand lawyers frequently commented on judicial variation when it came to relocation cases, and noted with a degree of professional embarrassment that their evaluation of whether a case was likely to succeed or not would sometimes change dramatically once they found out which judge was hearing the case. Judges themselves were aware of this variation, and some had attempted to standardise their own practice by developing their own sets of guidelines or checklists of factors to consider in relocation cases, because approaching each case with nothing but the welfare principle was too difficult.[30]

[29] Similar complaints are seen in Canada: see, eg, R Thompson, 'Ten Years After Gordon: No Law, Nowhere' (2007) 35 *Reports of Family Law* (6th) 307; N Bala and A Wheeler, 'Canadian Relocation Cases: Heading Towards Guidelines' [2012] *Canadian Family Law Quarterly* 271.

[30] These judges were well aware that the New Zealand High Court was opposed to such an approach (*Brown v Argyll* [2006] NZFLR 705 (NZHC) [38]; *S v L [Relocation]* [2008] NZFLR 237 (NZHC) [28]–[30]), but took the risk of being criticised on appeal because they found the checklists too useful to abandon. The New Zealand Supreme Court subsequently took the view that s 5 of COCA should be approached as a form of checklist (*Kacem v Bashir* [2010] NZSC 112, [2010] NZFLR 884 [19]), but that point cannot be seen as endorsement of the use of checklists derived from sources other than the statute.

It might well be thought that guidance of some kind is therefore both appropriate and valuable in relocation cases. However, looking at the position in England by way of contrast, it is apparent that there is a fine line to be walked, since the law in England has been criticised for giving too much guidance as to how judges and, by extension, legal advisers and others should approach relocation cases. The argument against the English approach was first made by academics,[31] and was reflected in the views of some participants in this research when interviewed in 2008–09.[32] At the same time, though, participants in this study acknowledged the value of guidance in general, since it allowed particularly relevant aspects of child welfare to be highlighted,[33] and meant that there was more conformity of practice between judges.[34]

Since the interviews for this research took place, the English Court of Appeal has clarified the role of guidance in child law cases, and in relocation cases in particular.[35] Given that the only legal principle applicable to relocation cases is the welfare principle, it follows that everything said in *Payne* and other appellate cases is judicial guidance, something akin to a judge-made version of the welfare checklist.[36] That does not mean that it is of no relevance: as Black LJ explained in *K v K*, the case law 'must be heeded . . . but as guidance not as rigid principle or so as to dictate a particular outcome in a sphere of law where the facts of individual cases are so infinitely variable'.[37] The same point was made by Moore-Bick LJ:

> Guidance of the kind provided in [appellate relocation cases] is, of course, very valuable both in ensuring that judges identify what are likely to be the most important factors to be taken into account and the weight that should generally be attached to them. It also plays a valuable role in promoting consistency in decision-making. However, the circumstances in which these difficult decisions have to be made vary infinitely and the judge in each case must be free to weigh up the individual factors and make whatever decision he or she considers to be in the best interests of the child.[38]

This decision, along with other reported cases,[39] may have settled some of the controversy over the guidance that was apparent when interviews for this research took place. Whether that is so or not, it is important not to conflate any arguments

[31] See, eg, M Hayes and C Williams, *Family Law: Principles, Policy and Practice*, 2nd edn (London, Butterworths, 1999) 311–16; M Hayes, 'Relocation Cases: Is the Court of Appeal Applying the Correct Principles?' [2006] *Child and Family Law Quarterly* 351.

[32] See above, pp 103–12.

[33] See above, p 106.

[34] See above, p 110.

[35] *K v K*; see discussion in R George, 'Reviewing Relocation?' [2012] *Child and Family Law Quarterly* 110, 115–20.

[36] *K v K* [40].

[37] *K v K* [142].

[38] *K v K* [86].

[39] See, eg, *Re H (Leave to Remove)* [2010] EWCA Civ 915, [2010] 2 FLR 1875 [21]; *J v S (Leave to Remove)* [2010] EWHC 2098 (Fam), [2011] 1 FLR 1694 [81]–[82]; *Re F (Relocation)* [2012] EWCA Civ 1364, [2013] 1 FLR 645.

that can be made against the particular guidance given in *Payne* with an argument that there should be no guidance at all in relocation cases. It was noted in chapter four that most of those who were critical of the guidance as it was being interpreted then went on to say that some guidance, albeit perhaps 'more light-handed' (EB5), was beneficial and important.

Some may suggest that, now that its role in judicial decision-making has been clarified by the Court of Appeal,[40] the *Payne* guidance is an appropriate way to approach relocation applications brought by primary carers. However, that case has been subjected to such sustained criticism over a number of years that, in the interests of maintaining confidence in the law, it seems worth considering whether alternative guidance can be formulated which is both practically useful and also sufficiently 'light-handed' that it does not risk being interpreted as overly directive. That is especially true if, as discussed earlier, there is to be a single set of guidelines applicable to all relocation cases.[41]

Rewriting the Relocation Guidance

Learning the lessons from this research means that there needs to be some degree of guidance as to which factors are important for a judge to consider; the guidance needs to apply equally to any relocation case, regardless of its factual variations; and it needs to be sufficiently 'light-handed' to avoid any appearance of having predetermined the outcome.

One reason why common law systems focus on resolving particular cases and then drawing general principles from them is that it is difficult to foresee the problems and complexities of real cases without having one to consider. That is why courts do not usually entertain hypothetical disputes, contrived facts, or cases in which there is no meaningful disagreement between the parties. Consequently, suggesting alternative approaches to relocation in the abstract is not without its limitations. However, the final section of this chapter addresses three possible alternative approaches to relocation guidance. The first suggests a list of factors to consider when determining a relocation dispute, drawn from the Washington Declaration on International Family Relocation 2010.[42] The second has emerged separately from both Canada and New Zealand, proposing presumed outcomes based on the child's existing care arrangements. The third proposes to consider a relocation dispute by asking a series of connected questions.

[40] *K v K*.

[41] See above, pp 138–43.

[42] Some of this discussion was previously published in R George, 'The International Relocation Debate' [2012] *Journal of Social Welfare and Family Law* 141.

Guidance in the Form of Factors to Consider

In March 2010, over 50 judges and other experts from 14 countries attended a three-day conference on international relocation in Washington DC. The purpose was 'to explore the development of common principles to guide the exercise of [judicial] discretion in granting or refusing a relocation'.[43]

From this conference came a 13-point statement, the Washington Declaration on International Family Relocation 2010. Although technically restricted to international relocation cases (since domestic relocation was considered to be outside the scope of the conference), there is little reason why the approach adopted could not be extended to all relocation cases. The crucial aspects, under the heading 'Factors Relevant to Decisions on International Relocation', are points 3 and 4:

> 3 In all applications concerning international relocation the best interests of the child should be the paramount (primary) consideration. Therefore, determinations should be made without any presumptions for or against relocation.
>
> 4 In order to identify more clearly cases in which relocation should be granted or refused, and to promote a more uniform approach internationally, the exercise of judicial discretion should be guided in particular, but not exclusively, by the following factors listed in no order of priority. The weight to be given to any one factor will vary from case to case:
>
> i) the right of the child separated from one parent to maintain personal relations and direct contact with both parents on a regular basis in a manner consistent with the child's development, except if the contact is contrary to the child's best interest;
> ii) the views of the child having regard to the child's age and maturity;
> iii) the parties' proposals for the practical arrangements for relocation, including accommodation, schooling and employment;
> iv) where relevant to the determination of the outcome, the reasons for seeking or opposing the relocation;
> v) any history of family violence or abuse, whether physical or psychological;
> vi) the history of the family and particularly the continuity and quality of past and current care and contact arrangements;
> vii) pre-existing custody and access determinations;
> viii) the impact of grant or refusal on the child, in the context of his or her extended family, education and social life, and on the parties;
> ix) the nature of the inter-parental relationship and the commitment of the applicant to support and facilitate the relationship between the child and the respondent after the relocation;
> x) whether the parties' proposals for contact after relocation are realistic, having particular regard to the cost to the family and the burden to the child;
> xi) the enforceability of contact provisions ordered as a condition of relocation in the State of destination;
> xii) issues of mobility for family members; and
> xiii) any other circumstances deemed to be relevant by the judge.

[43] M Thorpe, 'Relocation Development' [2010] *Family Law* 565, 565.

Put shortly, the Declaration's approach is to identify factors which are relevant to a welfare assessment and then leave judges to assess their weight in each individual case. However, there are two reasons to question whether this approach would mark an improvement to the current legal approaches adopted in various countries. One is that the Declaration's factors may simply be too general to offer any meaningful guidance. A jurisdiction (or individual judge) favouring relocation could focus on those factors which support a relocation application, while other factors could be highlighted by those opposed to relocation. It seems at least possible that the practical application of this approach would be open to much the same criticism as the current law in countries like New Zealand and Canada, namely that it allows individual decision-makers to impose their own values on relocation cases with no way to make that reasoning explicit.

The second difficulty is that the list of considerations highlighted by the Declaration, as well as the phrasing of some of them, is open to question. (It should be kept in mind that the Declaration was drafted by a large committee, which means, as Thorpe LJ noted in his report on the Conference, that 'the text is not a matter of satisfaction to any individual on the drafting committee'.[44]) On the one hand, there are those who note that the Declaration appears to overlook potentially important considerations, as Wilson LJ explained:

> In that the principal charge against [the English law's] guidance, as it stands, is that it ascribes too great a significance to the effect on the child of the negative impact upon the applicant of refusal of the application, one is interested to discern the way in which, in [4] of the declaration, that factor is addressed. One finds (does one not?) that it is not squarely addressed at all. The closest to any address of it is to be found in (viii), namely 'the impact of grant or refusal on the child, in the context of his or her extended family, education and social life, and on the parties.' Some may share my initial perplexity even at the terminology of (viii) in that it appears to train the consideration of the court upon impact not only 'on the child' but also, and by way of contradistinction, 'on the parties' apparently irrespective of impact on the child. It is axiomatic that our notion of paramountcy excludes from consideration all factors which have no bearing on the child. But, that possible curiosity apart, there is no square address in (viii) of the impact upon the child likely to flow from negative impact upon the applicant of refusal of the application. Indeed the reference to the child's extended family, education and social life, seems almost to draw attention away from such a factor. I wonder whether consideration might need to be given as to whether, if the present law of England and Wales does indeed place excessive weight upon that factor, paragraph [4] of the declaration, as presently drawn, by contrast places insufficient weight upon it.[45]

While some may disagree with Wilson LJ's criticism of the Declaration for considering the effect 'on the parties' separately from the child's welfare,[46] even the

[44] ibid.

[45] *Re H (Leave to Remove)* [2010] EWCA Civ 915, [2010] 2 FLR 1875 [27].

[46] One of the main criticisms of the welfare principle advanced by some critics is its alleged failure to take into account the interests of people other than the child concerned: see, eg, S Harris-Short, 'Family Law and the Human Rights Act 1998: Judicial Restrain or Revolution?' [2005] *Child and Family Law Quarterly* 329; S Choudhry and H Fenwick, 'Taking the Rights of Parents and Children

broader point about the importance of considering the effect of refusing leave to relocate has proved controversial.

On the other side of the debate, Mostyn J appeared rather more content with the limited focus on the applicant parent's well-being in the Declaration,[47] though his Lordship's remarks have a number of limitations which cast doubt on his view that the Declaration is 'a more balanced and neutral approach to a relocation application'.[48] In particular,[49] his Lordship's discussion of the relevance of the applicant parent's well-being in an assessment of the child's best interests is problematic. While acknowledging that the impact of refusing relocation on what he termed 'the thwarted primary carer'[50] should be acknowledged explicitly and 'deserves its due weight, no more, no less', Mostyn J was concerned that this factor 'appears to penalise selflessness and virtue, while rewarding selfishness and uncontrolled emotions'.[51] As his Lordship explained:

> The parent who stoically accepts that she would accept the decision, make the most of it, move on and work to promote contact with the other parent is far more likely to be refused leave than the parent who states that she will collapse emotionally and psychologically. This is the reverse of the Judgment of Solomon, where of course selflessness and sacrifice received their due reward.[52]

Respectfully, despite its later repetition by the Judge,[53] this approach should be rejected. The issue is not about punishing or rewarding the parent for being 'stoical' or 'uncontrolled', but about what effect her state of mind is likely to have on the child.[54] As one judge interviewed in this study made clear, the effect of refusal of leave is a question of fact 'that needs to be examined rigorously [and it is not] just someone expressing their view, expressed and taken at face value' (EJ2). The parent who is found by the judge to be able to 'accept the decision, make the most of it, move on', is, as a matter of fact, in a different position from the parent who is believed by the judge to be likely to 'collapse emotionally and psychologically'.

Seriously: Confronting the Welfare Principle under the Human Rights Act' [2005] *Oxford Journal of Legal Studies* 453; but *cf* below, pp 160–63.

[47] *Re AR (A Child: Relocation)* [2010] EWHC 1346 (Fam), [2010] 2 FLR 1577.

[48] ibid [11].

[49] For further criticism of Mostyn J's judgment, especially his comparison between the Washington Declaration and the welfare checklist in Children Act 1989 (England), s 1(3), see R George, *Ideas and Debates in Family Law* (Oxford, Hart Publishing, 2012) 114–17.

[50] Eleanor King J must be right to describe this phrase as 'not helpful' because 'such an expression carries with it pejorative overtones' and overlooks the fact that a would-be relocating parent must show a legitimate motivation for bringing the application: *J v S (Leave to Remove)* [2010] EWHC 2098 (Fam), [2011] 1 FLR 1694 [96].

[51] *Re AR (A Child: Relocation)* [2010] EWHC 1346 (Fam), [2010] 2 FLR 1577 [12].

[52] ibid.

[53] *Re TC And JC (Children: Relocation)* [2013] EWHC 292 (Fam), [2013] 2 FLR 484 [12].

[54] As with all factors, a parent's state of mind 'must be assessed and weighed in [its] bearing on the welfare of the child': *J v C* [1970] AC 668 (UKHL) 715. In the relocation context, see, eg, *S v T (Permission to Relocate to Russia)* [2012] EWHC 4023 (Fam), [2013] 2 FLR 457 [6(5)]: 'The court should scrutinise the impact on the applicant of the order being refused or on the respondent of the order being granted, but . . . this impact will be relevant generally only insofar as it impacts on the child.'

The impact of each state on the child will be different, and this differential impact is sidelined in Mostyn J's adult-centred analysis.

Regardless of the merits of either of these judicial conclusions, though, what is apparent is that the contents of any list of 'relevant considerations', as well as the phrasing of those factors which are to be listed, is a matter on which people may well differ, even at a national level. The Declaration was intended to start a discussion about an international consensus on relocation cases, but subsequent international discussions appear to have quashed such aspirations for now.[55] Consequently, while there may be value in giving further thought to developing the Declaration's approach, this is also a good time to consider alternatives.

Guidance in the Form of Presumptions

The use of presumptions in family law has a rather mixed history. On the one hand, presumptions are sometimes said to aid consistency and certainty of decision-making; on the other, they can be seen as detracting from the facts of individual cases, and as trying to standardise the heterogeneous experiences of family life. The courts of England at one time spoke of the approach to relocation as amounting to a presumption in favour of the bona fide application,[56] but later explicitly recanted from this view.[57] Likewise, Judge Boshier's initial interpretation of the Care of Children Act 2004 in New Zealand might be thought to have amounted to a presumption against relocation applications, though his Honour did not use the word 'presumption'.[58] Certainly some judges thought that the similar approach of the Court of Appeal in *Bashir v Kacem* had a presumptive effect.[59] Again, there has since been a retreat from that position and an affirmation of a non-presumptive approach.[60] Despite this judicial ambivalence about presumptions, scholars in both New Zealand and Canada have recently suggested approaches which explicitly or implicitly involve presumptions.

The Canadian work in question comes from Nicholas Bala and Andrea Wheeler.[61] Based on an analysis of 738 relocation cases reported between 2001 and 2011, they extrapolate certain patterns from the judicial decisions. These include:[62]

[55] See discussion of these developments in R George, 'The International Relocation Debate' [2012] *Journal of Social Welfare and Family Law* 141, 148–50.

[56] See, eg, *MH v GP (Child: Emigration)* [1995] 2 FLR 106 (EWHC), 110; *Re C (Leave to Remove from Jurisdiction)* [2000] 2 FLR 457 (EWCA), 464, 466 and 467.

[57] *Payne* [25] and [82]. For discussion of a similar judicial history in Canada, first favouring and then abandoning a presumption in favour of a primary carer in relocation cases, see *Gordon v Goertz* [1996] 2 SCR 27 (Supreme Court, Canada) [26]–[48].

[58] P Boshier, 'Relocation Cases: An International View from the Bench' [2005] *New Zealand Family Law Journal* 77.

[59] *Bashir v Kacem* [2010] NZCA 96, [2010] NZFLR 865; for the view that this decision amounted to a presumption, see, eg, *DJP v KDF [Relocation]* [2011] NZFLR 386 (NZFC) [16(d)].

[60] *Kacem v Bashir* [2010] NZSC 112, [2010] NZFLR 884.

[61] N Bala and A Wheeler, 'Canadian Relocation Cases: Heading Towards Guidelines' [2012] *Canadian Family Law Quarterly* 271.

[62] ibid 311–12 for a helpful summary of the trends and patterns found in the study.

- two significant factors in favour of a relocation application are that the applicant is the main carer of the child, and that there is significant family violence; shared care arrangements (40% or more of time for each parent) tend to work against relocation;
- the age of the child has no apparent effect on whether the application is allowed or not;
- there is no apparent effect of previous restrictions on relocation, whether agreed by the parties or ordered by a court on a previous occasion, on whether the application is allowed or not.

From these findings, and bearing in mind the criticism in Canada about the lack of guidance and consequent unpredictability found in the Canadian law,[63] Bala and Wheeler join a growing trend in Canada and elsewhere in calling for greater clarity.[64] The Bala and Wheeler approach – which they term *Relocation Advisory Guidelines* or RAGs[65] – is designed not as a normative statement about what should happen in relocation cases, but rather as a clearer articulation of what is happening in the Canadian courts already.[66] In short, they consider that there are two separate presumptions in operation, as they explain:

> There is a *presumption in favour of relocation* if
>
> - the parent opposing relocation has perpetrated acts of familial abuse;
> - the parent seeking relocation has sole custody (legal or *de facto*); or
> - the child wishes to move.
>
> There is a *presumption against relocation* if
>
> - the parent seeking relocation has made clearly unfounded allegations of familial abuse;
> - there is shared physical custody (each parent has at least 40 per cent of the time); or
> - the parent seeking relocation has unilaterally moved the child; or
> - the child does not wish to move; or
> - the case is at an interim stage.[67]

The only comment that is important about the detail of these factors relates to the inclusion of unilateral moves in the list of factors which engage the presumption against relocation. While there may be an argument that this factor ought, as a matter of policy, to militate against relocation – though there is also an argument the other way – it is difficult to see why it is included here, given that the list

[63] The leading case is *Gordon v Goertz* [1996] 2 SCR 27 (Supreme Court, Canada); for criticism, see, eg, R Thompson, 'Ten Years After Gordon: No Law, Nowhere' (2007) 35 *Reports of Family Law* (6th) 307.

[64] See, eg, R Thompson, 'Ten Years After Gordon: No Law, Nowhere' (2007) 35 *Reports of Family Law* (6th) 307; E El Fateh, 'A Presumption for the Best' [2009] *Canadian Journal of Family Law* 73.

[65] N Bala and A Wheeler, 'Canadian Relocation Cases: Heading Towards Guidelines' [2012] *Canadian Family Law Quarterly* 271, 316.

[66] ibid.

[67] ibid 317; *cf* R Zafran, 'Children's Rights as Relational Rights: The Case of Relocation' (2010) 18 *American University Journal of Gender, Social Policy and the Law* 164, 205–06, where Zafran proposes that there ought to be three categories of case: near-equal shared care with a presumption against relocation; low-involvement contact parents with a presumption favouring relocation; and a middle group with no presumption either way.

is based on the practice of the Canadian courts. The difficulty arises from the authors' analysis of the unilateral move issue earlier in their paper. They say:

> Although court decisions frequently condemn mothers who take unilateral action (relocate with their children without the approval of the other parent or permission of the court), in our study, applicants were successful in 70 out of 144 cases where they 'moved first and asked permission later' (49%).[68]

That 49 per cent compares with an overall success rate for all relocation cases of 51 per cent.[69] This factor probably ought therefore not to be included as indicating a presumption against relocation; it is a factor which does not predict the outcome either way.

Before considering the merits of the presumption system in general, we can consider the New Zealand research that leads to a similar approach, coming from Mark Henaghan.[70] This approach proposes to offer a discipline based on social science research and a degree of normative reasoning which prioritises the values that are at stake in a relocation dispute. Henaghan's model starts by asking about 'the degree of actual responsibility taken for the child',[71] and then gives priority to the child's emotional and physical safety, and to the child's views. So long as safety is not an issue, the attitude of the applicant parent towards the other parent is given emphasis 'because where parents work together, children inevitably benefit'.[72] However, the current psychological state of the parents is not given particular emphasis.[73]

This 'discipline' is intended to make the framework of relocation decisions more visible and predictable, helping lawyers to advise their clients as well as helping judges to make more consistent decisions.[74] The full discipline that Henaghan proposes is set out in Figure 6.1.[75] While Henaghan does not describe his approach as involving any presumptions,[76] his identification of factors, or combinations of factors, which should make applications more or less likely to be granted carries similar connotations.

[68] N Bala and A Wheeler, 'Canadian Relocation Cases: Heading Towards Guidelines' [2012] *Canadian Family Law Quarterly* 271, 303–04.

[69] ibid 288.

[70] M Henaghan, 'Relocation Cases: The Rhetoric and the Reality of a Child's Best Interests: A View from the Bottom of the World' [2011] *Child and Family Law Quarterly* 226.

[71] ibid 247.

[72] ibid.

[73] 'It puts the parent making such a case in a no-win bind. Establishing psychological devastation risks such a parent losing care of their child altogether': ibid.

[74] That aim, it may be noted, arises from the unpredictability seen in New Zealand relocation cases over the last decade, as discussed in ch 5. The *Payne* approach to relocation cases in England, also described as a 'discipline', may (partly) address those issues already, as discussed in ch 4.

[75] M Henaghan, 'Relocation Cases: The Rhetoric and the Reality of a Child's Best Interests: A View from the Bottom of the World' [2011] *Child and Family Law Quarterly* 226, 250. I am grateful to Jordan Publishing for permission to reproduce this diagram here.

[76] Though he does criticise the indeterminacy of having '[n]o rules or presumptions' in relocation cases: ibid 248.

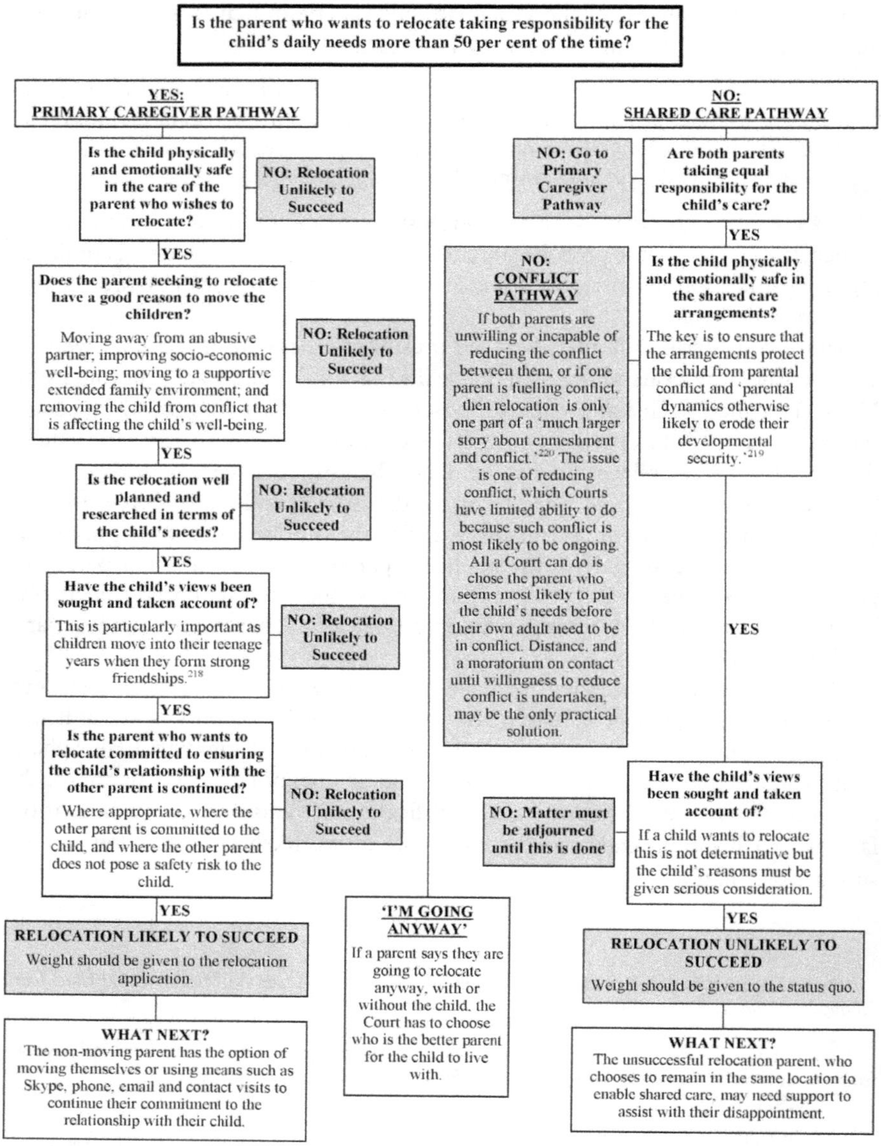

Figure 6.1 Mark Henaghan's proposed discipline for relocation cases

There is much to be said for both the Henaghan approach and the Bala and Wheeler approach, and their shared aim of increasing the predictability of relocation decision making is both laudable and increasingly widespread. However, there may be reasons to be cautious about any proposal which involves presumptions, whether introduced as a reflection of existing practice (the Bala and Wheeler model) or based on social science research with the aim of regulating power relations (the Henaghan model).

A useful first step may be to deconstruct what is meant by a presumption in this context. In general, the word 'presumption' is used in law to mean that if Fact A is proved by evidence, Fact B is then presumed ('proved by presumption'), and the legal conclusion flows from the presumed existence of Fact B.[77] The 'presumption of legitimacy' is a good example.[78] In that example, Fact A has two components: that the woman has had a child, and that X is that woman's husband (or was, within the normal gestational period of the child). When those facts are proved, the law presumes Fact B, namely that X is the father of the child. However, a person wishing to challenge X's status as the father can adduce evidence which rebuts the presumption by showing that X is not the father. Absent such rebuttal, though, the legal consequences that flow from Fact B are identical whether X's status as the father is proved by presumption or proved by evidence.

In the relocation context, this analysis is hard to apply. The facts to be proved by evidence (Fact A) are things like 'that the applicant is the primary caregiver' or 'that the child does not wish to move'. From this, Fact B should then be presumed, but it is difficult to understand what the fact would be, because any 'fact' which might be presumed is inherently a future outcome, rather than a past or present fact. The closest that one can get to constructing this secondary fact seems to be, put at its most basic, to say that the child's overall welfare will be better served by relocating or not relocating, as the case may be; describing that as a fact might be thought to stretch the language too far. A welfare conclusion is not a fact but an assessment of the likely future course of events. The proposed presumption therefore seems not to be a 'true' presumption at all, for it is the legal conclusion itself which is being presumed, not a fact on which the legal conclusion is to be based.[79]

Even if we adopt a looser understanding of what a presumption is, there are still reasons to be cautious of an approach which draws on presumptions. The first reason is purely technical, but it is important to be aware that imposing any presumption would be beyond the remit of the courts and constitute an unjustifiable judicial gloss on the welfare principle as set out by Parliament, so this approach could be implemented only through legislative change.[80]

[77] See generally C Tapper, *Cross and Tapper on Evidence*, 12th edn (Oxford, Oxford University Press, 2010) ch 3.

[78] See W Swadling, 'Explaining Resulting Trusts' [2008] *Law Quarterly Review* 72, 75.

[79] This appears to be most akin to Swadling's example of a 'false presumption' as one 'indicating a burden of proof', somewhat like the so-called presumption of innocence in criminal trials: ibid 75.

[80] In the relocation context, see most recently *Re F (Relocation)* [2012] EWCA Civ 1364, [2013] 1 FLR 645 [37], and *Kacem v Bashir* [2010] NZSC 112, [2010] NZFLR 884 [36]. See observations to similar effect in other contexts by Lord Hobhouse in *Dawson v Wearmouth* [1999] 1 FLR 1167 (UKHL) 1180–81, and Lord Nicholls in *White v White* [2000] 2 FLR 981 (UKHL) 990, the latter saying: 'A presumption of equal division would be an impermissible judicial gloss on the statutory provision. That would be so, even though the presumption would be rebuttable. Whether there should be such a presumption in England and Wales, and in respect of what assets, is a matter for Parliament.'

Another line of criticism calls into question the likely effectiveness of presumptions in the family law context.[81] The aim of enhancing certainty has a powerful rhetorical appeal, and similar arguments are seen in other areas of family law.[82] However, it might be said that certainty is a less powerful argument in family law cases than in many areas of the law, because finding the 'best solution' for this individual set of facts is more important than knowing in advance what the answer will be.[83] Moreover, regardless of that question, some have argued that presumptions will not produce the certainty that is claimed, because they will simply shift the argument.[84] Instead of arguing about what the child's welfare requires, the parties will argue about which presumption applies and then, regardless of the answer to that question, about whether that presumption has been rebutted by other evidence.

Another question is whether an approach involving presumptions would cause difficulties from a human rights perspective. The reason that the English courts rejected a presumptive approach in *Payne* was precisely that such an approach might breach 'not only [rights] under Art 8 [to respect for private and family life] but also . . . rights under Art 6 to a fair trial'.[85] This argument must work both ways: just as a presumption in favour of relocation risks breaching the human rights of the respondent, so a presumption against relocation must risk breaching the rights of the applicant.[86]

Finally, it might be said that a presumptive approach risks a focus on outcomes rather than on reasons. Indeed, one might go so far as to suggest that this approach risks something of an 'is/ought fallacy', drawing normative conclusions about

[81] Jonathan Herring has suggested that a presumption has a practical effect on the outcome of a case only where i) the presumption calls for an outcome that the judge would not otherwise have favoured under a welfare analysis, and ii) the judge's welfare decision was a marginal call, such that the judge did not have sufficient evidence to rebut the presumption: J Herring, 'The Welfare Principle Is Presumably About Welfare' (*A Seminar Celebrating Twenty-One Years of the Children Act 1989*, University of Sussex, 2012). While this argument has much force, it may also be possible that a presumption would have some effect, over time, on the way that decision-makers (and individuals outside the courts) conceive of welfare in general, thus changing the background against which the presumption is to be judged.

[82] Outside the child law context, the most obvious use of this argument in recent years has been in relation to financial provision after divorce.

[83] See, eg, *Kacem v Bashir* [2010] NZSC 112, [2010] NZFLR 884 [35]: 'Lack of predictability, particularly in difficult or marginal cases, is inevitable and the so-called wide discretion given to judges is the corollary of the need for individualised attention to be given to each case. . . . [T]he court is not in fact exercising a discretion; it is making an assessment and decision based on an evaluation of the evidence. It is trite but perhaps necessary to say that judges are required to exercise judgment. The difficulties which are said to beset the field are not conceptual or legal difficulties; they are inherent in the nature of the assessments which the courts must make.'

[84] J Herring, 'The Welfare Principle Is Presumably About Welfare' (*A Seminar Celebrating Twenty-One Years of the Children Act 1989*, University of Sussex, 2012); in another family law context, see also P Harris, 'The Miller Paradoxes' [2008] *Family Law* 1096; R George, P Harris and J Herring, 'Pre-Nuptial Agreements: For Better or For Worse?' [2009] *Family Law* 934, 935–36.

[85] *Payne* [40]. The same point was made by the Supreme Court in the context of children giving evidence in abuse cases: *Re W (Children) (Abuse: Oral Evidence)* [2010] UKSC 12, [2010] 1 FLR 1485 [3]. On human rights relating to relocation disputes in general, though not discussing this particular point, see J Herring and R Taylor, 'Relocating Relocation' [2006] *Child and Family Law Quarterly* 517.

[86] *Payne* [36].

what should be done from descriptive claims about what is done.[87] Taking the Bala and Wheeler model as an example, their analysis starts with the outcomes from 738 relocation cases, and uses them to suggest various circumstances in which they argue that there should be a presumption one way or the other about future cases. Using outcomes to create principles has a certain empirical attraction and, of course, '[t]hese are only presumptions, and can always be rebutted based on a multi-factoral best interests finding in an individual case'.[88] However, two risks might be highlighted.

The first of those risks is that the identification of 'patterns' might belie the highly individualised reasoning that led to the same outcome in different cases. As Rimer LJ said in a different child law context, '[t]hese cases may well follow a similar pattern but each will in fact be unique, [and] it should be recognised as such'.[89] The second risk, which follows from the first, is that the use of these presumptions may result in judges (or legal advisers) imposing 'default outcomes' on cases where those outcomes are not appropriate.[90] This point was made in relation to contact disputes by Thorpe LJ some years ago:

> There is a danger that the identification of a presumption will inhibit or distort the rigorous search for the welfare solution. There is also the danger that a presumption may be used as an aid to determination when the individual advocate or judge feels either undecided or overwhelmed.[91]

A similar point was made by Lady Hale when considering the circumstances in which a child should be called to give oral evidence in a case of alleged abuse: a careful balancing of all the relevant considerations 'may well mean that the child should not be called to give evidence in the great majority of cases, but that is a result and not a presumption or even a starting point'.[92] As her Ladyship later put it, 'rarity should be a consequence of the exercise rather than a threshold test'.[93]

[87] See generally D Hume, *A Treatise of Human Nature* (L Selby-Bigge ed, London, John Noon Publishing, 1968 [this edition first published 1888]) 455*ff*.

[88] N Bala and A Wheeler, 'Canadian Relocation Cases: Heading Towards Guidelines' [2012] *Canadian Family Law Quarterly* 271, 317.

[89] *Re W (Children) (Abuse: Oral Evidence)* [2010] EWCA Civ 57, [2010] 2 FLR 256 [64]; this decision was reversed on appeal (see *Re W (Children) (Abuse: Oral Evidence)* [2010] UKSC 12, [2010] 1 FLR 1485), but the Supreme Court judgment speaks with much the same voice as Rimer LJ, and his Lordship described himself as being on 'the brink of dissent' because of precisely the concerns that caused the Supreme Court to reach a different conclusion.

[90] A similar point is made about the appropriate use of research evidence in this context: see above, pp 13–14.

[91] *Re L, V, M and H (Contact: Domestic Violence)* [2000] 2 FLR 334 (EWCA), 364. In the relocation context, see also *Re F (Relocation)* [2012] EWCA Civ 1364, [2013] 1 FLR 645 [37]. In the leading relocation case in Canada, McLachlin J said: '[Parliament] entrusted the court with the best interests of the particular child whose custody arrangements fall to be determined. Each child is unique, as is its relationship with parents, siblings, friends and community. Any rule of law which diminishes the capacity of the court to safeguard the best interests of each child is inconsistent with the requirement of the Divorce Act for a contextually sensitive inquiry into the needs, means, condition and other circumstances of "the child" whose best interests the court is charged with determining': *Gordon v Goertz* [1996] 2 SCR 27 (Supreme Court, Canada) [44].

[92] *Re W (Children) (Abuse: Oral Evidence)* [2010] UKSC 12, [2010] 1 FLR 1485 [22].

[93] ibid [30].

While there is room to debate the issue, much the same logic might apply to the use of presumptions in the relocation context. It may be true that most relocation applications brought by parents who are providing the main care for the child are allowed, and that most applications brought by parents in shared care arrangements are refused, but that is an outcome and should not be allowed to predetermine any individual case. The characteristics identified – 'shared care', 'unilateral move', 'familial violence' and so on – are convenient labels, but reliance on them may belie the complexity of each case, and risk imposing a homogeneity of outcomes on cases with a heterogeneity of facts and circumstances.

Guidance in the Form of Questions

Finally, then, we turn to the idea of approaching relocation cases using a series of questions. The aim of this approach is to offer decision makers and advisers a structure with which to approach relocation decisions which identifies the main relevant issues and encourages a logical analysis of them without predetermining (or appearing to predetermine) the outcome. The idea for this approach comes from a Court of Appeal decision called *E v E (Shared Residence: Financial Relief: Yardstick of Equality)* in 2006.[94] Giving the judgment of the court in that case, Wall LJ put the matter like this:

> The [relocation issue] broke down into a number of essential components, best expressed, we think, by a series of questions. (1) Was it in the interests of the children for the shared residence order to continue? (2) Irrespective of the label put on the residence arrangements for the children, was it in their interests to move with their mother to [the new location], if the consequence of that move was a substantial disruption of their relationship with their father? (3) If they were not to move to [the new location] with their mother, what arrangements should be made for their residence? (4) If they did not move to [the new location], should they live with their father, and if so where? (5) If it was in the interests of the children for Mrs E to remain their primary carer, should she be required to remain in [the original location] and in the matrimonial home as a pre-condition of her retention of that role?[95]

While there may be merit in approaching relocation cases through a series of questions, the particular questions chosen by the Court of Appeal in *E v E* are problematic: the choice of questions, their phrasing, and their order are all debatable.[96] For example, since the child's welfare, or best interests, is the over-arching question into which these sub-questions feed, it is unhelpful to structure individual sub-questions in the form 'is it in the child's interests to do *x*?', as is seen in questions (2) and (5). The questions ought to be either about past or prevailing circumstances, or about likely future circumstances in the different possible scenarios

[94] *E v E (Shared Residence: Financial Relief: Yardstick of Equality)* [2006] EWCA Civ 843, [2006] 2 FLR 1228.

[95] ibid [25].

[96] See further R George, 'Re L (Internal Relocation: Shared Residence Order) [2009] EWCA Civ 20, [2009] 1 FLR 1157' (casenote) [2009] *Journal of Social Welfare and Family Law* 71, 77.

being contemplated; in either case, the answers are then used to determine the outcome which is in the child's best interests.

Inevitably every case will have its own idiosyncrasies, and therefore the questions proposed here are intended simply to help decision-makers to identify factors which are likely to be amongst those which are important in a relocation case. It should be noted, though, that similar cautionary statements are found in *Payne*,[97] and that did not stop that case becoming perceived as being a presumption in favour of relocation.[98]

So what might the questions look like? The following questions,[99] which are intended to give no indication as to the weight that each element would carry in an individual case, would seem to be relevant:

(1) **How are the care-giving responsibilities for the child (and other family members, if relevant) currently being discharged?** While this question would probably focus on the child's residence arrangements, whether mainly with one parent or shared, the inquiry should be broader than that, asking about the various contributions that each parent (and anyone else) is currently making to the child's welfare and well-being.

(2) **Why does Parent A wish to relocate, and why does Parent B oppose the relocation?** There are two primary objectives found in this question. The first is to ask whether either parent has an illegitimate motivation for their position. For Parent A, such a motivation could be a desire to get the child away from Parent B without objective justification for doing so. On the other hand, if applicable, family violence would be an important factor to consider.[100] For Parent B, an illegitimate motivation could be a desire to control Parent A's life, using the child simply as a ruse to do so with no regard for his or her interests. The second objective is simply to understand more about the case, since (for example) Parent A's reason for wanting to relocate with the child may be relevant when asking, in the next question, about the alternatives to the relocation plan.

[97] *Payne* [85]: 'In summary I would suggest that the following considerations should be in the forefront of the mind of a judge trying one of these difficult cases. They are not and could not be exclusive of the other important matters which arise in the individual case to be decided. All the relevant factors need to be considered, including the points I make below, so far as they are relevant, and weighed in the balance.'

[98] See, eg, C Geekie, 'Relocation and Shared Residence: One Route or Two?' [2008] *Family Law* 446.

[99] Earlier versions of these proposals were made in R George, 'Re L (Internal Relocation: Shared Residence Order) [2009] EWCA Civ 20, [2009] 1 FLR 1157' (casenote) [2009] *Journal of Social Welfare and Family Law* 71, 78–79 and R George, 'Regulating Responsibilities in Relocation Disputes' in J Bridgeman, H Keating and C Lind (eds) *Regulating Family Responsibilities* (Farnham, Ashgate, 2011) 166.

[100] While it will be very rare, Parent A may *legitimately* seek to relocate to get the child away from Parent B if Parent B presents an objective and on-going risk to the child's welfare. One such case is discussed briefly in R George, 'Relocation Research: Early Ideas from Ten County Court Cases' [2012] *Family Law* 700. The father had criminal convictions for child pornography offences and was considered an on-going risk to the child. The judge thought that the mother was acting responsibly in seeking to move away from the father and granted her permission to relocate, ordering indirect contact to take place after the move was complete.

(3) **Taking into account the answers to question (2), what scope is there for either parent to change their plans so that the child can remain in close proximity to both?** So for Parent A, the question is whether he or she is both able and willing not to relocate, while for Parent B the question is whether he could also move to the proposed relocation destination.[101] (That is not to say that the court could *order* Parent B to move to the new destination.[102] However, if Parent B is arguing that the child's welfare requires the close proximity of both parents, then his or her willingness to consider, at least, the possibility of moving as well ought to be relevant.) If one or both of these options is possible, the next question is what effect such a course of action would have on the parents and on the child (both directly on the child, and indirectly through the effect on the parents). The courts in England have long highlighted that stopping Parent A from relocating – even if that parent says that he or she will remain if leave to take the child is refused – has potential to be detrimental to the parent and to the child in the longer term,[103] and this issue should be assessed in a case-specific way. The right of each parent to freedom of movement (which includes the freedom not to move[104]) should be considered here, bearing in mind that the overall analysis involves the balancing of many (potentially conflicting) considerations.[105]

(4) **If the options in question (3) are either impractical or undesirable (meaning that Parent A is going to relocate and Parent B is not), what would be the likely effect on the child either of relocating with Parent A, or of remaining in the current location with Parent B?** This question requires a number of complex assessments of medium- and long-term consequences, all of which are hypothetical future issues that are liable to involve a degree of 'crystal ball-gazing'.[106] Some issues for each option will be similar, and may include considerations like

[101] The question of Parent B moving has long been a consideration in some jurisdictions (see, eg, *NW v MW [Parenting Order]* [2006] NZFLR 485 (NZFC) [10]), and has recently been highlighted explicitly in England by *K v K* [47]. It is fair to say, as an Australian judge once pointed out, that if Parent B follows Parent A once, it could mark the first of many moves if Parent A has a peripatetic lifestyle or if Parent A is in fact trying to get away from Parent B: see *G and A* [2007] FCWA 11 (Family Court, Australia).

[102] It is generally thought that the court has no jurisdiction to make such an order, though the Full Court of the Family Court of Australia did once say that it had power under Australia's Family Law Act 1975 (Cth), s 114(3), 'to enjoin a parent from relocating or to relocate, provided that that injunction is no more than is necessary to secure the best interests of a child': *Sampson v Hartnett* (No 10) [2007] Fam CA 1365 (Full Court of the Family Court, Australia) [58]. That section provides a general power to grant injunctions in child law cases, and it seems no more or less ambitious to use that provision to require a parent to relocate than it would to make a specific issue order to the same effect under Children Act 1989, s 8. For comment, see R Chisholm, 'To What Extent Can the Court Make Orders that Inhibit a Parent's Right to Relocate?' [2008] *Australian Journal of Family Law* 154.

[103] See, eg, *Payne* [41]; *Re B (Leave to Remove: Impact of Refusal)* [2004] EWCA Civ 956, [2005] 2 FLR 239.

[104] P Parkinson, 'Freedom of Movement in an Era of Shared Parenting: Differences in Judicial Approaches to Relocation' (2008) 36 *Federal Law Review* 145.

[105] See generally *Re S (Identification: Restrictions on Publication)* [2004] UKHL 47, [2005] 1 FLR 591.

[106] That matter cannot be a legitimate ground for criticising the judge's findings on this point, as happened in *Re H (A Child) (Removal from Jurisdiction)* [2007] EWCA Civ 222, [2007] 2 FLR 317 [27].

'the child's familial, educational and social environment, and the child's social, cultural, ethnic and religious community'.[107] Other issues may be different, and it is helpful to address them separately.

(a) **If the child were to move with Parent A, what would be the likely effect on the child?** This assessment needs to include things like (i) the long-term effect of reduced or even lost contact between the child and Parent B (and other family members that the child currently has a relationship with); (ii) the realistic ways in which those relationships could be maintained after relocation; (iii) the general disruption of relocating to a new location (such as different school, different language, different society, community and friends, and so on).

(b) **If the child were to stay with Parent B, what would be the likely effect of that on the child?** That assessment would require attention to be paid to issues like (i) the extent of the change of existing care arrangements (which would vary considerably based on the extent of sharing in the previous care arrangements); (ii) the long-term effect of reduced or even lost contact with Parent A; (iii) the realistic ways in which that relationship could be maintained after the parent's relocation; (iv) the extent of any changes in schooling, etc if living with Parent B involved such changes.

(5) **What are the wishes and feelings of each child involved?** In making this assessment, it is important to bear in mind that the issues at stake in a relocation case are complex and hard to understand: adults struggle to imagine accurately what it would be like to live in a different location or not to see someone that they love as often as they want to, and even older children may have little conception of the realities of the decision that is being taken. At the same time, for those children who do have understanding of the issues, their views may be of great significance.

These questions are certainly not exhaustive, and the weight that would be attached to the answers would likely vary considerably from case to case. At the end of the process, the judge will be required to bring all of the answers together and make whatever decision she believes is likely to advance the child's welfare best. 'The task is a difficult one. It must be performed without prejudice or preconceived ideas. But it is the task which we [as judges] are paid to perform to the best of our ability'.[108] We cannot expect judges always to get these decisions 'right', because 'in most of these cases there is no right answer'.[109] The aim is to help judges to have the right information and to be asking themselves the right questions in order to exercise their judgment carefully in such a way as is most likely to be 'reasonably satisfactory'.[110]

[107] *Re G (Education: Religious Upbringing)* [2012] EWCA Civ 1233, [2013] 1 FLR 677 [27].

[108] *Re B (Care Proceedings: Standard of Proof)* [2008] UKHL 35, [2008] 2 FLR 141 [31].

[109] *G v G (Minors: Custody Appeal)* [1985] FLR 894 (UKHL) 897.

[110] ibid 898.

A predictable criticism of this approach is that the entire line of questioning is based around the welfare principle, focusing the enquiry on the child's interests 'alone'. Some may say that this approach gives inadequate respect and attention to the rights of others involved in the case, most especially the parents.[111] There are two answers which may pre-emptively be offered to this criticism.[112] The first is that, from a practical perspective, there seems little prospect of relocation cases (or any other child law cases) being determined other than via the welfare approach in the near future. Indeed, adopting an alternative approach would require statutory change and, while a new Children and Families Bill was before the English Parliament when this book went to press, there was never any indication that it would not be based around the welfare principle.[113] New international documents relating to relocation similarly regard the welfare of the child as central.[114] Consequently, engaging with the question of reform at the present time necessarily means a welfare focus.

The second answer, though, goes further and asserts that the welfare principle is an appropriate approach to relocation cases. It is important to understand fully what the process involves, and not to allow the focus to become overly narrow. In 1970, Lord MacDermott in *J v C* described the welfare principle as:

> a process whereby, when all the relevant facts, relationships, claims and wishes of the parents, risks, choices and other circumstances *are taken into account and weighed*, the course to be followed will be that which is most in the interests of the child's welfare as that term has now to be understood. That is the first consideration because it is of first importance and the paramount consideration because it rules upon or determines the course to be followed. (Emphasis added.)[115]

Later, his Lordship explains that 'in applying [the welfare principle], the rights and wishes of parents, whether unimpeachable or otherwise, must be assessed and weighed in their bearing on the welfare of the child in conjunction with all other factors relevant to that issue'.[116] Put another way, the welfare principle allows, and indeed requires, that all factors relevant to the child's welfare be taken into consideration when assessing what would be best for the child.

More recently, Munby LJ has expanded upon the requirements of the welfare principle.[117] As his Lordship put it in *Re G (Children) (Education: Religious Upbringing)*, the idea of welfare:

[111] The argument for a human rights approach to relocation is made most explicitly in J Herring and R Taylor, 'Relocating Relocation' [2006] *Child and Family Law Quarterly* 517.

[112] It might be noted that, despite the many and varied criticisms levelled at relocation law by practitioners in this study, there was no mention of 'rights' as such.

[113] See, eg, Department for Education and Ministry of Justice, 'Co-operative Parenting Following Family Separation: Proposed Legislation on the Involvement of Both Parents in a Child's Life' (London, HMSO, 2012) [4.2].

[114] See most recently the Washington Declaration on International Family Relocation 2010, Art 3, discussed above, pp 146–49.

[115] *J v C* [1970] AC 668 (UKHL) 710–11.

[116] ibid 715.

[117] *Re G (Education: Religious Upbringing)* [2012] EWCA Civ 1233, [2013] 1 FLR 677.

> extends to and embraces everything that relates to the child's development as a human being and to the child's present and future life as a human being. The judge must consider the child's welfare now, throughout the remainder of the child's minority and into and through adulthood. . . . How far into the future the judge must peer – and with modern life expectancy a judge dealing with a young child today may be looking to the 22nd century – will depend upon the context and the nature of the issue.[118]

In the relocation context, it seems that the judge really may have to think over that kind of timeframe, since the decision in many cases is indeed life-altering. Moreover, the judge will need to consider 'a wide range of ethical, social, moral, religious, cultural, emotional and welfare considerations', which is likely to include 'the child's familial, educational and social environment, and the child's social, cultural, ethnic and religious community'.[119] Put shortly, the judge 'must adopt a holistic approach'.[120] That includes consideration of 'the child's network of relationships', since as Munby LJ explains, 'a child's relationships, both within and without the family, are always relevant to the child's interests; often they will be determinative'.[121]

All of that, of course, is easier said than done. Munby LJ goes on to explain that the judge, like a parent, will apply modern standards with the aim of achieving three separate but connected things:

> First, we must recognise that equality of opportunity is a fundamental value of our society: equality as between different communities, social groupings and creeds, and equality as between men and women, boys and girls. Second, we foster, encourage and facilitate aspiration: both aspiration as a virtue in itself and, to the extent that it is practical and reasonable, the child's own aspirations. Far too many lives in our community are blighted, even today, by lack of aspiration. Third, our objective must be to bring the child to adulthood in such a way that the child is best equipped both to decide what kind of life they want to lead – what kind of person they want to be – and to give effect so far as practicable to their aspirations. Put shortly, our objective must be to maximise the child's opportunities in every sphere of life as they enter adulthood.[122]

If this understanding of the welfare principle is adopted, it may start to address some of the challenges that this approach faces. In particular, the questions proposed in this section together with Munby LJ's approach may increase the 'transparency' of the welfare principle, helping us to see what values and interests are driving the decision.[123] That is not to say that this approach answers all the questions which critics make of the welfare principle. In particular, the apparent

[118] ibid [26].

[119] ibid [27].

[120] ibid.

[121] ibid [30]. See generally J Herring, 'Relational Autonomy and Family Law' in J Wallbank, S Choudhry and J Herring (eds), *Rights, Welfare and Family Law* (Abingdon, Routledge, 2010); J Herring and C Foster, 'Welfare Means Rationality, Virtue and Altruism' (2012) 32 *Legal Studies* 480.

[122] *Re G (Education: Religious Upbringing)* [2012] EWCA Civ 1233, [2013] 1 FLR 677 [80].

[123] On 'the *lack of transparency* objection' to the welfare principle, see J Eekelaar, 'Beyond the Welfare Principle' [2002] *Child and Family Law Quarterly* 237.

indeterminacy of the welfare approach,[124] and the objection that a welfare approach gives inadequate attention to the interests of people other than the child concerned,[125] may require further thought.

On this final point, the English courts have traditionally seen no conflict between a welfare approach and the requirements of human rights instruments, whether international or domestic.[126] While some commentators were unconvinced by this assessment,[127] recent European Court of Human Rights cases suggest that a similar view is now being taken by that Court. The most obvious example might be *YC v United Kingdom*,[128] which involved a mother's application following a decision of the domestic court to make a final care order and an adoption placement order in relation to her child. The key legislative provision in that case was section 1 of the Adoption and Children Act 2002, with its list of matters to be considered in search of a welfare outcome.[129] The European Court of Human Rights said that 'the considerations listed in s 1 of the 2002 Act . . . broadly reflect the various elements inherent in assessing the necessity under Art 8 of a measure placing a child for adoption'.[130] According to Claire Simmonds, the case 'reflects the changing attitude of the ECtHR towards children's rights in public law, and shows that paramountcy, in the English sense, may not be so alien to the ECtHR as it once was'.[131]

The Court in *YC* explained that the involvement of the parents in the decision-making process was a very significant factor, but went on to say that the overall assessment of the domestic court's decision involved asking

> whether the domestic courts conducted an in-depth examination of the entire family situation and of a whole series of factors, in particular of a factual, emotional, psychological, material and medical nature, and made a balanced and reasonable assessment of the respective interests of each person, with a constant concern for determining what would be the best solution for the child.[132]

[124] The classic explanation is in R Mnookin, 'Child Custody Adjudication: Judicial Functions in the Face of Indeterminacy' (1975) 39 *Law and Contemporary Problems* 226; but *cf Kacem v Bashir* [2010] NZSC 112, [2010] NZFLR 884, [35], quoted above, n 83.

[125] See, eg, J Eekelaar, 'Beyond the Welfare Principle' [2002] *Child and Family Law Quarterly* 237, 238–39; S Choudhry and H Fenwick, 'Taking the Rights of Parents and Children Seriously: Confronting the Welfare Principle Under the Human Rights Act' [2005] *Oxford Journal of Legal Studies* 453.

[126] See, eg, *Re KD (A Minor) (Access: Principles)* [1988] 2 FLR 139 (UKHL); *Payne* [35]–[37] and [82]; *Re C (Direct Contact: Suspension)* [2011] EWCA Civ 521, [2011] 2 FLR 912 [43].

[127] See, eg, S Choudhry and H Fenwick, 'Taking the Rights of Parents and Children Seriously: Confronting the Welfare Principle Under the Human Rights Act' [2005] *Oxford Journal of Legal Studies* 453; S Harris-Short, 'Family Law and the Human Rights Act 1998: Judicial Restrain or Revolution?' [2005] *Child and Family Law Quarterly* 329.

[128] *YC v United Kingdom* (Application No 4547/10) [2012] 2 FLR 332 (ECtHR); see also *R and H v United Kingdom* (Application No 35348/06) [2011] 2 FLR 1236 (ECtHR) esp at [77].

[129] Adoption and Children Act 2002, s 1(4).

[130] *YC v United Kingdom* (Application No 4547/10) [2012] 2 FLR 332 (ECtHR) [135].

[131] C Simmonds, 'Paramountcy and the ECHR: A Conflict Resolved?' [2012] *Cambridge Law Journal* 498. For a longer discussion and analysis of how a welfare analysis can be seen to be compatible with a rights analysis, see R George, 'The Child's Welfare in European Context' in J Scherpe (ed) *Research Handbook on European Family Law* (Cheltenham, Edward Elgar, 2014).

[132] *YC v United Kingdom* (Application No 4547/10) [2012] 2 FLR 332 (ECtHR) [138].

YC was concerned with adoption and therefore with public law proceedings, but there is reason to think that a similar view might be taken in the private law context. For example, the *YC* formulation of the overarching assessment was identical to that used in *Neulinger and Shuruk v Switzerland* in July 2010, which was a child abduction case.[133] It might be said that a welfare assessment which is informed by consideration of 'the entire family situation' and the factors identified in the welfare checklist is, in effect, a means of conducting the balancing exercise that is required when there is a conflict of rights.[134]

The attraction that such an interpretation has is that it allows a full rights-based analysis and careful, individualised balancing exercise to take place, while also recognising that some important matters cannot adequately be framed in a rights discourse. Rights are important because they protect valuable interests,[135] but some considerations which can and should be taken into account are not readily analysed as a question of rights, such as whether a particular course of action is *responsible*,[136] and what the reasonable *expectations* of the parties might be.[137]

It is for this reason that the questions proposed in this section represent an attempt to incorporate a wider range of relevant matters into the decision than might previously have been expressly recognised in the law, using both broad welfare questions and explicit reference to rights. For example, part (3) of this proposed analytical framework makes explicit reference to certain rights of the parents, but all relevant parental rights and interests can and should be considered. The questions in part (4) relating to disruption to, and continuation of, parent–child relationships, for example, must include both the child's and each parent's Article 8 rights to respect for their private and family life. Consequently, this approach might both pursue a solution based on the welfare of the child, and at the same time express more clearly the necessary separate consideration of and respect to the important rights of all those involved which feed into a welfare analysis.

[133] *Neulinger and Shuruk v Switzerland* (Application No 41615/07) [2011] 1 FLR 122 (ECtHR) [139]. Indeed, in *YC* the court referenced its earlier use of this formulation, saying 'see, mutatis mutandis, *Neulinger and Shuruk v Switzerland* . . . para 139'.

[134] On the balancing exercise, see generally *Re S (Identification: Restrictions on Publication)* [2004] UKHL 47, [2005] 1 FLR 591.

[135] J Raz, *The Morality of Freedom* (Oxford, Clarendon Press, 1986) 166; J Eekelaar *Family Law and Personal Life*, paperback edition (Oxford, Oxford University Press, 2007) 135.

[136] See generally J Eekelaar, *Family Law and Personal Life*, paperback edn (Oxford, Oxford University Press, 2007) 127–31, on 'a fuller concept of responsibility'.

[137] See further R George, 'Regulating Responsibilities in Relocation Disputes', in J Bridgeman, H Keating and C Lind (eds), *Regulating Family Responsibilities* (Farnham, Ashgate, 2011); R George, *Ideas and Debates in Family Law* (Oxford, Hart Publishing, 2012) 32–34.

Concluding Remarks

It is really only in the last 10 years or so that relocation law has entered the mainstream of family law scholarship.[138] We have come a long way in that time in advancing our understanding of relocation disputes, both in terms of the legal principles,[139] the human experience,[140] and the application of those legal principles to individual cases by the professionals tasked with implementing the law.

This book offers insight into the current working of relocation law in two jurisdictions. The findings presented here help us to understand more about what is currently happening, and about the benefits and difficulties experienced by the professionals working within the system. Drawing from those findings, I have discussed possible models for reforming relocation law. I have endeavoured to find a way of asking the questions which seem important in most relocation cases in such a manner as to present 'as neutral a set of guidelines as possible',[141] while allowing the balancing exercise inherent in all relocation cases to be as transparent as possible. Whether I have succeeded or not is for others to judge.

One of the difficulties facing all of family law, but perhaps relocation law in particular, is the rapid pace of changes taking place in many societies. Families are 'increasingly heterogeneous' and, for children, the concept of *family* 'increasingly involves absent and re-partnered parents'.[142] More generally, conceptions of family forms and family norms have shifted, and traditional gender roles are changing.[143] The particular manifestation and extent of these changes has varied between different countries, though in general there is a shift towards co-parenting.[144] For relocation cases in particular, the rapid increase in international migration has huge consequences. In 2010, it was estimated that there were 215 million international migrants globally, with the number typically increasing by around 10 per cent every five years.[145]

[138] When I began my DPhil in 2007, it was common to have to explain what relocation disputes were when I attended conferences and seminars. Many people seemed to think of relocation as the less interesting alter ego of international child abduction!

[139] See especially M Hayes, 'Relocation Cases: Is the Court of Appeal Applying the Correct Principles?' [2006] *Child and Family Law Quarterly* 351.

[140] See especially N Taylor, M Gollop and M Henaghan, *Relocation Following Parental Separation: The Welfare and Best Interests of Children* (University of Otago, Dunedin, 2010).

[141] S Gilmore, 'The Payne Saga: Precedent and Family Law Cases' [2011] *Family Law* 970, 976.

[142] J Masson, 'Caring for Our Future Generations' in G Douglas and N Lowe (eds), *The Continuing Evolution of Family Law* (Bristol, Jordan Publishing, 2009) 221–22.

[143] J Lewis, 'Introduction: Children in the Context of Changing Families and Welfare States' in J Lewis (ed), *Children, Changing Families and Welfare States* (Cheltenham, Edward Elgar, 2006). On the changing roles of fathers, see R Collier and S Sheldon, *Fragmenting Fatherhood: A Socio-Legal Study* (Oxford, Hart Publishing, 2008).

[144] See, eg, I Théry, '"The Interests of the Child" and the Regulation of the Post-Divorce Family' (1986) 14 *International Journal of the Sociology of Law* 341; P Parkinson, *Family Law and the Indissolubility of Parenthood* (Cambridge, Cambridge University Press, 2011).

[145] United Nations, 'Trends in Total Migration Stock: The 2008 Revisions', available online at www.un.org/esa/population/migration/UN_MigStock_2008.pdf.

As these changes take place and debates continue about the appropriate norms for the law to set down for separated parents in general, relocation cases are likely to continue to represent one of the clearest tensions in child law. There are many reasons why this is so: the parties are usually very conflicted, the interests at stake are of the highest order, the possibilities for compromise are severely limited, and the outcomes are often irreversible. More so than any other area of private child law, relocation disputes offer a problem with no right answer. As the opening quotation in this book said, '[a]ll practicable answers are to some extent unsatisfactory and therefore to some extent wrong, and the best that can be done is to find an answer that is reasonably satisfactory'.[146] In the relocation context, even a 'reasonably satisfactory' answer seems a lot to ask, and the increasingly varied ways in which post-separation families live their lives, coupled with the increasingly international world in which we live, will not make it any easier to find a satisfactory legal approach. However, the more we learn, the more chance we have of developing an approach to relocation cases that gives full respect and weight to the important interests of all those involved in the search for a solution that promotes the best interests of each child.

[146] *G v G (Minors: Custody Appeal)* [1985] FLR 894 (UKHL) 897–98.

Methodological Appendix

Overview of Research Methodology

This study involved qualitative interviews with family law professionals, and was given ethical clearance by the University of Oxford's Central University Research Ethics Committee.[1] Qualitative research is exploratory, used to obtained detailed insight into individuals' experiences. As Carol Smart and colleagues explain, qualitative research is 'a systematic, rigorous and theoretically sound method for investigating and understanding the social world' and, as a methodological approach, 'is grounded in the interpretative tradition in that it is concerned with how the social world is interpreted, understood, experienced and produced'.[2] Qualitative research 'is flexible and sensitive to the social context in which the data is produced',[3] and typically draws its sample of participants in a purposive, rather than representative, way.[4]

Qualitative empirical research in this study focused on the legal process involved in resolving relocation disputes in the courts. This study looked only at the experiences and views of legal practitioners, since its aim was to obtain information about the day-to-day practice of relocation law in the trial courts. The specialisation and complexity of the legal issues involved mean that the issues lent themselves to the kind of in-depth qualitative research which interviews provide.

Selecting a Sample of Legal Professionals to Interview

There were four main categories of professional involved in the legal resolution of relocation disputes: Family Court judges, family barristers, family solicitors, and specialists who provide expert evidence to the court about the children and families involved (usually social workers or psychologists).[5]

Judges and court welfare officers, in general, do not specialise in particular areas of child law. With regard to barristers and solicitors, while a small number

[1] Central University Research Ethics Committee Approval No. SSD/CUREC1/08-216.

[2] C Smart, B Neale and A Wade, *The Changing Experience of Childhood: Families and Divorce* (Cambridge, Polity Press, 2001) 174–75.

[3] ibid 175; see also J Mason, *Qualitative Researching* (London, Sage, 1996); M Miles and M Huberman, *Qualitative Data Analysis: An Expanded Sourcebook*, 2nd edn (London, Sage, 1994); N Denzin and Y Lincoln, *The Sage Handbook of Qualitative Research*, 3rd edn (London, Sage, 2005).

[4] Studies vary in the extent to which they attempt to be representative.

[5] See further below, pp 168–70.

of practitioners specialise in relocation cases, most of those working on relocation are 'child law' practitioners more generally.[6] Because of this lack of specialisation within the professions, the population of potential participants is large, but many of its members have only limited experience. The aim, therefore, was to obtain a range of experiences, both from those who specialise in relocation and from those who do not; but in order to ensure that participants had a reasonable experience of relocation, they were invited to participate if they had done three or more cases in the last two years.

In order to obtain a full range of experience, the aim was to interview five participants in each of the four professional categories in each country. In fact, to obtain this range of participants, and in particular because of difficulties in obtaining a reasonably even gender split, the numbers in each group varied slightly. In the end, participants comprised: seven English judges and six New Zealand judges; seven barristers in each country; five English solicitors and six New Zealand lawyers who worked as both solicitors and barristers; and three court experts in each country (in England, court welfare advisors; in New Zealand, psychologists who work for the Family Court).

Table A1 provides a full list of participants, divided by nationality and professional group, and also showing their sex,[7] approximate time in practice,[8] and the approximate number of relocation trials done each year. The table also shows the identity tags which are used to identify individuals in the thesis. These tags have three components, identifying i) the country in which the individuals work,[9] ii) their professional group,[10] and iii) an allocated number within that group. So, for example, EJ2 is an English judge, NB5 is a New Zealand barrister, ES1 an English solicitor and NC3 a New Zealand court expert (psychologist). In terms of participant recruitment, the approach in the two countries was broadly similar but, since there was some variation, will be explained in turn. Starting with the English sample, relocation cases can be filed in either the High Court or the County Court, and so trial judges from both levels of court were recruited. The seven judicial participants included five men and two women;[11] two sat in the Family Division

[6] One solicitor in this study explained that relocation 'is not exactly our bread and butter – it's slightly off the beaten track for us. We do it because we feel comfortable enough doing it, but . . . [we] have never done enough of them to major in them' (ES1).

[7] In the interests of preserving anonymity, the sex of the judges who participated in this research is not shown on the table. There were five men and two women amongst the English judges, and three men and three women amongst the New Zealand judges.

[8] In the interests of preserving anonymity, the time that judges who participated in this research had been on the bench is not shown on the table; the average time sitting full-time for English judges was 9.5 years, and for New Zealand judges was 8.5 years.

[9] 'E' for England and Wales, 'N' for New Zealand.

[10] 'J' for judges, 'B' for barristers, 'S' for solicitors in England and for lawyers who worked as both solicitors and barristers in New Zealand, 'C' for court experts (welfare officers in England, court-appointed psychologists in New Zealand).

[11] This gender split (29% women) approximates that found on the English bench: see J Neuberger, *The Report of the Advisory Panel on Judicial Diversity 2010* (London, Ministry of Justice, 2010) 15.

Table A1 – List of participants by identifying tag, showing nationality, professional group, sex, time in practice, and approximate number of relocation trials per year

English participants					New Zealand participants				
Identifying tag	Professional group	Sex	Time in practice (years)	Approximate number of relocation trials per year	Identifying tag	Professional group	Sex	Time in practice (years)	Approximate number of relocation trials per year
EJ1	Judge			4	NJ1	Judge			9–14
EJ2				1	NJ2				5–6
EJ3				2	NJ3				3–4
EJ4				3	NJ4				5–6
EJ5				2–3	NJ5				5–6
EJ6				3–4	NJ6				10–12
EJ7				2–3	NB1	Barrister	F	23	2–3
EB1	Barrister	M	7	1	NB2		M	25	1–2
EB2		M	18	2–3	NB3		F	15	1–2
EB3		M	19	2–3	NB4		M	40	3–4
EB4		F	8	1	NB5		F	35	3–4
EB5	Barrister, QC	M	30	2–3	NB6		F	21	3
EB6		F	24	5–6	NB7		M	25	1–2
EB7		F	24	1–2	NS1	Solicitor/ barrister	M	23	2–3
ES1	Solicitor	M	28	1	NS2		F	30	1–2
ES2		F	9	1–2	NS3		F	22	3
ES3		M	15	2	NS4		F	18	2–3
ES4		F	18	1–2	NS5		F	19	2–3
ES5		M	12	6-8	NS6		F	31	1
EC1	Court welfare officer	F	20	1–2	NC1	Psychologist	M	25	7–8
EC2		M	25	3–4	NC2		F	25	12
EC3		F	33	1–2	NC3		M	13	6

of the High Court,[12] and five were County Court Judges,[13] who either were or had been Designated Family Judges.[14] Judges in the High Court are all specialists and highly experienced; they were contacted in no particular order, and the seventh and ninth to be contacted were the ones who participated. Circuit Judges were contacted by writing to the Designated Family Judges of courts in a variety of locations, including large cities and smaller towns.

Family barristers were selected by drawing up a list of all those who were named as having represented litigants in reported relocation cases between 2000 and 2008. This produced a list of some 50 individuals, with few names coming up more than once. Since most reported cases are from the Court of Appeal, it was not uncommon for leading counsel to be engaged for the appeal. Since most cases do not reach an appeal, however, it was important to see juniors as well as Silks, so as to gain a more rounded impression of 'normal' relocation cases (rather than ones which are appealed). Barristers were shortlisted if their name appeared on this list and their chambers' website listed relocation (or leave to remove) as one of their areas of practice. Two of those interviewed also made specific recommendations of other people to interview. Seven barristers were interviewed (four men, three women), three of whom were QCs (one man, two women).[15]

Family solicitors were also selected by listing firms which had been named in the law reports in relocation cases between 2000 and 2008. This produced a rather shorter list, since the names of solicitors are often omitted in the interests of preserving litigant anonymity. The websites of firms which were mentioned were searched, and five individuals who specifically stated that relocation cases were one of their specialisms were interviewed (three men, two women).[16]

The standard source of expert input to the court in England is a report from the Child and Family Court Advisory and Support Service (CAFCASS). Five CAFCASS offices were contacted, and three individuals participated (one man, two women).

Turning to New Zealand, relocation cases start in the Family Court, which is where all judicial participants worked. Six judges were interviewed (three men, three women).[17] These judges were contacted by virtue of their being the Family Judges of their courts, and were spread across a variety of locations, including both urban and rural areas.

In New Zealand, there is no split legal profession amongst lawyers, but there is an increasing trend for some family lawyers to specialise in advocacy work, and to be referred to as specialist family law barristers. In total, 13 lawyers were

[12] A further seven declined to participate.
[13] A further two declined to participate.
[14] Designated Family Judges are responsible for the administration of family justice from their court, and work predominantly on family cases.
[15] A further three, all juniors, declined to participate.
[16] A further four declined to participate.
[17] Of the 48 Family Court judges in New Zealand, 19 (40 per cent) were women at the time of interviewing.

interviewed,[18] of whom seven identified themselves as specialist barristers (three men, four women); the other six worked as both solicitors and barristers (one man, five women).

Most New Zealand lawyers were selected in the same way as the English, by listing those who had appeared in reported cases between 2000 and 2008. This group was supplemented using snowball sampling, with several participants also suggesting colleagues whom they thought would be willing to participate. As well as acting for parties in relocation cases, most of these lawyers (in both categories) did some of their work as Lawyer for Child, representing the child's views to the court.[19] Three psychologists experienced in working for the Family Court were also interviewed (two men, one woman).

In all cases, participants were initially contacted by letter or email. This initial communication explained the nature of the research and what was being asked of the person, and included a copy of the informed consent form. If no reply was received within two weeks, follow-up telephone calls were made.

Participants were told that interviews would be entirely anonymous, and that they would be identified using only their professional group, their gender, the approximate time they had been in practice, and the approximate number of relocation cases they did each year. All participants were also given the option, on the informed consent form, of asking to see any direct quotations taken from their interviews to ensure that they were happy with the material that was used; 24 participants exercised this option.[20]

Conduct of Interviews

Most English interviewees (18 participants) were seen between November 2008 and January 2009, with the remainder (four participants) seen in May and June 2009. All New Zealand interviews took place in February and March 2009. All interviews were digitally audio recorded, and an anonymised transcript produced of the interview. Each transcript was identified with the participant tag which was to be used in the thesis itself.

Interviews lasted between 36 and 81 minutes (the mean was 53 minutes), and were divided into three broad sections. First, a number of background questions were asked, designed to elicit information about the participant's experience of relocation disputes, and to learn more about those disputes. The second section asked participants about their experiences of the law in practice and their

[18] A further five declined to participate.

[19] Care of Children Act 2004 (New Zealand), s 7.

[20] When quotations were sent to these participants for checking in mid-2010, one participant asked that a few words be removed from one quotation, and another asked that a few words that were originally to be quoted twice (though in different chapters) be used only once. The other 22 participants who saw quotations made no requests for changes.

evaluations of it. The final section looked at three hypothetical cases, presented in the form of 350-word vignettes. (Vignettes are 'short stories about hypothetical characters in specified circumstances, to whose situation the interviewee is invited to respond'.[21])

Analysis of Interviews

Analysis of the transcripts was conducted using a broadly grounded methods theory approach, which involves 'coding' data in several 'phases', though the phases are not linear nor entirely distinct from one another.[22] The first stage of analysis involved familiarisation with the data and identification of emerging issues. These issues were used to develop a thematic framework, enabling the views and experiences of respondents to be explored within a common analytical framework, grounded in and driven by participants' own accounts.[23] Key themes, largely coming from the interview schedule but also arising out of the data, were used to organise ideas, and were arranged so as to retain their source and keep national and professional groups separate for ease of comparison.

In addition to the general methodological discussion, it is necessary to look at the methodology around the use of vignettes. Vignettes offer a number of advantages as a research tool in socio-legal research. In particular, they ground discussion in specific examples and so avoid 'a series of answers which are simply bland generalisations'.[24] For comparative work, they also provide a standard stimulus for different groups of participants (ie English and New Zealand practitioners), enabling the effect of the legal background to be examined when applied to the same sets of facts. For participants in this research, there is also the particular advantage of more closely approximating legal practitioners' daily work: whereas critical analysis of the law in the abstract may be an unusual activity for practitioners, a detailed analysis of how the law would be applied to a set of facts resembles their everyday work.

To assist with 'the need to construct vignettes in which both the characters and the story line[s] are believable',[25] the three vignettes were based on the facts of reported English cases,[26] though in each case the facts were modified. These modifications were intended both to distance the vignettes from the reported cases,

[21] J Finch, 'The Vignette Technique in Survey Research' (1987) 21 *Sociology* 105, 105.

[22] R LaRossa, 'Grounded Theory Methods and Qualitative Family Research' (2005) 67 *Journal of Marriage and Family* 837, 840.

[23] L Spencer, J Ritchie, J Lewis and L Dillon, *Quality in Qualitative Evaluation: A Framework for Assessing Research Evidence* (London, Cabinet Office, 2003).

[24] J Finch, 'The Vignette Technique in Survey Research' (1987) 21 *Sociology* 105, 110.

[25] ibid 111.

[26] The cases were *Re H (Children) (Residence Order: Condition)* [2001] EWCA Civ 1338, [2001] 2 FLR 1277; *Re Y (Leave to Remove from Jurisdiction)* [2004] 2 FLR 330 (EWHC); and *Re B (Leave to Remove: Impact of Refusal)* [2004] EWCA Civ 956, [2005] 2 FLR 239.

since expert practitioners were likely to know a large number of cases, and also to ensure that a wide range of factors was present in the three vignettes. Each vignette was about 350 words long. This length was designed to strike a balance between the amount of time available in each interview, and the need for detail in order for meaningful analysis to be forthcoming.

Participants themselves frequently commented on the use of vignettes as a research tool. Some said that the 'case scenarios are very well put' (NJ2), but others pointed out that analysing 350-word summaries was 'quite an unreal task' (EC1), with the information provided offering more questions than answers. Almost all participants identified aspects about which they needed more detail, and a common theme was that the personalities of the parties as they presented themselves to the court could be crucial. As one English judge explained, 'it is the difference between [reading the vignette] and walking in there and seeing them' (EJ7).

These methodological criticisms are important, and it should be recognised that vignettes can only approximate the work which practitioners undertake in real cases. However, given the time constraints of interviews, and the amount of work which volunteer participants can be asked to do, these limitations are unavoidable. Moreover, the primary purpose of the vignettes is to identify differences between English and New Zealand practitioners' analyses; since all participants received identical information, the comparison is internally consistent, even though not a perfect replica of participants' day-to-day work.

The analysis of the vignettes looked qualitatively at participants' discussions. This work involved the same grounded methods framework analysis used for the general parts of the interviews.[27] In addition, an assessment was made of participants' predictions of the likely outcomes of each vignettes. To make participants' views comparable, their predictions of the likely outcomes were standardised on a 0–10 scale, with 0 representing participants who thought the relocation certain to be refused and 10 those who thought it certain to be allowed.

Some participants gave a specific numerical estimate of the chances that relocation would be allowed in each case; where that happened, these numerical estimates were converted onto the 0–10 scale. In other cases, the chances of success were estimated based on non-numerical indicators which participants gave in their discussions. To give examples, participants who said that an applicant 'hasn't got a hope' (NS2) were allocated 0; at the other end, when an opposition to relocation was 'bound to fail' (EB5), the participant was allocated 10. Participants who said that cases 'could go either way' (NJ6) were put at 5, while those who said that a case might succeed or fail 'by a narrow margin' (EJ1) were given 6 or 4 respectively. Cases which were 'probably' going to succeed or fail were given 7 or 3 respectively; participants who described 'a strong case' (EB3) were given 8 or 2, while a very strong case was given 9 or 1. Given that not all participants expressed

[27] L Spencer, J Ritchie, J Lewis and L Dillon, *Quality in Qualitative Evaluation: A Framework for Assessing Research Evidence* (London, The Cabinet Office, 2003).

specific numerical chances, it is important to treat these numbers with caution, and they should be seen as indicative of participants' strength of feeling, rather than as mathematical predictions.

BIBLIOGRAPHY

Amato, P, Meyers, C and Emery, R, 'Changes in Nonresident Father-Child Contact from 1976 to 2002' (2009) 58 *Family Relations* 41.

Bailey-Harris, R, Barron, J and Pearce, J, 'From Utility to Rights? The Presumption of Contact in Practice' [1999] *International Journal of Law, Policy and the Family* 111.

Bainham, A, 'Taking Children Abroad: Human Rights, Welfare and the Courts' [2001] *Cambridge Law Journal* 489.

Bala, N and Wheeler, A, 'Canadian Relocation Cases: Heading Towards Guidelines' [2012] *Canadian Family Law Quarterly* 271.

Baker, H, Hirsch, J and Sauvage, N, 'International Family Relocation from an English, French and German Perspective' [2012] *International Family Law* 97

Barton, C, 'Emigration After Divorce: (Not) the Children Act 1989' (1990) 24 *The Law Teacher* 81.

Barton, C, 'When Did You Next See Your Father? Emigration and the One-Parent Family' [1997] *Child and Family Law Quarterly* 73.

Beatson, K and Turrell, S, 'Leave to Remove: The Carer's Prerogative?' (2005–06) 52 (Dec/Jan) *Family Law Journal* 9.

Behrens, J, 'A Feminist Perspective on *B and B* (The Family Court and Mobility)' (1997) 2 *Sister in Law* 65.

Behrens, J, '*U v U*: The High Court on Relocation' [2003] *Melbourne University Law Rev* 572.

Behrens, J, Smyth, B and Kaspiew, R, 'Outcomes in Relocation Decisions: Some New Data' [2010] *Australian Journal of Family Law* 97.

Bingham, J, '"Barbaric" Family Courts Behind "State Sponsored Kidnap" – Bob Geldof', *The Telegraph* (7 December 2009).

Bishop, G, 'Brookside or Stateside: A Residence Battle' (1993) 137 *Solicitors Journal* 556.

Boshier, P, 'Relocation Cases: An International View from the Bench' [2005] *New Zealand Family Law Journal* 77.

Bowermaster, J, 'Relocation Custody Disputes Involving Domestic Violence' (1998) 46 *University of Kansas Law Review* 433.

Boyd, S, 'Autonomy for Mothers? Relational Theory and Parenting Apart' (2010) 18 *Feminist Legal Studies* 137.

Boyd, S, 'Gendering the Best Interests Principle: Custody, Access and Relocation in a Mobile Society' in Niman, H and Sadvari, G (eds), *Family Law: 'The Best Interests of the Child'* (Ottawa, Law Society of Upper Canada, 2000).

Brasse, G, 'The Payne Threshold: Leaving the Jurisdiction' [2005] *Family Law* 780.

Bridge, C, 'Comment: Re H (A Child) (Removal from Jurisdiction) [2007] EWCA Civ 222, [2007] 2 FLR 317' [2007] *Family Law* 707.

Bryant, D, 'Freedom of Movement in an Era of Shared Parenting: The Difference in Judicial Approaches: A Critique' [2010] *International Family Law* 11.

Champion, T, 'Population Movement within the UK' in *Focus on People and Migration* (London, Office for National Statistics, 2005).

Chisholm, R, 'A Brief Reply to Professor Parkinson' [2007] *Australian Journal of Family Law* 229.

Chisholm, R, 'Making It Work: The Family Law Amendment (Shared Parental Responsibility) Act 2006' [2007] *Australian Journal of Family Law* 143.

Chisholm, R, 'To What Extent Can the Court Make Orders that Inhibit a Parent's Right to Relocate?' [2008] *Australian Journal of Family Law* 154.

Choudhry, S and Fenwick, H, 'Taking the Rights of Parents and Children Seriously: Confronting the Welfare Principle Under the Human Rights Act' [2005] *Oxford Journal of Legal Studies* 453.

Choudhry, S and Herring, J, *European Human Rights and Family Law* (Oxford, Hart Publishing, 2010).

Collier, R and Sheldon, S, *Fragmenting Fatherhood: A Socio-Legal Study* (Oxford, Hart Publishing, 2008).

Daly, M and Rake, K, *Gender and the Welfare State: Care, Work and Welfare in Europe* (London, Polity Press, 2003).

Denzin, N and Lincoln, Y, *The Sage Handbook of Qualitative Research*, 3rd edn (London, Sage, 2005).

Department for Education and Ministry of Justice, 'Co-operative Parenting Following Family Separation: Proposed Legislation on the Involvement of Both Parents in a Child's Life' (London, HMSO, 2012).

Doughty, S, 'Bob Geldof Accuses "Barbaric" Family Courts of "Kidnapping Children from Their Fathers"', *The Daily Mail* (8 December 2009).

Easteal, P and Harkins, K, 'Are We There Yet? An Analysis of Relocation Judgments in Light of Changes to the Family Law Act' [2008] *Australian Journal of Family Law* 259.

Eekelaar, J, 'Beyond the Welfare Principle' [2002] *Child and Family Law Quarterly* 237.

Eekelaar, J, *Family Law and Personal Life*, paperback edn (Oxford, Oxford University Press, 2007).

Eekelaar, J, 'The Interests of the Child and the Child's Wishes: The Role of Dynamic Self-Determinism' [1994] *International Journal of Law and the Family* 42.

El Fateh, E, 'A Presumption for the Best' [2009] *Canadian Journal of Family Law* 73.

Ermish, J, Iacovou, M and Skew, A, 'Family Relationships', in McFall, S, and Garrington, C (eds), *Understanding Society: Early Findings from the First Wave of the UK's Household Longitudinal Study* (Colchester, Institute for Social and Economic Research, 2011).

Finch, J, 'The Vignette Technique in Survey Research' (1987) 21 *Sociology* 105.

Fischhoff, B and Kadvany, J, *Risk: A Very Short Introduction* (Oxford, Oxford University Press, 2011).

Foley, T, 'International Child Relocation: Varying Approaches Among Member States to the 1980 Hague Convention on Child Abduction' (London, Court of Appeal, 2006).

Freeman, M, *Relocation: The Reunite Research* (London, Reunite, 2009).

Freeman, M and Taylor, N, 'The Reign of Payne' (2011) 2 *Journal of Family Law and Practice* 20.

Geekie, C, 'Relocation and Shared Residence: One Route or Two?' [2008] Family Law 446.

George, R, 'Changing Names, Changing Places: Reconsidering Section 13 of the Children Act 1989' [2008] *Family Law* 1121.

George, R, *Ideas and Debates in Family Law* (Oxford, Hart Publishing, 2012).

George, R, 'International Relocation, Care Arrangements, and Case Taxonomy' [2012] *Family Law* 1478.

George, R, 'Practitioners' Views on Children's Welfare in Relocation Disputes: Comparing Approaches in England and New Zealand' [2011] *Child and Family Law Quarterly* 178.

George, R, 'Principles Relevant to Child's Welfare and Best Interests' [2011] *New Zealand Family Law Journal* 26.

George, R, 'Re F (Children) (Internal Relocation) [2010] EWCA Civ 1428' (casenote) [2011] *Journal of Social Welfare and Family Law* 169.

George, R, 'Re L (Internal Relocation: Shared Residence Order) [2009] EWCA Civ 20, [2009] 1 FLR 1157' (casenote) [2009] *Journal of Social Welfare and Family Law* 71.

George, R, 'Regulating Responsibilities in Relocation Disputes', in Bridgeman, J, Keating H and Lind, C (eds), *Regulating Family Responsibilities* (Farnham, Ashgate, 2011).

George, R, 'Relocation Disputes in England and Wales: First Findings from the 2012 Study' (Oxford Legal Studies Research Paper, 2013), online at http://ssrn.com/abstract=2306097.

George, R, 'Relocation Research: Early Ideas from Ten County Court Cases' [2012] *Family Law* 700.

George, R, 'Reviewing Relocation?' [2012] *Child and Family Law Quarterly* 110.

George, R, 'The Child's Welfare in European Context' in Scherpe, J (ed) *Research Handbook on European Family Law* (Cheltenham, Edward Elgar, 2014)

George, R, 'The International Relocation Debate' [2012] *Journal of Social Welfare and Family Law* 141.

George, R, 'The Shifting Law: Relocation Disputes in New Zealand and England' [2009] *Otago Law Review* 107.

George, R, Harris, P and Herring, J, 'Pre-Nuptial Agreements: For Better or For Worse?' [2009] *Family Law* 934.

George, R, Judd, F, Garrido, D and Worwood, A, *Relocation: A Practical Guide* (Bristol, Jordan Publishing, 2013).

Gilligan, C, *In A Different Voice* (London, Harvard University Press, 1982).

Gilmore, S, 'The Payne Saga: Precedent and Family Law Cases' [2011] *Family Law* 970.

Hale, B, 'Relocation' (*International Child Abduction, Forced Marriage and Relocation Conference*, London Metropolitan University, 2010).

Hankivsky, O, *Social Policy and the Ethic of Care* (Vancouver, University of British Columbia Press, 2005).

Harris, P, 'The Miller Paradoxes' [2008] *Family Law* 1096.

Harris, P and George, R, 'Parental Responsibility and Shared Residence Orders: Parliamentary Intentions and Judicial Interpretations' [2010] *Child and Family Law Quarterly* 151.

Harris-Short, S, 'Family Law and the Human Rights Act 1998: Judicial Restraint or Revolution?' [2005] *Child and Family Law Quarterly* 329.

Harris-Short, S, 'Resisting the March Towards 50/50 Shared Residence: Rights, Welfare and Equality in Post-Separation Families' [2010] *Journal of Social Welfare and Family Law* 257.

Hayes, M, 'Relocation Cases: Is the Court of Appeal Applying the Correct Principles?' [2006] *Child and Family Law Quarterly* 351.

Hayes, M and Williams, C, *Family Law: Principles, Policy and Practice*, 1st edn (London, Butterworths, 1995).

Hayes, M and Williams, C, *Family Law: Principles, Policy and Practice*, 2nd edn (London, Butterworths, 1999).

Henaghan, M, 'Care of Children Act Cases: Where Are We, Where Are We Going?' (*LexisNexis Annual Child Law Conference*, Auckland, 2008).

Henaghan, M, 'Care of Children Act Cases: Where Are We, Where Are We Going?' (*LexisNexis Annual Child Law Conference*, Auckland, 2008).

Henaghan, M, 'Going, Going . . . Gone – To Relocate Or Not To Relocate, That Is The Question' (*New Zealand Family Law Conference*, Auckland, 2009).

Henaghan, M, 'Legally Rearranging Families: Parents and Children After Break-Up' in Henaghan, M and Atkin, W (eds), *Family Law Policy in New Zealand*, 3rd edn (Wellington, LexisNexis, 2007).

Henaghan, M, 'Relocation Cases in Australia Post The Family Law Amendment (Shared Parental Responsibility) Act 2006 – Considerations Not Rules Determine the Best Interests of the Child' (*Sixth Annual Family Law Summit*, Brisbane, 2009).

Henaghan, M, 'Relocation Cases: The Rhetoric and the Reality of a Child's Best Interests: A View from the Bottom of the World' [2011] *Child and Family Law Quarterly* 226.

Henaghan, M, Klippel, B and Matherson, D, 'Relocation Cases' (*New Zealand Law Society Seminar*, Wellington, 2000).

Herring, J, 'Relational Autonomy and Family Law' in Wallbank, J, Choudhry, S and Herring J (eds) *Rights, Welfare and Family Law* (Abingdon, Routledge, 2010).

Herring, J, 'The Welfare Principle and the Rights of Parents' in Bainham, A, Day Sclater, S, and Richards, M (eds), *What Is A Parent? A Socio-Legal Analysis* (Oxford, Hart Publishing, 1999).

Herring, J, 'The Welfare Principle Is Presumably About Welfare' (*A Seminar Celebrating Twenty-One Years of the Children Act 1989*, University of Sussex, 2012).

Herring, J and Foster, C, 'Welfare Means Rationality, Virtue and Altruism' (2012) 32 *Legal Studies* 480.

Herring, J and Taylor, R, 'Relocating Relocation' [2006] *Child and Family Law Quarterly* 517.

Hetherington, M and Kelly, J, *For Better or For Worse: Divorce Reconsidered* (New York, Norton, 2002).

Hill, A, 'Mothers Lose Out as Expat Parents Fight for Custody in Foreign Courts', *The Guardian* (20 October 2012).

Hodson, D, 'Every Family Matters: An In-Depth Review of Family Law in Britain' (London, Centre for Social Justice, 2009).

Hodson, D, *A Practical Guide to International Family Law* (Bristol, Jordan Publishing, 2008).

Holman, J, 'Emigration and Leave to Remove from the Jurisdiction' [1983] *Family Law* 92.

Horsfall, B and Kaspiew, R, 'Relocation in Separated and Non-Separated Families: Equivocal Evidence from the Social Science Literature' [2010] *Australian Journal of Family Law* 34.

Hume, D, *A Treatise of Human Nature* (L Selby-Bigge (ed), London, John Noon Publishing, 1968 [this edition first published 1888]).

Hunt, J with Roberts, C, *Child Contact With Non-Resident Parents* (Oxford, University of Oxford, 2004).

Hunter, R, McGlynn, C and Rackley, E, 'Feminist Judgments: An Introduction', in Hunter, R, McGlynn, C and Rackley, E (eds) *Feminist Judgments: From Theory to Practice* (Oxford, Hart Publishing, 2010).

Inglis, D, 'The Care of Children Act and Separated Parents' [2005] *New Zealand Law Journal* 233.

Jollimore, E and Sladic, R, 'Mobility: Are We There Yet?' [2008] *Canadian Family Law Quarterly* 341.

Judd, F and George, R, 'International Relocation: Do We Stand Alone?' [2010] *Family Law* 63.

Junk, J, 'Your Number's Up, Payne v Payne: Time for Change?' (2010), online at http://www.mckenziefriend.com/2010/04/27/your-numbers-up-payne-v-payne-time-for-change.

Kaspiew, R, Behrens, J and Smyth, B, 'Relocation Disputes in Separated Families Prior to the 2006 Reforms: An Empirical Study' (2011) 86 *Family Matters* 72.

Kielty, S, 'Mothers Are Non-Resident Parents Too: A Consideration of Mother's Perspectives on Non-Residential Parenthood' [2005] *Journal of Social Welfare and Family Law* 1.

Kirkconel, A, 'Removing Children from the Jurisdiction' [1999] *Family Law* 333.

Lamont, R, 'Free Movement of Persons, Child Abduction and Relocation Within the European Union' [2012] *Journal of Social Welfare and Family Law* 231.

LaRossa, R, 'Grounded Theory Methods and Qualitative Family Research' (2005) 67 *Journal of Marriage and Family* 837.

Lewis, J, 'Introduction: Children in the Context of Changing Families and Welfare States' in Lewis, J (ed), *Children, Changing Families and Welfare States* (Cheltenham, Edward Elgar, 2006).

Lowe, N, 'Note on Lonslow v Hennig (Formerly Lonslow)' [1986] *Family Law* 304.

Lowe, N, 'Where in the World Is International Family Law Going Next?' in Douglas, G and Lowe, N (eds), *The Continuing Evolution of Family Law* (Bristol, Jordan Publishing, 2009).

Lowe, N and Douglas, G, *Bromley's Family Law*, 10th edn (Oxford, Oxford University Press, 2007).

Lowe, N, Everall, M and Nicholls, M, *International Movement of Children: Law Practice and Procedure* (Bristol, Jordan Publishing, 2004).

Mackenzie, F, *Uneasy Trends in Relocation Law* (unpublished LLM Thesis, Victoria University of Wellington: 2009).

Mason, J, *Qualitative Researching* (London, Sage, 1996).

Masson, J, 'Caring for Our Future Generations' in Douglas, G and Lowe, N (eds), *The Continuing Evolution of Family Law* (Bristol, Jordan Publishing, 2009).

McCallum, L, 'Shared Residence: Just a Label?' [2004] *Family Law* 528.

Mears, M, 'Removal of Children from the Jurisdiction' [1989] *Family Law* 322.

Metge, J and Ruru, J, 'Kua Tutū Te Puehu, Kia Mau: Māori Aspirations and Family Law Policy' in Henaghan, M and Atkin, W (eds), *Family Law Policy in New Zealand*, 3rd edn (Wellington, LexisNexis, 2007).

Miles, M and Huberman, M, *Qualitative Data Analysis: An Expanded Sourcebook*, 2nd edn (London, Sage, 1994).

Mnookin, R, 'Child Custody Adjudication: Judicial Functions in the Face of Indeterminacy' (1975) 39 *Law and Contemporary Problems* 226.

Mnookin, R and Kornhauser, L, 'Bargaining in the Shadow of the Law: The Case of Divorce' (1979) 88 *Yale Law Journal* 950.

Morley, J and Maguire, J, 'International Relocation of Children: American and English Approaches' [2006] *International Family Law* 77.

Neuberger, J, *The Report of the Advisory Panel on Judicial Diversity 2010* (London, Ministry of Justice, 2010).

Newark, F, 'Twine v Bean's Express Ltd' (casenote) (1954) 17 *Modern Law Review* 102.

O'Flinn, C, 'Back in the Fold' (2009) 159 *New Law Journal* 1416.

Overington, C, 'Divorced Mums Forced to Stay Put', *The Australian* (1 June 2009).

Parkinson, P, *Family Law and the Indissolubility of Parenthood* (Cambridge, Cambridge University Press, 2011).

Parkinson, P, 'Family Law and the Indissolubility of Parenthood' (2006) 40 *Family Law Quarterly* 237.

Parkinson, P, 'Freedom of Movement in an Era of Shared Parenting: Differences in Judicial Approaches to Relocation' (2008) 36 *Federal Law Review* 145.
Parkinson, P, 'The Realities of Relocation: Messages from Judicial Decisions' [2008] *Australian Journal of Family Law* 35.
Parkinson, P, Cashmore, J and Single, J, 'Mothers Wishing to Relocate with Children: Actual and Perceived Reasons' (2011) 27 *Canadian Family Law Journal* 11.
Parkinson, P, Cashmore, J and Single, J, 'The Need for Reality Testing in Relocation Cases' (2010) 44 *Family Law Quarterly* 1.
Perry, A, 'Leave to Remove Children from the Jurisdiction: Payne v Payne' [2001] *Child and Family Law Quarterly* 455.
Polak, L, 'Note on Bevan v Bevan' [1974] *Family Law* 127.
Pressdee, P, 'Relocation, Relocation, Relocation: Rigorous Scrutiny Revisited' [2008] *Family Law* 220.
Probert, R, Gilmore, S and Herring, J (eds), *Responsible Parents and Parental Responsibility* (Oxford, Hart Publishing, 2009).
Rathus, Z, 'A Call for Clarity in the Use of Social Science Research in Family Law Decision-Making' [2012] *Australian Journal of Family Law* 81.
Raz, J, *The Morality of Freedom* (Oxford, Clarendon Press, 1986).
Robinson, M, 'Relocation and Leave to Remove' (2009), online at www.thecustodyminefield.com.
Robinson, M, *Relocation: The Case for Reform* (The Custody Minefield/Families Need Fathers, 2010), online at http://www.thecustodyminefield.com/Reports/FamilyLaw-Relocation_The_Need_For_Reform.pdf.
Rogers, L, 'Fathers to Fight Removal of Children Overseas', *The Telegraph* (11 February 2007).
Ruru, J, 'Indigenous Peoples and Family Law: Issues in Aotearoa/New Zealand' [2005] *International Journal of Law, Policy and the Family* 327.
Salkeld, L, 'Let Them Use Skype! Judge Sends Children to Australia with Mother and Tells Father to Talk to Them Via the Internet', *The Daily Mail* (31 March 2011).
Seymour, J, 'Parens Patriae and Wardship Powers: Their Nature and Origin' [1994] *Oxford Journal of Legal Studies* 159.
Smart, C, 'The Ethic of Justice Strikes Back: Changing Narratives of Fatherhood' in Diduck, A and O'Donovan, K (eds), *Feminist Perspectives on Family Law* (Abingdon, Routledge-Cavendish, 2007).
Smart, C, Neale, B and A Wade, *The Changing Experience of Childhood: Families and Divorce* (Cambridge, Polity Press, 2001).
Spencer, L, Ritchie, J, Lewis, J and Dillon, L, *Quality in Qualitative Evaluation: A Framework for Assessing Research Evidence* (London, The Cabinet Office, 2003).
Spon-Smith, R, 'Relocation Revisited' [2004] *Family Law* 191.
Swadling, W, 'Explaining Resulting Trusts' [2008] *Law Quarterly Review* 72.
Tapp, P and Taylor, N, 'Relocation: A Problem Or A Dilemma?' [2008] *New Zealand Family Law Journal* 94.
Tapper, C, *Cross and Tapper on Evidence*, 12th edn (Oxford, Oxford University Press, 2010).
Taylor, N and Freeman, M, 'The Gender Agenda and Relocation Disputes' [2012] *International Family Law* 184
Taylor, N, Gollop, M and Henaghan, M, *Relocation Following Parental Separation: The Welfare and Best Interests of Children* (University of Otago, Dunedin, 2010).

Taylor, R, 'Poels Apart: Fixed Principles and Shifting Values in Relocation Law' in Gilmore, S, Herring, J and Probert, R (eds), *Landmark Cases in Family Law* (Oxford, Hart Publishing, 2011).

Théry, I, '"The Interests of the Child" and the Regulation of the Post-Divorce Family' (1986) 14 *International Journal of the Sociology of Law* 341.

Thomas, A, 'Relocation Dispute Resolution Hearings' [2010] *Family Law* 872.

Thompson, R, 'Heading for the Light: International Relocation from Canada' [2011] *Canadian Family Law Quarterly* 1.

Thompson, R, 'Ten Years After Gordon: No Law, Nowhere' (2007) 35 *Reports of Family Law* (6th) 307.

Thorpe, M, 'Relocation Development' [2010] *Family Law* 565.

United Nations, 'Trends in Total Migration Stock: The 2008 Revisions', available online at www.un.org/esa/population/migration/UN_MigStock_2008.pdf.

Wallbank, J, 'Getting Tough on Mothers: Regulating Residence and Contact' (2007) 15 *Feminist Legal Studies* 189.

Webb, D, Henaghan, M, Atkin, B, Clarkson, D, Caldwell, J and Partridge, D, *Family Law in New Zealand*, 14th edn (Wellington, LexisNexis, 2009).

Weiner, M, 'Inertia and Inequality: Reconceptualizing Disputes Over Parental Relocation' (2007) 40 *University of California Davis Law Review* 1747.

Young, L, 'Resolving Relocation Disputes: The "Interventionist" Approach in Australia' [2011] *Child and Family Law Quarterly* 203.

Zafran, R, 'Children's Rights as Relational Rights: The Case of Relocation' (2010) 18 *American University Journal of Gender, Social Policy and the Law* 164.

INDEX